national allocation plans in the EU emissions trading scheme

LESSONS AND IMPLICATIONS FOR PHASE II

T0314595

EDITORS:
**Michael Grubb,
Regina Betz and
Karsten Neuhoff**

climate policy

VOLUME 6 ISSUE 4 **2006**

Taylor & Francis Group

LONDON AND NEW YORK

First published 2006 by Earthscan

Published 2014 by Routledge
2 Park Square, Milton Park, Abingdon, Oxfordshire OX14 4RN
711 Third Avenue, New York, NY 10017

First issued in paperback 2014
Routledge is an imprint of the Taylor & Francis Group, an informa business

ISBN 978-1-84407-472-3 (hbk)
ISBN 978-1-13801-220-2 (pbk)
ISSN: 1469-3062

Typeset by Domex

Cover design by Paul Cooper Design

Contents

Preface

In its six-year history, *Climate Policy* has now carried four special issues on emissions trading. The first was a broad survey of design issues sponsored by the International Emissions Trading Association. The other three have been largely focused on the EU ETS: an overview collection associated with the launch of the EU ETS in January 2005 (5:1); the analysis of economic principles around allocation and competitiveness (6:1); and this collection, in which several articles critically examine how these principles compare against the actual experience of phase I allocations and phase II proposed allocation plans in the EU.

To the uninitiated, four special issues in as many years may seem like overkill. Those concerned with actual climate change policy will recognize that it is not. Emissions trading has emerged as the instrument of choice for controlling core industrial emissions not only in Europe – where the EU ETS caps almost half of European CO_2 emissions – but increasingly in a number of other parts of the world, including North America. At present the EU scheme is the largest emissions control scheme in the world, eclipsing most pollution control efforts by an order of magnitude. Its financial impact is to be measured in tens, even hundreds, of billions of euros. EU policymakers increasingly like to see it as the centrepiece of an emergent global emissions-trading architecture. It is also a key driver of global low-carbon investments through its links to the Kyoto mechanisms.

In Issue 5:1, my own article with Azar and Persson (2005) described allocation as the 'Achilles heel' of emissions trading. We concluded that phase I allocations were 'excessive on all [these] measures', and predicted parallels with the UK pilot trading scheme, with 'a price spike early in its operation, before prices collapsed to near zero towards the compliance date'. Sadly, the tumultuous events of Spring 2006 bore out that prediction, and made it plain that the key to emissions trading is indeed allocation – hence the focus of Issue 6:1. In the present issue, we include two articles commissioned by Climate Strategies to examine the draft allocation plans, following on from the material in 6:1, together with a broad-ranging separate analysis by Betz et al. The depressing general conclusion, illuminated particularly in the Betz et al. article, is that governments did not learn nearly quickly enough from the fiasco of phase I allocation: and that, accordingly, the European Commission had little choice but to step in and reject almost all the initial proposed allocation plans as inadequate.

In the articles in this volume you can find some of the key analyses that helped to inform that decision, and which give extensive insights into the struggle over allocations that may continue throughout at least the first half of 2007. Other articles put lessons from phase I under the microscope – with conclusions that other regions contemplating emissions trading would do well to heed.

But learning must be in all directions. The article by Palmer et al., on the US RGGI scheme, reminds us all that CO_2 emissions trading is actively and rapidly developing in the USA, and that the European approach to auctioning is timid compared with analyses and developments elsewhere. Several other regions are moving rapidly towards implementing emissions trading schemes.

Inevitably, these schemes will all differ in their design and detail: the idea in some European circles that the EU ETS provides a 'blueprint' design are way off the mark. *Climate Policy* is already considering a future special issue on these regional schemes, and whether and how they might link. Prepare for a fifth in the series.

Michael Grubb
Imperial College, London
7 February 2007

www.climatepolicy.com

Emissions trading: lessons learnt from the 1st phase of the EU ETS and prospects for the 2nd phase

Regina Betz[1]*, Misato Sato[2]

[1] *Centre for Energy and Environmental Markets (CEEM), School of Economics, University of New South Wales (UNSW), Sydney 2052, Australia*
[2] *Faculty of Economics, University of Cambridge, Sidgwick Avenue, Cambridge CB3 9DE, UK*

1. Introduction

In January 2005, the European Union launched an EU-wide emissions trading scheme (EU ETS) for CO_2 emissions. It covers approximately 45% of total CO_2 emissions and is thus the largest 'cap-and-trade' carbon trading scheme in the world – an ambitious and highly challenging policy experiment.[1] As it emerges from its pilot phase and prepares for phase II, the EU ETS now stands at a crossroad: will it quickly address the problems experienced in phase I and establish strong price signals in Europe, or will the prevailing uncertainty continue into phase II?

Phase I has indeed proved how much market design matters to its operation and signalling. Unlike normal markets, emissions trading schemes are designed markets, where the demand and supply are dependent on government decisions. The volume of allowance allocation determines scarcity levels and thus the *effectiveness* of the scheme. Furthermore, the various provisions in the allocation plans can influence investment and operational choices and thus the *efficiency* of the scheme. Decisions on auctioning and free allocation, as well as on how to split the allocation pie across sectors and installations, will also have *distributional consequences*.

This special issue presents seven articles that consider the influence of allowance allocation, and inform the debate surrounding 'National allocation plans in the EU ETS: lessons and implications for phase II'. Five articles focus on recent experience with the design of national allocation plans (NAPs) for the period 2008–2012 and provide qualitative and quantitative assessments. These are complemented by two numerical simulations of trade and distributional effects. We summarize their findings in the context of the debate, which we structure into the three key criteria for ETS assessment: market efficiency; distributional effects, and environmental effectiveness.

* Corresponding author. Tel.: +61-2-9385-3354; fax: +61-2-9313-6337
E-mail address: r.betz@unsw.edu.au

2. Allocation plans in relation to three key criteria

2.1. Is the EU ETS efficient?

Kemfert et al. (2006, this issue), using a general equilibrium multi-sector model, estimate significant efficiency gains from trading under the EU ETS in phase I compared with a situation without inter-sectoral or inter-regional trade. This gives net welfare gains in most countries, except for the Netherlands and Italy. They find that efficiency gains from inter-sectoral trading are greater than those from inter-regional trading.

This study assumes, as simplified economic models suggest (Montgomery, 1972), that the approach to allocation – either auctioning or free allocation – has no impact on cost-efficiency. Yet, as demonstrated by the phase I experience, certain design features of the ETS can in fact act to prevent the realization of the theoretical efficiency gains.

The 'updating' dilemma

This describes the perverse incentives created by the iterative approach to allocation – if allocation is 'updated' between trading periods and the level of an installation's future allowance is a function of today's emission levels. Thus, an installation that expects high future prices has an incentive to abate less today. Neuhoff et al. (2006a, this issue) show that most NAP-2s use the years 2004/2005 as part of their base period to decide on volume of allowances at the installation level. The NAPs have thus not solved the early-action problem.

New entrant and closure rules

As analysed in detail by Åhman and Holmgren (2006, this issue), free distribution of allowances to new entrants coupled with the withdrawal of allocation from 'ceasing installations' creates further perverse incentives to keep inefficient plants in operation. This reduces the efficiency of the overall system. Yet Betz et al. (2006, this issue) find that there has been resistance to change in most Member States, and allocation rules for new installations have mainly remained unchanged in NAPs for phase II. Only slight amendments have been forced by the EU Commission, e.g. *ex-post* adjustments of load factors have been replaced with fixed standardized load factors.

We underline the seriousness of this pitfall together with allocation updating, as they affect investment decisions. Anecdotal evidence has shown that this has already had an adverse impact on both operational and investment behaviour, and hence dynamic efficiency is being compromised.

Price volatility and uncertainty

Price volatility has profound impacts on long-term investment risk and therefore also reduces dynamic efficiency. In addition, sharp price decreases lead to a loss in overall market value, which can reduce confidence in the market itself. EU allowance (EUA) prices are by their nature influenced by a number of factors (e.g. fuel prices, weather) as well as political decisions (e.g. international negotiation on future targets). Spot prices have been volatile since the beginning of the scheme; in extreme cases experiencing a price decline of over €10/EUA in the space of 2 days following the release of verified emissions data in April 2006. Forward and futures trading of EUAs is also active, enabling companies to manage at least short-term volatility.

To prevent such extreme price volatility in the future, greater transparency as well as more structured and regular information disclosure are necessary. More certainty beyond 2012 is also needed for the EU ETS to drive long-term investment, including banking into post-2012 as well as setting a minimum price-floor in auctions (Hepburn et al., 2006).

2.2. Is the EU ETS distributionally fair?

Distributing allowances for free avoids directly increasing costs for firms. Advocates of this approach have claimed that giving all installations free allowances according to their need will, whilst maintaining efficient incentives in the emissions market, address *distributional* and *competitiveness* concerns of the covered sectors and prevent firms from increasing product prices.

Windfall profits

Phase I experience has proved such claims to be naïve and false. Power-sector players have indeed responded to CO_2 opportunity costs both by actively trading in the emissions market and adjusting pricing strategies. Empirical studies on Germany and the Netherlands show opportunity cost pass-through rates varying between 60% and 100% for the wholesale electricity market (Sijm et al., 2006). The windfall profits are financed from the pockets of electricity consumers (both domestic and industrial) who are not compensated by the scheme. Whilst there are genuine cases of competitiveness concerns in cases of high trade exposure and very price-sensitive demand, in aggregate, most sectors, including cement, iron and steel, refining, and pulp and paper, have the potential to profit from free allocation on aggregate sector levels, by adjusting output and pricing (Smale et al., 2006).

To complement Sijm's earlier analysis of selected EU countries, Palmer et al. (2006, this issue) use a power-sector model for the north-east of the USA to assess the amount of free allocation needed to compensate the electricity sector for the costs associated with the implementation of the US RGGI scheme. Looking at the electricity sector as a whole, 100% auctioning would not reduce profitability. The share of auctioning declines if the objective is to maintain profitability of individual power producers or individual power stations. The article discusses possible metrics that are both sufficiently objective as a basis for governments' allocation decisions and sufficiently differentiated to effectively target free allocation as a compensation for expected costs.

However, only four Member States included auctioning in phase I. For phase II, most Member States seem to acknowledge distributional aspects, but seek to address them through reduced free allowance allocation mainly to the power sector, where cost pass-through has been readily demonstrated. The draft plans propose a very limited extension of auctioning – an issue discussed further below.

Sectoral burden-sharing

An additional distributional aspect concerns the level of burden-sharing across sectors. As stated earlier, the EU ETS covers 45% of CO_2 emissions in the EU. However, when taking the reduction potential and abatement costs into account, in aggregate, EU ETS sectors have been let off easily in terms of sharing the burden of Kyoto targets relative to non-covered sectors. As shown in Figure 1 and described by Betz et al. (2006, this issue), the burdens applied to the non-covered sectors are – apart from the UK – disproportionately higher. Consequently, while many EU ETS-covered firms enjoy a significant increase in their profitability induced by free allocation, non-covered sectors or government treasuries, through purchase of Kyoto credits, must pick up the slack in order to reach their Kyoto targets.

2.3. Is the EU ETS environmentally effective?

Evaluation of the scheme's effectiveness both *ex ante* and *ex post* is not a simple task. This is not least because of trade-offs in criteria of assessment, e.g. between market efficiency and lack of political assertiveness, and that there are no firm agreements on how to draw the distinction between over-allocation and real abatement (Ellerman and Buchner, 2006).[2]

Phase I ET budget

The official data on verified emissions for 2005 revealed that the volume of EUAs allocated exceeded real emissions by around 100 million (Kettner et al., 2007).[3] How can this be explained?

A scrutiny by Rogge et al. (2006) reveals that phase I allocation was severely constrained by **technical and time constraints**, which further complicate the application of an 'effectiveness' criteria for its assessment. For example, there are a number of technical issues which increase the probability that over-allocation may have occurred in the first phase, some of which are due to the enormous time pressure to develop the scheme:

1. Existing sector definitions for data collection (e.g. energy balances or national inventory reports) that create noise when using a top-down approach to determine emissions of the covered installations;
2. Interpretations regarding installation coverage of the EU ETS Directive – especially regarding installations such as combustion processes involving crackers in the chemical industry or furnaces in integrated steelworks;
3. Monitoring methodologies applied to gathering historic data prior to 2005;
4. Emissions verification requirements by Member States and other measures to prevent companies from overstating their historic emissions.

Because of these problems, the uncertainties in the base data were significant compared to the size of the (generally small) cutbacks targeted by the Member States. Thus, even those Member States which aimed to reduce emissions with respect to their past emissions had difficulties in doing so. In many cases, the total ET budget was in fact determined before more detailed information on the above had been gathered.

Furthermore, most Member States based the size of their ET budget on a reduction compared to **emission trajectories**. In these cases, the uncertainties outlined above were compounded by often over-optimistic economic or sector growth rates. This is a common problem for projections of any sort, since governments and the business sector like to believe in strong economic growth. Thus, aiming for only marginal reductions against inflated projections is likely to result in over-allocation (Grubb and Neuhoff, 2006; Grubb and Ferrario, this issue).

Compared with phase I, in phase II the availability of verified and more accurate data as well as specific guidelines on installation coverage, in theory facilitate better targeting of ETS budgets by Member States. However, the debate about the use of projections to measure emission reductions is far from over. It is crucial that their underlying assumptions are assessed carefully and that they are compared to historic trends – as analysed for the EU total by Neuhoff et al. (2006b, this issue).

3. Strengthening phase II and beyond

Whether phase II is effective will depend upon both its design and the overall cap, as considered below.

3.1. The phase II EU ETS budget

Uncertainty over the environmental effectiveness of phase I puts a spotlight on the parallel question – will the EU ETS deliver credible emissions reductions in phase II? In 2006, considerable analyses have been conducted to first inform and then assess the proposed phase-II national allocation plans in the light of emerging evidence and lessons from phase I. Presented in this Special Issue are the key results emerging during this period. The conclusion on which opinions probably most firmly converged, however, is not a positive one – the NAP-2s first submitted to the Commission demonstrated little evidence of learning during the pilot phase of the scheme, undermining hopes for improvement in the *effectiveness* of the EU ETS in cutting GHG emissions.

Articles in this issue compare the original NAPs submitted to the EU Commission by Member States against the EU ETS Directive's own assessment criteria:

1. The total quantity of allowances to be allocated shall not be more than is likely to be needed
2. The allocation needs to be in line to reach the Kyoto target
3. Reduction potential of installations should be taken into consideration when setting the cap
4. Use of Kyoto Mechanisms should be supplementary to domestic action.

Although many Member States are using higher quality 2005 data to determine the ETS budget (Neuhoff et al., 2006a, this issue), most submitted NAPs demonstrated little commitment to substantial emissions reductions in the EU ETS sectors. Figure 1 compares allocation volumes proposed under 12 NAPs, relative to reductions required to meet Kyoto targets domestically. The diagonal line indicates the 'proportional share line', i.e. if the emission reductions for covered sectors were proportional to those of non-covered sectors required to meet the Kyoto targets.

Figure 1 shows that out of the Member States assessed, only the UK's allocation is in accordance with criteria 1 and 2. Poland and France, whilst on track for meeting their Kyoto targets, proposed over-allocation to their ET sectors, thus violating criterion 1. The plans submitted by Austria, Germany and proposed in draft by Italy, the Netherlands and Spain meet neither criterion.

Betz et al. (2006, this issue) estimate that phase II ET budgets for the 18 NAPS assessed are only 3% below the budgets in phase I (2005–2007). They also reveal a dichotomy between new and old Member States, to the extent that the envisaged reductions by EU-15 are almost over-compensated by the generous allocations by the 10 new members.

The large volume of emission credits emerging from JI and CDM could amplify these problems if NAPs do not implement viable constraints on their use. Betz et al. (2006, this issue) conclude that the potential volume of imports could mean that there would be no need for domestic reductions at all, although substantial differences exist across Member States; thus the supplementarity criterion (criterion 4) would be violated by the EU ETS sector in aggregate. As stated above, this increases the burden share for non-covered sectors or government treasuries in meeting Kyoto targets. By comparing NAPs with emissions projections derived from detailed electricity model analysis and taking account of inflows from JI and CDM markets, Neuhoff et al. (2006b, this issue) similarly conclude that proposed allocation volumes would be incompatible with sustaining EUA prices in the EU ETS.

3.2. Addressing efficiency and distributional issues through auctions

As indicated, several of the articles note that the very high level of free allocation creates a multitude of both incentive and distributional problems. Greater use of auctioning could alleviate several of these problems, and help to establish more cost-reflective prices than was evident in phase I, thereby improving price stability. Auctioning can also be seen as fundamentally implementing the 'polluter pays' principle, and it also raises revenue for governments which could be recycled creatively, for example to ease the distributional inequalities or to help fund low-carbon investments (Grubb and Neuhoff, 2006; Palmer et al., 2006, this issue).

None of proposed allocation plans fully used the option to auction up to 10% of issued allowances, even though this is far below the levels found in the Palmer et al. (2006, this issue) analysis, and indeed the *minimum* 25% proposed for the RGGI scheme. However, the Commission decision on assessment of the first 10 NAP-2s left this open – it allows each Member State to increase the share of auctioning after the Commission's assessment and prior to the finalization of the allocation process at national level (CEC, 2006).

Politically, it may not be easy for Member States to introduce significant auctioning whilst also cutting back on their initially proposed total volumes; but there are strong grounds for doing so. Recent discussions suggest that at least some major Member States may use this flexibility around auctioning. This also raises the possibility of sufficient auction volumes to enable a coordinated minimum auction reserve price in phase II, which could bring big benefits in terms of increased price security (Hepburn et al., 2006).

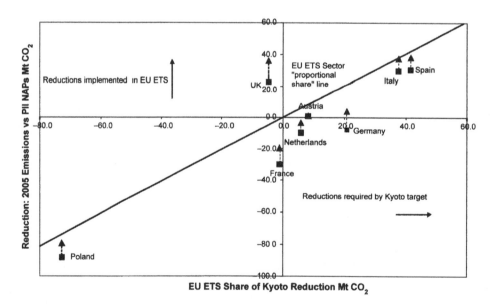

Figure 1. Comparison of proposed phase II EU ETS national allocation plants (NAPs) with estimated cutbacks required for Kyoto compliance. Note that some of the NAPs have been assessed by the Commission (end November 2006) but other NAPs were still drafts (Italy, Austria) and not officially submitted.
Source: Carbon Trust (2006) and ENTEC, with minor adaptations. (Carbon Trust, 2006).

Beyond phase II, auctioning well above 10% could be considered, and may ironically offer more effective ways than extensive free allocation to address competitiveness and leakage aspects (Demailly and Quirion, 2006) – critical issues that will need to be considered in the EU ETS review.

4. So where do we now stand?

Following the EUA price crash in May 2006, the EU Commission has come under intense pressure to restore credibility of the scheme through their review of phase II NAPs and to demonstrate that cap-and-trade schemes can deliver real environmental benefits.

The EU Commission's announcement of their decision on the first set of 10 NAPs assessed (Germany, Greece, Ireland, Latvia, Lithuania, Luxembourg, Malta, Slovakia, Sweden and the UK) did not shirk this challenge. Following a rigorous assessment,[4] the Commission asked all those Member States – except the UK – to reduce their proposed total allocation volume. The required reductions varied, but amounted to almost 7% in aggregate (including the UK) relative to the proposed allocation volume for phase II, and to their 2005 emissions. As shown in the Epilogue of Betz et al. (2006, this issue), this will lead to substantial cuts in the ET budget, especially for the new Member States. In addition, the Commission has introduced a quantitative supplementarity provision which protects the EU ETS from excessive inflows of Kyoto units should their international market price drop, e.g. with changing demands of other regions.[5]

In publishing its Communication (CEC, 2006), the Commission has indicated its intention to move away from the more qualitative guidelines in Annex 3 of the EU ETS Directive to a more rigorous quantitative process. This move is a bold step towards a harmonized allocation at the macro level. NAPs are evaluated with regard to the newly introduced transparent and objective approval process using the same formulas, and most prominently, a uniform method for calculating each Member State's ET budget has been set. Thus, the harmonization of allocation advocated by del Rio Gonzáles (2006, this issue) has started already, although so far it is more on the macro than the micro level. However, whether Member States will accept the decisions by the Commission – especially by new Member States, since they are on track to meet their Kyoto targets but still need to cut back their allocation substantially – remains to be seen.

Getting the design right is not only a significant issue for the EU ETS but for emissions trading in general. It is highly likely that other national schemes will be linked to the EU ETS in the future and will be influenced by it. Thus, the EU ETS has the opportunity of contributing to the emergence of an efficient and effective global trading. Conversely, an inefficient and ineffective EU scheme would set a dangerous international precedent.

Therefore it is very important that the European Commission rigorously evaluates the proposed second-phase NAPs and that both Member States and the EU Commission work together to solve the more fundamental design issues – such as a higher proportion of auctioning or the rules for new entrants and closure – in the long run. Only by drawing on the lessons learned can emissions trading in Europe develop to realize its full potential.

Notes

1   Recently, proposals for similar schemes have followed in other countries and States, e.g. Norway, and the north-eastern US states known as the Regional Greenhouse Gas Initiative (RGGI).

2   Ellerman and Buchner (2006) point out that a long position of the market *per se* does not provide evidence of over-allocation, as installation that undertook abatement in order to sell allowances also appear in the 'excess' data. In addition, it has been argued that equal distribution of the total allocation over the 3-year trading period has resulted in a surplus of allowances in the first year of the trading phase. This may be true for new Member States if ongoing growth was assumed during allocation, in which case there may be a deficit of allowances towards the end of the 3-year period.

3   To the author's knowledge, this comprehensive study by Kettner et al. (2007) uses the most recent and detailed database. Their figures on excess volume fall in the range quoted publicly, e.g. 80 million tons (Ellerman and Buchner, 2006) and 200 million tons (CEC 2006). However, the figures do not include the allowances that will enter the phase I market via new entrants allocation out of reserves and auctioned directly by a few MS.

4   According to the Communication published in November 2006 (CEC, 2006), a much more consistent, transparent and objective approval process was launched for NAP-2s compared with NAP-1s, based on the following process. (1) Each MS cap is assessed using a generic formula based on verified 2005 data, growth factors and reduction potential estimates, ensuring that criteria 2 and 3 are fulfilled. The factors are all derived from the same source, thus trying to counteract exaggeration of the emissions budget driven by national self-interest. (2) At least a 'fair' proportion of the 'remaining effort' (2004 GHGs compared with the Kyoto target) should be borne by the sectors covered by the ETS. (3) The substantiation of expected government purchase of Kyoto units, reliance on other policies and measures, as well as the projections of the transport sector's CO_2 emissions, are separately assessed. If those are not acceptable, the 'remaining effort' will be increased.

5   Supplementarity is assessed taking government and private-sector use of Kyoto mechanisms into account, based on three different formulas used to calculate the 'effort', where the formula that results in the greatest effort is selected. A maximum of half of that amount can be met by the government and private sector using Kyoto mechanisms. Where the government intends to meet more than 40% of its 'effort' using Kyoto mechanisms, the private sector can still use up to a maximum of 10% (CEC, 2006). The three formulas are:

A = base year emissions – emissions allowed under Kyoto target
B = greenhouse gas emissions in 2004 – emissions allowed under Kyoto target
C = projected emissions in 2010 – emissions allowed under Kyoto target

References in this Special Issue of *Climate Policy*

Åhman, M., Holmgren, K., 2006. New entrant allocation in the Nordic energy sectors: incentives and options in the EU ETS. Climate Policy 6(4), 423–440.

Betz, R., Rogge, K., Schleich, J., 2006. EU emissions trading: an early analysis of national allocation plans for 2008–2012. Climate Policy 6(4), 361–394.

del Rio González, P., 2006. Harmonization versus decentralization in the EU ETS: an economic analysis. Climate Policy 6(4), 457–475.

Grubb, M., Ferrario, F., 2006. False confidences: forecasting errors and emission caps in CO_2 trading systems. Climate Policy 6(4), 495–501.

Kemfert, C., Kohlhaas, M., Truong, T., Protsenko, A., 2006. The environmental and economic effects of European emissions trading. Climate Policy 6(4), 441–455.

Neuhoff, K., Åhman, M., Betz, R., Cludius, J., Ferrario, F., Holmgren, K., Pal, G., Grubb, M., Matthes, F., Rogge, K., Sato, M., Schleich, J., Sijm, J., Tuerk, A., Kettner, C., Walker, N., 2006a. Implications of announced phase II national allocation plans for the EU ETS. Climate Policy 6(4), 411–422.

Neuhoff, K., Ferrario, F., Grubb, M., Gabel, E., Keats, K., 2006b. Emission projections 2008–2012 versus national allocation plans II. Climate Policy 6(4), 395–410.

Palmer, K., Burtraw, D., Kahn, D., 2006. Simple rules for targeting CO_2 allowance allocations to compensate firms. Climate Policy 6(4), 477–493.

References

Carbon Trust, 2006. EU ETS News Flow for an Investor Audience: Analysis of Available Phase II NAP Data. Report prepared by ENTEC UK Limited, London.

CEC, 2006. Communication from the Commissions to the Council, and the European Parliament on the Assessment of National Allocation Plans for the Allocation of Greenhouse Gas Emission Allowances in the Second Period of the EU Emissions Trading Scheme. CEC, Brussels.

Demailly, D., Quirion, P., 2006. CO_2 abatement, competitiveness and leakage in the European cement industry under the EU ETS: grandfathering versus output-based allocation. Climate Policy 6(1), 93–114.

Ellerman, D., Buchner, B., 2006. Over-Allocation or Abatement? A Preliminary Analysis of the EU ETS based on the 2005 Emissions Data. FEEM Working Paper 139.2006.

Grubb, M., Neuhoff, K., 2006. Allocation and competitiveness in the EU emissions trading scheme: policy overview. Climate Policy 6(1), 7–30.

Hepburn, C., Grubb, M., Neuhoff, K., Matthes, F., Tse, M., 2006. Auctioning of EU ETS phase II allowances: how and why. Climate Policy 6(1), 137–160.

Kettner, C., Köppl, A., Schleicher, S.P., Therius, G., 2007. Stringency and distribution in the EU Emissions Trading Scheme – the 2005 evidence. Climate Policy 7, forthcoming.

Montgomery, D.W., 1972. Markets in licenses and efficient pollution control programs. Journal of Economic Theory 5, 395–418.

Rogge, K., Schleich, J., Betz, R., 2006. An Early Assessment of National Allocation Plans for Phase 2 of EU Emission Trading. Working Paper Sustainability and Innovation No. S1/2006, Karlsruhe, Germany.

Sijm, J., Neuhoff, K., Chen, Y., 2006. CO_2 cost pass-through and windfall profits in the power sector. Climate Policy 6(1), 49–72.

Smale, J., Hartley, M., Hepburn, C., Ward, J., Grubb, M., 2006. The impact of CO_2 emissions trading on firm profits and market prices. Climate Policy 6(1), 31–48.

EU emissions trading: an early analysis of national allocation plans for 2008–2012

Regina Betz[1], Karoline Rogge[2,3], Joachim Schleich[2,4]*

[1] *Centre for Energy and Environmental Markets (CEEM), School of Economics, University of New South Wales (UNSW), Sydney 2052, Australia*
[2] *Fraunhofer Institute for Systems and Innovation Research (Fraunhofer ISI), Breslauer Strasse 48, 76139 Karlsruhe, Germany*
[3] *Swiss Federal Institute of Technology Zürich (ETH Zürich), Department of Management, Technology and Economics, Group for Sustainability and Technology (SusTec), Zürich, Switzerland*
[4] *Virginia Polytechnic Institute and State University, Blacksburg, Virginia, USA*

Abstract

Based on 18 national allocation plans (NAPs) submitted to the European Commission for phase II (2008–2012) of the EU Emissions Trading Scheme (EU ETS), we find that, on average, the ET budgets in phase II are only about 2.6% below historical emissions in 2005, about 3.1% lower than the budgets in phase I (2005–2007), and 3% below projected emissions in 2010. While the EU-15 Member States (MS) intend to reduce emissions by about 8–11%, the implied excess allocation in the new Member States lies between 17% and 31%. Compared with a cost-efficient split of the required emission reductions, the ET budgets in the EU-15 MS are generally too large. Thus, in total, the burden for the non-trading sectors (households, tertiary and transport) is too high. Furthermore, the high shares of governments' intended and companies' possible use of Kyoto mechanisms challenge the supplementarity principle. Our detailed analyses of the allocation methods of these NAPs (across countries and phases) suggest that MS should adhere to the concepts and methodologies developed in phase I. This implies that only a little progress has been made towards achieving more efficient and more harmonized allocation rules across MS. Untapped potentials to improve environmental effectiveness and economic efficiency crucially hinge on the outcome of the Commission's review process.

Keywords: Climate policy; Emissions trading; Economic efficiency; Environmental effectiveness; National allocation plan

1. Introduction

As its key climate policy instrument, in January 2005 the European Union launched an EU-wide trading scheme (EU ETS) for CO_2 emissions from companies in the energy industry and other carbon-intensive industry sectors. In total, the approximately 11,500 installations covered by the

---

* Corresponding author. Tel.: +49-721-6809-203; fax: +49-721-6809-272
E-mail address: Joachim.Schleich@isi.fraunhofer.de

EU ETS account for nearly 45% of total CO_2 emissions, and about 30% of all greenhouse gases in the EU (CEC, 2005b). The EU ETS is supposed to help its Member States (MS) meet their greenhouse gas emission targets cost-efficiently, i.e. to achieve their Kyoto targets at minimum cost. This emission reduction target for the greenhouse gases CO_2, CH_4, N_2O, SF_6, PFCs and HFCs for the EU-15 MS is 8% by 2008–2012 compared with 1990/1995 base-year levels. In the Burden-Sharing Agreement this target was broken down into differential targets for individual MS. The reduction target for the 10 new MS is usually 8%, with the exceptions of 6% for Hungary and Poland, and no targets at all for Cyprus and Malta.

The costs of reducing emissions will eventually be reflected in the market price for EU emission allowances (EUA) and will induce a demand for innovative, energy/carbon saving processes, products and services. This increased demand should in turn lead to more research and development, and the invention, adoption and market diffusion of such innovations. The extent of the technological change induced by the EU ETS crucially depends on the scheme's design (Gagelmann and Frondel, 2005; Schleich and Betz, 2005). In general, this is governed by the EU Emission Trading Directive 2003/87/EC (CEC, 2003b) and country-specific design features are determined by the national allocation plans (NAPs) of the individual MS for each trading period. The first trading period of the EU ETS is from 2005 to 2007 (phase I); the second trading period (phase II) coincides with the Kyoto commitment period from 2008 to 2012. At the macro level, NAPs state the total quantity of allowances available in each period (ET budget); at the micro level, they determine how these allowances will be allocated to individual installations. Thus, at the macro level, the NAPs determine to what extent the individual MS may rely on the EU ETS to achieve their emission targets. In particular, the NAPs establish how to 'split the pie': How many allowances should be allocated to the installations covered by the EU ETS trading sectors (i.e. from energy and industry sectors), and which emission reductions are expected from the household, services and transport sectors, which are not covered by the EU ETS (non-trading sectors)? The combined emission budgets for trading and non-trading sectors also determine to what extent MS rely on domestic efforts and to what extent on the Flexible Mechanisms of the Kyoto Protocol to meet their emission targets, i.e. International Emission Trading, the Clean Development Mechanism (CDM) and Joint Implementation (JI). Finally, macro plans provide a first indication of the additional efforts necessary to meet medium- and long-term emission reduction targets. For example, the EU Council considers greenhouse gas emission reductions of 15–30% (compared to 1990 levels) by 2020 a necessary mid-term target for industrialized countries in order to limit the mean global temperature increase to 2° Celsius compared with pre-industrialized levels (European Council, 2005).

The size of the ET budget at the macro level of the NAPs indicates whether the EU ETS is environmentally effective in terms of reducing CO_2 emissions. The allocation rules specified at the micro level for existing and new installations and for closures shape the incentives for innovation and long-term investments in low-carbon energy technologies and in energy efficiency in the industry sectors. In terms of distribution, the micro plan also predetermines the winners and losers of emissions trading. All NAPs need to be approved by the EC, based on the criteria specified in Annex III of the Emission Trading Directive (CEC, 2003b) and in the NAP guidance (CEC, 2004a, 2005a).

In this article, we provide a comprehensive first analysis and evaluation of the NAPs submitted at the time of writing (mid-October 2006). Even though the deadline for submission of phase-2 NAPs was 30 June 2006, only 16 NAPs had been submitted by mid-October (Belgium, Cyprus (first submitted version), Estonia, France (first submitted version), Germany, Greece, Ireland, Latvia, Lithuania,

Luxembourg, Malta, the Netherlands, Poland, Slovakia, Sweden and the UK). To be more representative in terms of the emissions covered, we also include, whenever possible, data from the draft NAPs of Italy and Spain. To save space, at times we omit information on Cyprus and Malta, which are not subject to a Kyoto obligation and only have a very limited number of installations covered by the EU ETS. Therefore this article covers 16 NAPs and two draft NAPs with a total proposed budget of EUA for approx. 1,892 million tonnes of CO_2e per annum (one EUA corresponds to 1 tonne of CO_2e). In phase I, these 18 countries hold 87% of all allowances allocated in the EU ETS.

The structure of the article is as follows. Section 2 consists of the macro-level analysis. This includes a brief assessment of Member States' progress towards meeting their Kyoto targets and governments' intended and companies' possible use of credits from Kyoto mechanisms. Then we evaluate the stringency of the ET budgets using historical emissions, the size of the ET budgets in phase I, and projected emissions in 2010 as benchmarks. We also appraise the split of the required emission reductions between the ET sectors and the remaining sectors (including non-CO_2 sources) from a cost-efficiency perspective. Section 3 includes the micro-level analysis and assesses the allocation rules for existing and new installations, for closures and for clean technologies, based on insights from economic theory. We also survey provisions for process-related emissions, early action, small emitters and special reserves. The rules at the micro level are also compared with those applied in phase I. A summary table in the Appendix provides a comprehensive overview of the micro plans. Finally, the concluding Section 4 briefly summarizes the main results, points to areas of improved harmonization and efficiency, and offers guidance for the future design of the EU ETS and its possible application to other sectors and regions. In the Epilogue, we present the European Commission's decisions on the phase-II budgets of the first 10 NAPs published on 29 November 2006, and relate these to the findings of our article at the macro level.

2. Macro-level analysis of national allocation plans

2.1. Progress towards Kyoto: distance-to-target analysis

To set the stage, we first examine whether MS are on track to meet their individual burden-sharing or Kyoto targets and to which extent governments intend to rely on Kyoto mechanisms (KM). The black bars in Figure 1 reflect each EU Member State's burden-sharing or Kyoto commitment (as a percentage of base-year emission levels), while the white bars indicate the distance to achieving these targets as of 2004 (as a percentage and in $MtCO_2e/a$ in Figure 2).

Accordingly, apart from the new MS, which are clearly on a path towards reaching their Kyoto emission targets, only France, Greece, Sweden and the UK appear to be on target, while most other EU-15 MS will need to make substantial additional efforts to meet their targets. The striped bars in Figures 1 and 2 reveal how this distance-to-target (DTT) indicator improves for MS intending to use KM, i.e. in our sample for Belgium, Italy, Ireland, Luxembourg, the Netherlands, Spain and Sweden.[1] In total, these MS intend to purchase CERs, ERUs or AAUs for emissions of approx. 114 $MtCO_2e/a$, which represent a share of 3.1% of the assigned amount of the 11 EU-15 MS under consideration (for the seven MS using KM: 8.8% of the assigned amount) or 45.5% (50.3%) of these Member States' aggregate gap to reach the Kyoto target in 2004 (DTT_{2004} approx. –251 $MtCO_2e/a$, or –227 $MtCO_2e/a$, respectively). Data are based on the most recent UNFCCC national inventory reports for 2004 (UNFCCC, 2006) excluding land use, land-use change and forestry (LULUCF).

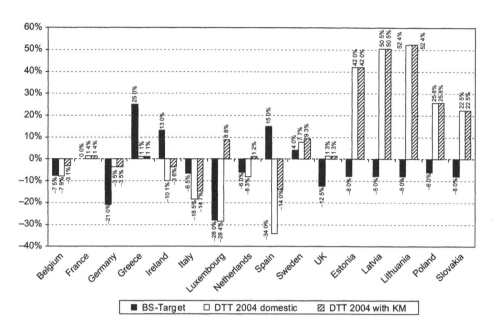

Figure 1. Kyoto burden-sharing and distance-to-target analysis (as a percentage of base-year emissions) (as of 2004).
Source: Fraunhofer ISI, based on UNFCCC national inventory reports and its common reporting format 2006 (NIR/CRF).

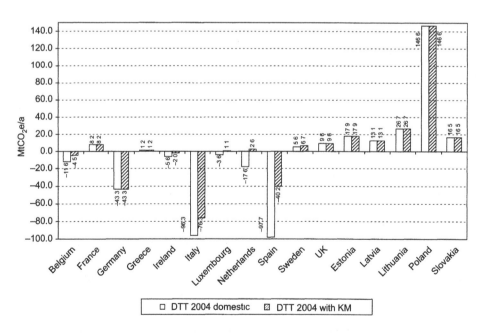

Figure 2. Distance-to-target analysis (in MtCO$_2$e/a) (as of 2004).
Source: Fraunhofer ISI, based on UNFCCC national inventory reports 2006 (NIR/CRF).

In addition, the Linking Directive (CEC, 2004b) allows companies to use credits from projects under Joint Implementation (JI) and the Clean Development Mechanism (CDM) to cover their emissions under the EU ETS. Based on the supplementarity requirements of the Marrakech Accords and the Kyoto Protocol, the EU ETS Directive also requires that the use of these mechanisms must be supplemental to domestic action (see Art. 30.3, CEC, 2004b). In line with the Linking Directive, MS specified the use of the mechanisms by companies as a percentage of allocation in their NAPs (KM limit) (Art. 5, CEC, 2004b). Since these credits and EUA can be traded without restriction between companies, the total available amount within the EU (including Bulgaria and Romania) will be the overall limit. For a supplementarity analysis, credits from CDM and JI projects used by domestic firms need to be added to the amount of Kyoto units (AAUs) that the governments intend to use to meet their Kyoto/burden-sharing targets.

As shown in Figure 3, the KM limits differ substantially across countries and range from 0% in Estonia and Malta to 50% in Ireland and Spain. There are also differences in how the limits will be implemented. First, some MS (e.g. the UK) require the limits to be met each year, but permit banking. Other countries (e.g. Germany, Luxembourg) permit banking and borrowing, so that the limit has to be met for the 5-year trading period only. Second, most limits are implemented at the level of installations but some are applied at the level of the entire ET sector (e.g. Slovakia) under a first-come-first-served policy. Greece allows these limits to be transferred across companies, i.e. operators may use the remainders of other installations' percentages. Third, in some instances, different limits for the power and industry sectors have been set in order to compensate the power sector for a more stringent allocation (e.g. Flanders). Since companies may trade credits from JI or CDM projects for EUA, restrictions imposed by individual MS on the use of these credits will only be binding at the aggregate level (in the 18 MS included in this article, the total would be approx. 289 $MtCO_2e/a$).

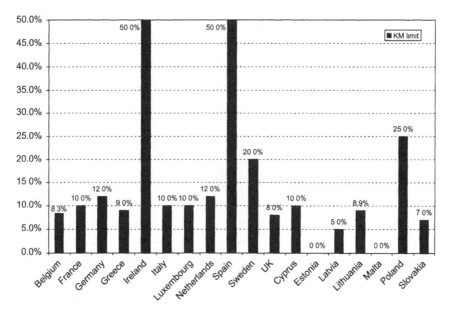

Figure 3. Limit for use of Kyoto mechanisms at installation level across countries (as a percentage of allocation).
Source: Fraunhofer ISI, based on phase 2 NAPs.

The sum of companies' maximum use (289 MtCO$_2$e/a) and governments' intended purchases (114 MtCO$_2$e/a) from the Kyoto mechanisms are approximately 403 MtCO$_2$e/a. This figure relates to a distance-to-target (as of 2004) of the 18 MS examined, of some 30 MtCO$_2$e/a only, which clearly shows that there would be no need for domestic reductions at all for these MS; but there are substantial differences across MS. Whether governments and companies will actually be able to use some or all of the KMs as stated in the NAPs depends on prices (and thus on sufficient supply) and also on the Commission's ruling. In particular, some MS (notably Ireland, the Netherlands and Luxembourg) appear to be at odds with existing interpretations of the supplementarity rule. The supplementarity requirement referred to by the criteria specified in Art. 30.3 of the EU ETS was originally formulated in the Kyoto Protocol (e.g. Art. 17) and the Marrakech Accords, but it is qualitative rather than quantitative. The EC will have to develop and apply new quantitative criteria, or it may refer to the one it originally proposed in the international negotiations (European Council, 1999) leading to the Marrakech Accords.

2.2. Stringency of national ET budgets

The stringency of the combined national ET budgets determines the relation between supply and demand and therefore also the prices of EUA in the market. Most notably, prices for EUA hovered around €26/EUA from January 2006 until the end of April 2006, but plummeted to around €10/EUA in response to the publication of verified emissions data for 2005, which indicated a surplus of about 44 million EUA for 2005 (CEC, 2006d). Figure 4 compares actual allocation[2] and actual emissions in 2005[3] using CITL data as of 23 October 2006, and shows an even increased excess allocation of almost 100 million EUA for 2005 or 4.7%.[4] Only very few countries allocated numbers of EUA in 2005 below the actual 2005 emission levels of the ET sector (Austria, Greece, Italy, Ireland, Spain and the UK).

We assess the stringency of the ET budgets for NAP 2 based on the following criteria.

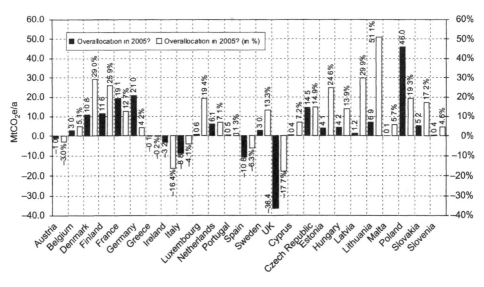

Figure 4. Allocation for 2005 compared to emissions in 2005 (in MtCO$_2$e/a and as a percentage).
Source: Fraunhofer ISI, based on NAP and registry data (CITL as of 23 October 2006).

Criterion 1: Second-phase ET budgets compared to verified emissions for 2005

As a first criterion, we compare the proposed phase-2 ET budget (without NER) with historical emissions of the EU ETS. Since it provides verified recent historical emissions data for the ET sector, we use the 2005 VET data (verified emissions table) rather than other measures for historical emissions such as those published in the NAPs for the various country-specific base periods. For the assessment we compare the VET 2005 data with the ET budget for 2008–2012 (without the New Entrant Reserve for installations going online in 2008–2012). There are three major caveats in using VET 2005 data and interpreting the results. First, the VET 2005 data do not incorporate the extended scope of the EU ETS in most Member States in phase II, an outcome of the EC's efforts to harmonize the types of installations included in the EU ETS across countries.[5] So far, these additional installations correspond to an increase of approximately 45.9 million EUA p.a. in the allocation for 2008–2012.[6] We address this issue by adjusting the phase-II budget downwards by the proposed allocation of these additional installations. Second, the Netherlands and the UK have applied opt-out rules in phase I, so that their VET 2005 data do not include the emissions of installations that have been temporarily excluded from the scheme. For phase II, the EU ETS Directive does not foresee such opt-outs. As a consequence, we subtract the estimates for opt-outs from the proposed phase-II budgets in these countries.[7] Third, Art. 24.1 of the EU ETS Directive allows MS to include further sources and gases in addition to the opt-in possibilities in phase I, depending on approval by the Commission.[8] To compute the share of the ET sector, we divide total (verified) CO_2 emissions from the ET installations in 2005 (CEC, 2006c) – adjusted upward by the emissions of additional installations and opt-outs – by the total GHG emissions of a country using national inventory data for 2004 (UNFCCC, 2006), excluding (as always) emissions from LULUCF. In order to arrive at consistent comparisons of the data across phases, we did not consider the allocation intended for these new opt-ins. In our assessment, a MS is considered to meet criterion 1 if the adjusted ET budget in phase II is below the verified emissions for 2005 in this MS.

Criterion 2: Second-phase ET budgets compared to first-phase ET budgets

For the second criterion, we compare the phase-II ET budget with that for phase I. We include the reserve for new entrants (and reserves for other purposes, such as legal claims, but not JI set-asides) in both ET budgets. Also, we again exclude the allocation foreseen for additional installations from the ET budget for phase II. Furthermore, both ET budgets need to equally incorporate the allocation levels for opt-in and opt-out installations, which we address in the same way as described in criterion 1. A Member State is said to fulfil this criterion if its adjusted ET budget for phase II is lower than the ET budget for phase I.

Criterion 3: Second-phase ET budgets compared to projected emissions for 2010

As a third criterion, we compare the phase-II ET budget (including NER) with the projected CO_2 emissions of the ET sector. If a projection is not provided in the NAP, we estimate it using the country's projection for all GHG from its NAP (Ireland, the Netherlands, Spain's draft NAP) and the ratio of CO_2 emissions of the ET sector to total GHG emissions in 2004/05. This procedure implicitly assumes that this ratio will remain constant in phase II, which might not be the case, especially in economies undergoing structural change. We used projection figures from external sources only if the NAP did not provide any data on projected emissions for 2008–2012.[9] This criterion is met if the ET budget for phase II is lower than the projected emissions.

The results of the evaluation using these three criteria are displayed in Figures 5 and 6, where negative figures mean that the ET budget in phase II is lower than verified emissions in 2005, the ET budget in 2005 and projected emissions for 2010, respectively. In general, for all three criteria,

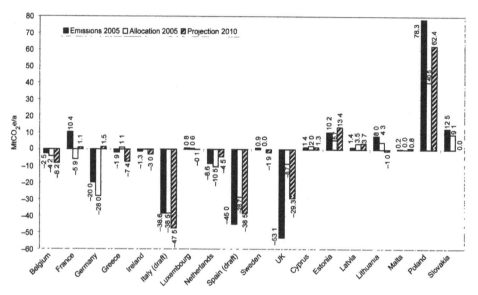

Figure 5. ET budget for phase II compared with emissions in 2005, allocation for 2005 and emission projection for 2010 (in MtCO$_2$e/a).
Source: Fraunhofer ISI based on CEC (2006c) and registry data (CITL as of 23 October 2006), EEA (2006), UNFCCC (2006) and NAPs I+II of MS.

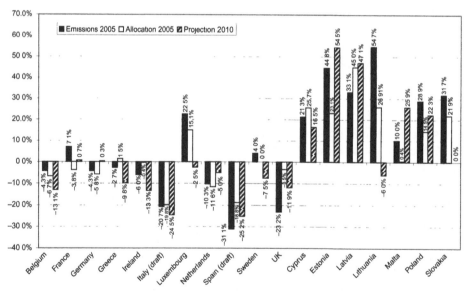

Figure 6. ET budget for phase II compared with emissions in 2005, allocation for 2005 and emission projection for 2010 (as a percentage).
Source: Fraunhofer ISI based on CEC (2006c) and registry data (CITL as of 23 October 2006), EEA (2006), UNFCCC (2006) and NAPs I+II of MS.

our assessment for the EU-15 MS differs substantially from our assessment for the new MS. More specifically, the results may be summarized as follows.

– *Historical emissions in* 2005 (black bar in Figures 5 and 6). With the exceptions of France, Luxembourg and Sweden, all EU-15 MS reduced their phase-II ET budget compared with actual emissions in 2005, while the new MS included in this article decided in favour of a budget larger than VET 2005 data. The MS with the most significant decreases in their new ET budgets compared with actual emissions in 2005 are Italy (draft NAP), Spain (draft NAP) and the UK (both in terms of absolute figures and percentages). Notably, these MS were (together with Ireland and Greece) the only MS in our sample where allocated quantities in phase I were below VET data in 2005 (see Figure 4). In addition, Poland has the largest overshoot of 2005 emissions in absolute terms, but this figure needs to be interpreted with caution as it is based on estimated data for 2005 (see note 3).
– *ET budget for phase I* (white bar in Figures 5 and 6). In the EU-15, only Greece and Luxembourg, and both only to a limited extent, increased their phase-II ET budget compared with the budget in phase I. All other EU-15 MS have decided in favour of a stricter (or evenly strict) ET budget compared with the previous one. The analysis reveals that, in absolute terms, Italy, Spain (both draft NAP) and Germany have the largest reductions. In percentage terms, Italy, Spain (both draft NAP) and the Netherlands show the largest cuts in their ET budgets. In contrast, all new MS show large upward deviations in their ET budgets, led by Poland (in absolute terms) and Latvia (in relative terms).
– *Projected emissions* (striped bar in Figures 5 and 6), While EU-15 MS chose an ET budget that is lower than projections (with the exception of France and Germany), most new MS intend to allocate more than projected emissions (with the exception of Lithuania and Slovakia). This appears particularly troublesome, as we used – whenever available – the projections provided in the NAP.[10]

Only six MS, all of them EU-15, meet all three criteria, namely Belgium, Ireland, Italy, Spain (the latter two according to their draft NAPs), the Netherlands and the UK. The results at the aggregate level of all NAPs appear in Table 1 and generally suggest that the intended allocation for the ET sector in 2008–2012 will not require significant reductions. Table 1 also portrays the dichotomy between new MS and EU-15 MS with respect to the three criteria at the aggregate level.

Table 1. Results for three criteria at aggregate level of 18 NAPs

	ET-budget in phase II compared to					
	VET 2005 (criterion 1)		ET-budget in phase I (criterion 2)		Emission projections for 2010 (criterion 3)	
	in million EUA	in % of VET 2005	in million EUA	in % of ET-budget phase I	in million EUA	in % of projected emissions
EU-15 (11)	−158.9	−11.1%	−122.8	−8.1%	−138.0	−9.1%
new MS (7)	112.1	31.1%	65.1	17.1%	80.5	21.1%
Total (18)	−46.8	−2.6%	−57.7	−3.1%	−57.5	−3.0%

Source: Fraunhofer ISI based on CEC (2006c) and registry data (CITL as of 23 October 2006), EEA (2006), UNFCCC (2006) and NAPs I+II of MS

2.3. Cost-efficiency of ET budget

To examine the extent to which MS rely on the EU ETS to meet their Kyoto burden-sharing targets, we examine whether the sizes of the ET budgets are consistent with an efficient distribution of reduction efforts between trading and non-trading sectors. From an economic perspective, the size of the budgets for the ET sector and the non-ET sector should be determined such that (before international trading starts) the total abatement costs are minimized, i.e. that the marginal costs of the abatement measures which are realized in the trading sectors and the non-trading sectors are equal. Thus, sectors with cheaper reduction measures should contribute more reductions (relatively) to achieving a country's emission target. To some extent, criterion 3 of Annex III of the EU ETS Directive – i.e. the potential to reduce emissions – addresses this issue. According to the NAP guidance (CEC, 2004a), this 'criterion will be deemed as fulfilled if the allocation reflects the relative differences in the potential between the total covered and total non-covered activities', where 'potential' also means economic, and not simply technical, potential.

Criterion 4: Hypothetical allocation scenario (HAS) between ET and non-ET sectors for 2008–2012

To derive an indicator for the cost-effectiveness of the ET budgets, we relate the size of the ET budget in the NAPs to a 'hypothetical allocation scenario between ETS and non-ETS' (HAS). To calculate this HAS, we multiply a Member State's burden-sharing or Kyoto target by the share of the ET sector's CO_2 emissions relative to total greenhouse gas emissions for 2004/05. Thus, the HAS represents the budget resulting for the trading sector (biggest parts of energy and industry), assuming that all sectors contribute proportionally to achieving a country's emission target. A similar approach was applied, for example, by Zetterberg et al. (2004), and implicitly by Betz et al. (2004), to assess the NAPs in phase I. In principle, the same caveats as described in the previous criteria apply with respect to calculating the share of ETS emissions relative to all GHG emissions.

In our analyses of the HAS of those MS intending to purchase KM (Belgium, Italy, Ireland, Luxembourg, the Netherlands, Spain and Sweden),[11] we distinguish two scenarios: a *domestic action scenario*, where we calculate the HAS without the governments' intended use of KM; and a scenario where these mechanisms result in an increase in the national emission budgets (and consequently also in the HAS). In our assessment, the NAP of a MS is considered to meet this criterion if the ET budget is not larger than the budget which corresponds to a proportional reduction of emissions to reach the Kyoto target (with and without the use of KM).

Figures 7 and 8 show the differences between the actual ET budgets and the HAS (in $MtCO_2e/a$ and as a percentage). Apart from the UK, the emission budgets for the ET sectors in all other MS are significantly larger than those which would result from a proportional contribution. Even if the governments' intended use of the Kyoto mechanisms is taken into account, in addition to the UK, only the ET budgets of the Netherlands and Spain (draft NAP) pass this test. In terms of cost efficiency, this result insinuates that the 'pie split' is not optimal in most countries. According to many studies (including Criqui and Kitous, 2003; Böhringer et al., 2005, 2006; Peterson, 2006), the marginal abatement costs of the ET sector are lower than the abatement costs of other sectors in the economy (even without considering the ETS companies' option to use 'cheap' credits from CDM or JI projects to fulfil their obligation under the EU ETS). Thus, from a cost-efficiency perspective, the ET sectors should actually make an over-proportional contribution. One obvious remedy here would be to extend the scope of the ETS to all sectors and sources.

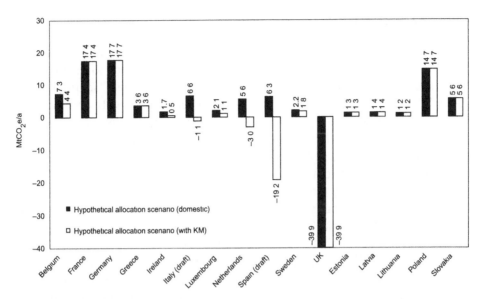

Figure 7. ET budget for phase II compared with 'hypothetical allocation scenario' (in MtCO$_2$e/a).
Source: Fraunhofer ISI based on CEC (2006c) and registry data (CITL as of 23 October 2006), UNFCCC (2006) and NAPs I+II of MS.

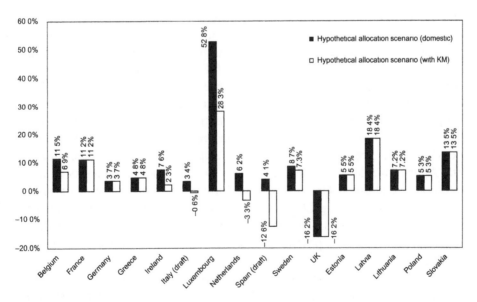

Figure 8. ET budget for phase II compared with 'hypothetical allocation scenario' (as a percentage).
Source: Fraunhofer ISI based on CEC (2006c) and registry data (CITL as of 23 October 2006), UNFCCC (2006) and NAPs I+II of MS.

3. Analysis of allocation rules at the micro level

Similar to phase I of the EU ETS[12], most MS allocate the entire ET budget for free in phase II (see Appendix). Likewise, the majority of MS again apply a two-step approach to determine the quantities of EUA to be allocated to individual installations. In the first step, sector budgets (SB) are determined, usually based on a combination of historical emission levels or average benchmarks, growth projections, emission-saving potentials (EF = efficiency factor) and a compliance factor (CF) required to reach the overall ET budget. In the second step, the sector budgets are then allocated to individual installations (IA = installation allocation), typically based on their share of emissions in a base period (rather than on output or capacity). Technically, most EU-15 MS apply sector-specific compliance factors (see Appendix) to guarantee the consistency of the bottom-up allocation to individual installations with the sector budgets. In the simplest case, there are only two budgets: one for energy and one for industry.[13] Since most of the new MS (e.g. Estonia, Latvia and Slovakia) will easily reach their Kyoto targets, they will not need to use either sector budgets or compliance factors at installation level. In all MS, these basic allocation rules are supplemented by special provisions serving particular distributional purposes, for example to account for clean technologies, process-related emissions, early action or small emitters. In addition, the micro plans include KM limits and may also provide information on special reserves. In the remainder of this section, we analyse the allocation rules for existing installations, for new projects (including new entrant reserves) and for closures in more detail, drawing primarily on arguments from economic theory. The section also covers special provisions and special reserves.

3.1. Basic allocation rules for existing installations

As can be seen from the Appendix, most MS allocate allowances to existing installations for free based on historical emissions in a fairly recent base period which typically consists of several years (conventional grandfathering). Most MS in our sample use data from the year 2005 to determine the number of EUAs to be allocated to individual installations (through base periods extending to 2005). One reason for this violation of the guidance provided by the EC (CEC, 2005a) may be that verified emissions data at the level of installations were readily available for 2005. Only a few MS avoided such updating and employed earlier years (e.g. Ireland, Sweden and the UK) or projected data (e.g. Greece). Several countries, such as Belgium, Italy, Latvia, Spain, Sweden and the UK, base their allocation for some existing installations – mostly power installations – on benchmarks (BM), and France and Poland use average benchmarks to determine the size of the sector budgets. Apart from France, these countries did not use benchmarks to allocate EUA to existing installations in phase I. Under benchmarking, allocation is based on specific emission values per unit of production (e.g. kg CO_2/MWh electricity or t CO_2/t cement clinker) for a particular group of products or installations. The actual number of allowances can be derived from the specific benchmark multiplied by past or predicted individual-specific or standardized activity rates for individual installations.

A benchmarking allocation at installation level favours carbon-efficient installations over less carbon-efficient installations, since operators of the latter need to purchase missing allowances on the market or will have fewer excess allowances. Average benchmarks are calculated as the activity-weighted average of emission values for a particular group. Therefore benchmarks based on the average technology installed result in a higher allocation for all companies than benchmarks based on the best available technology (BAT benchmarks). Benchmarks may be uniformly applied to all installations in a group or differentiated according to fuel inputs, technologies or products. Both types of benchmarks may be associated with high distributional effects compared with conventional grandfathering. Benchmarks used to determine the sector budget will not have these effects if allocation at the level of installations is based on the share of historical emissions.[14]

The majority of benchmarks are fuel- and/or technology-specific average benchmarks rather than uniform benchmarks or BAT benchmarks.[15] Exceptions include Flanders and Wallonia in Belgium, where a uniform BAT benchmark is applied for power installations, and Sweden, where allocation for basic oxygen steel furnaces is based on an EU-wide average benchmark.

Assessment: benchmarking versus grandfathering for existing installations

As long as full auctioning is not feasible (see next subsection), benchmarking may be preferable to conventional grandfathering for reasons of perceived fairness and efficiency. Since benchmarking to existing installations accounts for early action, it may lead to the desired distributional effects. The use of differentiated benchmarks cushions these effects. Also, as argued by Cremer and Schleich (2006), the deficit and surplus may be capped by upper and lower bounds. If companies can directly affect their allocation (updating), benchmarking leads to more efficient outcomes than conventional grandfathering (Cremer and Schleich, 2006; Sterner and Muller, 2006). For example, for installations receiving fewer free allowances under benchmarking than under conventional grandfathering, benchmarking provides a greater incentive to substitute inefficient installations if closures result in a termination of allocation (see also Section 3.4 on closures). The tighter the benchmark, the higher this incentive would be. Finally, benchmarking would facilitate comparison across EU MS and may be seen as a first step towards harmonized allocation rules throughout the EU (Kruger and Pizer, 2004).

The potential drawbacks of benchmarking include more stringent data requirements and the need to form benchmarking groups (see, for example, Radov et al., 2005). Also, distributional effects may be high even if differentiated benchmarks are used which might render them politically unfeasible (Cremer and Schleich, 2006). As in phase I, distributional aspects and the lack of sufficient data prevented the use of benchmarks for existing installations in several countries. In the NAP guidance for phase II, the EC stated that

> EU-wide benchmarking is not a sufficiently matured allocation method to be used for phase 2. Member States may, however, find appropriate use for benchmarking at national level for the installation level allocation in certain sectors and for new entrants, e.g. in the electricity sector (CEC, 2005a, p. 8).

The observation that benchmarks tend to be applied to power installations supports the view that the electricity sector is particularly well suited to benchmarking, since its output is fairly homogeneous and it is relatively easy to assign installations to benchmarking groups.

3.2. Auctioning

While in phase I of the EU ETS, only four MS (Denmark, Hungary, Ireland and Lithuania) chose to auction off parts of their ET budget (with an annual total of only 4.5 million EUA); more MS will do so in phase II. Similarly, the shares will usually be larger but tend to be well below the maximum share of 10% allowed by the ETS Directive in phase II. More specifically, in our sample of 18 NAPs, seven include auctioning for phase II, ranging from a share of 0.5% in Ireland and Flanders to 7% in the UK. In five of those MS, there was no auctioning in phase I.[16] Compared to the first period where the total number of EUA auctioned p.a. is 4.5 million, this share is now about 24.5 million EUA, which corresponds to 1.3% of the ET budgets (including reserves) for the MS included in this survey. The auction share would have been even higher if the French NAP, which now shows an auction share of zero, had kept the high share of up to 10% originally proposed in the draft NAP. The current NAPs provide sufficient information on the intended use of the revenues, but no information is given on the actual auctioning rules such as types, timing or frequency. In Flanders, Lithuania, Luxembourg and Poland, auction revenues are supposed to finance further emission reductions internally or externally (via buying Kyoto units); in the Netherlands they are to benefit 'low-volume users' of electricity in the ET sector and other sectors (Dutch NAPII, p. 14), and in Ireland to finance the scheme's administrative costs. Poland and Luxembourg have plans to restrict participation in the auction to domestic operators, but this may violate EU competition regulations.

Assessment: auctioning versus free allocation

While the method of allocation does not – at least under ideal conditions such as in the absence of market power – affect the market price for EUA, participating companies are better off if allowances are allocated for free, since their wealth increases by the total value of these allowances. Thus allocating all allowances free of charge is politically more palatable which may explain the observed low shares of the ET budgets that MS intend to auction off.

From an economics perspective, auctioning is generally preferred to conventional grandfathering (e.g. Pezzey and Park, 1998; Cramton and Kerr, 2002; Dinan and Rogers, 2002; Böhringer and Lange, 2005); auctioning off all allowances could avoid most, if not all, of the problems and distributional aspects which result in inefficient and complex rules in several MS. These aspects include accounting for early action, excess allocation at installation level,[17] or the treatment of new installations and closures (see subsequent sections for further details). Thus, if all allowances were auctioned off, the NAPs would be much simpler, more transparent and more efficient. In addition, the outcome of an auction may be perceived as 'fair' because – in contrast to a free allocation of allowances – the 'polluter pays' principle holds. Auctioning off part of the budget right at the beginning of the trading period may also generate robust early price signals for the actual scarcity in the market, since participants base their bidding behaviour on their marginal abatement costs (and expected prices in the secondary market) (e.g. Schmalensee et al., 1998; Ehrhart et al., 2005).

Auctioning off allowances would also address 'windfall profits'. Since companies try to pass on any additional marginal costs (opportunity costs) associated with emissions (i.e. price of allowances) to customers, extra profits (windfall profits) accrue if allowances are allocated for free. Opportunity cost pricing is not only sensible from an economic perspective, it is also essential for an ETS to send the correct price signals to provide adequate incentives to cut emissions and minimize total reduction costs. Thus, any attempts to directly regulate the price for EUA, for example by setting a cap, would be counterproductive. Whether allowances are auctioned off or allocated for free does not alter the opportunity costs (of additional emissions), but leads to very different outcomes in terms of the distribution of the scarcity rents associated with allowances. Empirical observations for the first phase suggest that the power sector, which faces a fairly inelastic demand (at least in the short run), has managed to pass on a large part of the opportunity costs to its customers. As a consequence, the power sector was able to secure high windfall profits. According to Sijm et al. (2006), the pass-through rates vary between 60% and 100%, depending on the country, market structure, demand elasticity and CO_2 price considered. Also, under (at least partially) free allocation, companies' profits in the product market (e.g. electricity) may rise if prices for EUA increase (above competitive prices) and if these increases can be passed on to consumers in the product markets. The observation that the price for EUA in the (rather thin) spot market did not drop to zero, but instead remained around or above €10 – 15 per EUA once the size of the surplus of allowances became common knowledge, has led to speculations that some large power companies exerted market power to support a high price of allowances in order to be able to charge a higher price for their entire electricity production (Misiolek and Elder, 1989). Of course, there are alternative or complementary explanations, including uncertainty about future demand, or regulatory uncertainty from pending legal procedures concerning allocation rules in several MS.

Although not all countries use auctioning, most of the EU-15 MS address windfall profits by splitting the reduction burden unequally between the industry and energy sectors. In principle, Germany, Italy, the UK and Sweden, for example, determine the size of the budget for the power sector as the residual of the ET budget once allocation to other installations has been determined. The Netherlands apply an additional specific reduction factor of 0.15 to existing power installations to correct for windfall profits.

3.3. Allocation rules for new projects

As was already the case in phase I, in the second period all MS will establish a New Entrant Reserve to allocate allowances to new projects (i.e. new installations and capacity extensions of existing installations) for free, usually on a first-come-first-served basis. The only exceptions are non-CHP plants in the Swedish power sector, which have to buy all their allowances on the market. As in phase I, gratis allocation in most MS is typically based on BAT values for individual installations or on BAT benchmarks for homogeneous products (or technologies). Benchmarks are common in the energy sector, where they tend to be differentiated by fuel inputs. So far only Luxembourg, Sweden, Flanders and Wallonia in Belgium, and the UK are applying uniform benchmarks. If BAT benchmarks are used for new projects in industry sectors, they tend to be technology-specific, and often assume gas as the fuel input (e.g. Latvia, UK). Sometimes, product groups are further split into subgroups (e.g. different types of tiles or glass in Germany). France, which has applied average benchmarks for allocation to new projects in phase I, now also plans to draw on BAT benchmarks.

Assessment: allocation rules for new projects

Neither the Emissions Trading Directive nor the NAP guidance make any recommendations on how new projects should be treated, even though the Commission would have preferred newcomers to buy allowances on the market, e.g. European Commission DG Environment (CEC, 2003a). In principle, three methods are acceptable under the Directive: auctioning from a set-aside reserve, purchasing EUA on the market, or free allocation (from a reserve for new entrants). The logic of emissions trading requires that all allowances for new projects be purchased at market prices, since investment decisions can then be based on the full social costs (i.e. private costs plus environmental cost). As already pointed out by Spoulber (1985), allocating allowances for free to new projects amounts to subsidizing investments (and output), and thus increases – *ceteris paribus* – the total costs to society of achieving climate targets. However, under the current closure rules, which essentially provide an output subsidy to incumbent installations (see Section 3.4), free allocation to new entrants may be considered second-best (Åhman and Holmgren, 2006, this issue).

Having to buy allowances for new projects on the secondary market or at an auction would provide strong monetary incentives to implement energy-efficient, low-carbon technologies, since these technologies require the purchase of fewer allowances. Allocating allowances to new projects based on uniform BAT benchmarks and uniform standardized projections of production or utilization rates for homogeneous products would only be second-best. In this case, investments in technologies which generate fewer specific emissions than the benchmark generate extra allowances that can be sold on the market. Thus, uniform benchmarks create strong incentives to invest in the most efficient technology within a given product group, independent of the level of the benchmark. In contrast, technologies which are less efficient than the benchmark cause additional costs through the necessary purchase of allowances. Any additional differentiation (e.g. by fuels, processes, or by utilization rates) implies additional subsidization of particular installations and further reduces the cost-saving potential of the EU ETS. In particular, the more sub-benchmarks there are within a product group or within a technology group, the smaller the innovation effects, since innovation incentives are limited to the subgroups.

As shown by Neuhoff et al. (2006a) and by Åhman and Holmgren (2006, this issue), applying the BAT benchmark rules across MS to the same new power plant would result in substantial differences in terms of allocation. To a large extent, these differences are the result of differences in the BAT values and activity rates applied (projected output, standardized load factors). Thus, inefficiencies not only arise from differentiated benchmarks but also from differences in the activity rates used. Ideally, to avoid this additional source of inefficiency, identical activity rates would have to be used for all technologies or fuels. For example, Germany, Luxemburg and the UK apply the same activity rates for allocation to all power installations (connected to the grid) of 7,500 hours in Germany, 6,500 hours in Luxembourg and 5,600 hours in the UK. In addition, there are differences in the compliance factors applied to new projects across MS (e.g. Wallonia, Spain, UK), if these are applied at all to new projects.

The increased use of standardized activity rates in phase II compared with phase I also avoids the risk of 'optimistic' projections by operators. Such installation-specific projections are primarily found in the NAPs of new MS. Germany has switched from relying on such individual projections to standardized utilization rates. However, if these rates are rather high – as, for example, for energy installations in the German power and some industry sectors – the use of standardized rates does not necessarily conserve the NER.

NER – size and rules

If new entrants receive allowances for free, the amount of the reserve needs to be determined and rules drawn up on how to proceed if the reserve is too large (cancel remaining allowances, sell them on the market) or too small (e.g. first-come-first-served, buy further allowances to replenish the reserve).

The reserves vary substantially in size (see Appendix) ranging from circa 2% of the ET budget in Germany to approximately 45% in Latvia. Germany again plans to replenish its NER reserve if it proves to be too small. In this case, an independent agency will purchase a sufficient amount of allowances on the market so that all new entrants receive allowances for free; part of the reserve in the third trading period will be earmarked to finance the agency. A similar set-up exists in Lithuania and Luxembourg, while France and the Netherlands may follow.

In cases where the NER turns out to be too large, some countries, such as the UK and Poland, will auction off their surplus, while others, like Ireland, intend to cancel any surplus allowances from the ET budget. However, some countries, including France, Latvia, the Netherlands and Sweden, have not yet made a final decision.

Finally, for France, Latvia and Lithuania, double counting may be a problem, since it is not clear from the NAPs whether the size of the NER was determined by adding projected growth at the aggregate level and bottom-up information on planned new installations/capacity expansions.

3.4. Allocation rules for closures

In most MS, the distribution of allowances ends with the year in which an installation closes. For phase II, Cyprus, Flanders and Malta, among others, joined Germany, Greece, Luxembourg, the Netherlands, Poland and the UK, which continue to include so-called transfer rules. To provide additional incentives for investments, a transfer rule allows the allocated allowances from a closed installation to be reassigned to a new installation. In most countries, allowances may only be transferred to the same activity or product (e.g. Germany, Poland), in some countries to the same operator, while countries such as Cyprus or Greece require both these criteria to be met. Member States continue to struggle with regard to the formal definition of a closure, and definitions vary widely across MS.

Assessment: closure rules

From an economic perspective, terminating the allocation of EUA after a closure implies inefficiencies and disincentives for new investments. Since the opportunity costs of a closure are not accounted for properly, old plants may continue to be operated for too long and new investments may be postponed. In fact, stopping allocation for closures corresponds to an output subsidy, and consequently there will be too many companies in the market (Spulber, 1985; Graichen and Requate, 2005; Åhman et al., 2007). Instead, operators should continue to receive the intended quantity of allowances, as is typically the case in other cap-and-trade systems (e.g. Ellerman et al., 2003).

The Emission Trading Directive requires that allowances can only be allocated to installations which operate under a permit to emit greenhouse gases (Art. 11 in combination with Art. 4; CEC, 2004b). Thus, if closed installations cease to adhere to the permit or no longer hold a permit to emit GHG, allowances may no longer be allocated to that installation. Technically, the ETS Directive would have allowed independent permits for operation and for GHG emissions. Then, a closure would not have resulted in a loss of the permit to emit GHG and allocation could have continued. In practice, however, MS have decided to link existing operating permits with the permit to emit GHG. In some MS, a tight schedule for implementing the ETS Directive in phase I may have prevented the required changes in legislation. Also, MS may have been concerned that operators might shut down their installations, keep the allocation, and open a new plant in another country. For phase II, no change could be observed in the national implementations of the permit rules.

3.5. Other special features

Combined heat and power

As in phase I, several MS decided to include special provisions for clean technologies in phase II, notably for new combined heat and power (CHP) plants, but in some cases also for existing CHP (see Appendix). The number and types of rules to compensate existing CHP have even increased.

In phase II they include applying a different compliance factor (e.g. Belgium, Germany, Greece, Sweden and the UK) or a bonus (e.g. Lithuania), excluding CHP from special cuts to account for windfall profits (e.g. the Netherlands), special early action provisions for CHP (e.g. Estonia), or a 'double benchmark' for heat and electricity (e.g. Latvia, Poland). Double benchmarks are used by other MS (e.g. Belgium, Germany, Ireland, Lithuania and Luxembourg) for new CHP plants only. Some MS (e.g. the UK, Wallonia and Flanders in Belgium) apply a less stringent compliance factor to new CHP installations. Finally, some MS which allocate gratis allowances to new projects on a first-come-first-served basis have established a special reserve for new CHP plants only (e.g. UK, Ireland).

Early action

Allocating allowances based on a recent base period implies that companies which invested in reductions prior to this period will receive fewer allowances than those which did not invest. Therefore some countries (e.g. the Czech Republic, Germany and Hungary) included special provisions using a higher compliance factor or an early-action bonus to directly compensate this 'early action' in phase I, since the lack of data prevented the use of earlier base periods. A larger number of MS accounted for early action in a more indirect way by using longer or earlier base periods (e.g. Ireland, Luxembourg and Slovenia), applying efficiency factors (e.g. Netherlands, Italy) or benchmarks (Belgium, UK). In phase II, none of the EU-15 MS accounts for any new early action directly (Germany has retained the early action rules for those installations which were subject to the rules in phase I). Only some of the new MS (Estonia and Poland) have kept special early action rules, and Lithuania has even introduced a special early action bonus although it did not directly account for early action in phase I.

Process-related emissions

The reduction of process-related emissions is believed to be either very expensive or technically not feasible for many applications, at least in the short term. Therefore, in phase I of the EU ETS, some MS have special provisions for installations emitting a higher proportion of process-related CO_2 (e.g. lime, cement clinker, steel or glass). In the first phase, these provisions are applied either at the level of individual installations via less stringent compliance factors (e.g. Germany), or at the level of sectors (e.g. France, the UK). Most countries continue their special treatment of process-related emissions in phase II in the same way as before. Only Germany has switched from an installation-level to a sector-level approach. Luxembourg now applies a uniform CF for all installations and no longer uses a special CF for process-related emissions. The Netherlands and Lithuania have introduced new, special rules for process-related emissions.

Assessment: special provisions for CHP, early action and process-related emissions

Provisions for CHP, early action or process-related emissions for existing installations are neither required by the Directive nor do they affect the economic efficiency of the EU ETS. Instead they may be justified for distributional reasons and to improve political acceptance of the system. However, no clear-cut rule exists by which installations 'worthy' of these special provisions can be defined. Accordingly, a wide range of criteria are used across MS. Also, particularly if special provisions are implemented specifically for each installation, they add to the complexity of the system and tend to be associated with higher transaction costs compared with special provisions which are implemented indirectly, i.e. at the sector level or as part of the general allocation rules (like benchmarking). Since, in phase II, political acceptance should play a lesser role than in phase I, the introduction of special provisions (in particular for early action) in some MS is somewhat surprising. In cases where operators are able to pass on the additional (including opportunity) costs from participating in the EU ETS, these special provisions result in additional windfall profits and can hardly be justified for distributional reasons. From the perspective of transaction costs, MS switching from direct rules applied at the installation level to indirect rules have to be commended.

Treatment of small emitters

The inclusion of small emitters in the EU ETS has often been criticized on efficiency grounds (e.g. Betz and Ancev, 2006). In particular, it was questioned whether the overall benefits from including small emitters would justify the transaction costs for data collection, reporting, monitoring and verifying (RMV) emissions, actual trading etc. In phase I, only a few countries used the opt-out provisions of the ETS Directive (Art. 27) for small emitters. In particular, the Netherlands exempted emitters with annual emissions below 25,000 tCO_2e/a from participating in phase I of the EU ETS. Since, from phase II onwards, the ETS Directive no longer allows opting out, several EU-15 countries have introduced provisions to either exclude or compensate small-scale installations. For example, the UK and the Flemish region in Belgium apply a *de minimis* threshold for installations below 3 MW and for emergency plants if no installation on the site exceeds 20 MW_{th}.[18] The aggregation rule for capacities (Annex I, EU ETS Directive) is not applied to these installations. The Netherlands interpret the aggregation rule in such a way that it applies only to a site where at least one installation exceeds 20 MW_{th} but not to sites where several installations are below this threshold. If each individual installation is below 20 MW_{th} but would exceed 20 MW_{th} in the aggregate, their operators may choose to include these installations in the EU ETS voluntarily. Finally, in Germany, the allocation for installations with average base period emissions below 25,000 tCO_2e/a is subject to a compliance factor of 1.0 rather than 0.9875 (industry, CHP) or 0.85 (power sector).[19]

In terms of the distribution of allowances, exempting 50% of the smallest installations would still leave 98% of the allowances in the EU ETS (e.g. Betz and Ancev, 2006). Thus, a threshold in the Directive based on emissions rather than on installed capacity (20 MW_{th}) might have been more appropriate from the very beginning. However, the EC decided not to proceed in this respect, possibly since changing the coverage of the scheme prior to phase II would have put other regulations in the ETS Directive at risk. Also, installations with low emissions are not necessarily small or owned by small companies. For example, energy installations may be large but only operated during peak hours or as reserve capacity. Likewise, they may be only one of several power plants operated by a large utility. In addition, as for example argued by Buchner et al. (2006), some of the transaction costs are sunk (historical data collection), decrease over time (RMV), or may be lowered by outsourcing. Thus, the economics for judging whether small emitters should be included have changed since phase I. In addition, alternative regulations would also incur transaction costs. So far, there is no broad empirical basis for a conclusive assessment on whether small emitters should be excluded or not. Future decisions need to be seen in the light of the intended inclusion of other greenhouse gases and sectors into the EU ETS. If there are only numerous small emitters for some gases,[20] an upstream regulation may be more appropriate, where a few producers rather than many emitters would participate in the scheme.

Special reserves

Some of the new MS (e.g. Estonia, Latvia, Lithuania and Poland) have included 'set-asides' in their NAPs to avoid double counting for JI projects. These reserves are a requirement under the Linking Directive to avoid possible double counting if JI projects in these countries reduce CO_2 emissions from installations covered by the ETS Directive. These projects would generate ERU and free up EUA. The NAPs of Estonia, Latvia, Lithuania and Poland suggest that the JI reserves have simply been added to the overall allocation. Since an equivalent number of EUA has not been subtracted from the ET budget, double counting results in inflated ET budgets in these countries.

Strangely, Poland already plans to set up a special reserve for forestry in the event that a change in the Directive should include this sector in the EU ETS. But, so far, there has been no indication that this is likely to happen in phase 2 or in phase 3 (CEC, 2006b).

Several EU-15 MS also created special reserves to cover additional allocations resulting from legal claims (e.g. NL: 0.5 million EUA p.a. and UK: 0.47 million EUA p.a.). These reserves may not be approved, since legal claims – if not finalized before the actual allocation – may require *ex-post* allocations which are opposed by the EC.

4. Conclusions

Our analysis of the notified and draft NAPs for phase II suggests that, for many NAPs, there is ample potential for improvement in terms of environmental effectiveness and economic efficiency. In terms of environmental effectiveness, our analyses on the stringency of the ET budgets for the 18 NAPs included in this article suggest that, on average, the ET budgets in phase II are only 2.6% below historical emissions in 2005, about 3.1% lower than the budgets in phase I (2005–2007), and 3% below projected emissions in 2010. A separate analysis of EU-15 MS and the new MS reveals significant differences between EU-15 and the new MS: the ET budgets in phase II are 11.1% below historical emissions in 2005 for EU-15 MS, but +31.1% for new MS; about 8.1% lower than the budgets in phase I (2005–2007) for EU-15 MS, but above 17.1% for new MS; and 9.1% below projected emissions in 2010 for EU-15 MS, but 21.1% above projections for the new MS. As shown by the aggregated figures for the 18 EU MS considered in this paper, the intended allocation for the ET sector in 2008–2012 would not require significant reductions. Unless the ET budgets are adjusted downwards, the price for EUA, innovation incentives for low-carbon technologies, and demand for ERUs and CERs by companies, are all expected to be low as well. Of course, prices in phase II also depend on expected future ET budgets, since EUAs may be transferred into phase III. The analyses also indicate a dichotomy between old and new MS. While, on average, the EU-15 MS intend to reduce emissions by about 8–11% for all three criteria, the implied average surplus of allowances in the new MS is substantial, ranging from 17% to 31% depending on the criterion applied. In addition, several governments of EU-15 MS – notably Belgium, Ireland, Italy, the Netherlands and Spain – plan to purchase credits from Kyoto mechanisms corresponding to about 114 $MtCO_2e/a$. Assuming a price of €15/tCO_2e, these purchases correspond to about €1.7 billion p.a., which would have to be financed by the federal budgets. In these MS, the credits from KM contribute substantially to meeting the burden-sharing targets, and easing the reduction burden for installations covered by the ETS Directive. Since companies are also allowed a generous use of KM in most MS, and because of the heavy reliance of some MS on KM, the Commission's interpretation and possible application of new or existing quantitative criteria for supplementarity will be crucial (European Council, 1999).

From the perspective of cost efficiency, we find that, with the possible exception of the UK, the non-trading sectors have to bear a disproportionately high share of the reduction efforts in all EU-15 MS. Thus, while the ETS enables the trading sector to cost-efficiently achieve its ET budget, the economy as a whole pays a premium for giving a more generous share of the Kyoto budget to the ET sector rather than to those sectors where it would cost more to achieve emission reductions.

Based on the NAPs included in this survey, a comparison of the allocation rules between phases I and II yields mixed results in terms of increased harmonization and improved efficiency. Even though the Directive, which sets the general rules for allocation in phase I and phase II, remained unchanged, MS were able to alter allocation rules across phases within the constraints of the Directive. As a general observation, MS tend to stick to the allocation concepts and methodologies applied in phase I. This path dependency of policies helps to explain the observed small progress in the implementation of more efficient and more harmonized rules across MS. Of course, as a result of the NAP guidance for phase II, the types of installations covered in almost all MS have been harmonized.[21] Likewise, the efficiency of the system has been improved because the NAP guidance bans *ex-post* adjustments.

Areas of harmonization which were not triggered by EC rules or guidelines include the *use of benchmarks* for existing and new energy installations, in particular (but not limited to) the power sector in EU-15 MS. The benchmarks and standard utilization rates continue to differ substantially across MS. To limit distributional effects, these benchmarks are typically differentiated by fuels, technologies or sub-product groups; only a few MS (e.g. for new power installations in Luxemburg and the UK) intend to use undifferentiated BAT benchmarks and standard load factors. For existing installations, differentiated benchmarks may limit the incentives to replace energy-inefficient technologies in the case of updating, but they are less harmful in terms of providing the correct incentives for dynamic efficiency than is the case with regard to new installations. The intended use of differentiated benchmarks or activity rates for new technologies are, in essence, technology- or fuel-specific subsidies to preserve existing production structures, which distort the dynamic innovation incentives and result in higher reduction costs for society in the long run. They run counter to the logic of emission trading systems, where market prices and flexibility should guide investment decisions rather than subsidies for particular types of installations. Nevertheless, from an economic, environmental and distributive perspective, basing allocation to new projects on differentiated benchmarks and standardized activity rates is still preferable to using installation-specific emission values together with projected activity rates for which operators have an incentive to predict 'optimistic' data. Harmonization of the allocation rules for new projects aiming at levelling the playing field across MS would have to include not only benchmarks but also activity rates and compliance factors. Naturally, this would still leave the differences in other, potentially more relevant, investment criteria across MS.

Distributing free allowances to new projects and stopping allocation after closure in all MS are examples where implicit harmonization has prevailed (see also Del Río González, 2006, this issue), but the outcome is not economically efficient. In particular, since MS competing for new investments may have an incentive to use generous allocation rules to attract new projects, a change in the ETS Directive seems indispensable to solve this potential 'prisoner's dilemma' situation. Arguably, the most flagrant example for this type of strategic use of the NER reserve is the reserve replenishment mechanism, which essentially allows EUA to be borrowed from future trading periods. If future reduction costs are lower than current costs, such a mechanism would actually reduce total costs for emission reductions over time, but the opposite may actually be more likely.

Another area of improved harmonization concerns the increased use of transfer rules in the case of closures, but the transfer terms vary across MS. In addition, in the EU-15 MS (apart from

Luxembourg), allocation to the power sector is more stringent than the allocation to industry, but the relative stringency still differs widely across MS. Similarly, most EU-15 MS (including Germany) now use a two-step approach to determine allocation to installations, but the logic applied to arrive at sector budgets varies considerably.

Several MS now include 2005 VET data to determine the allocation to installations. To avoid strategic behaviour leading to inefficient decisions on production and emission levels, the Directive may have to be changed accordingly, and MS should commit as soon as possible to abstain from such updating in the future.

A further example for improved efficiency is the higher share of allowances to be auctioned off in phase II. Compared with phase I, this share will increase by more than five times to 1.3%, but this still falls short of the maximum level of 10% permitted by the Directive. In the long run, the auction share should rise to 100% because auctioning is able to avoid most, if not all, of the problems and distributional aspects, such as early action, windfall profits or rules for new projects and closures of installations. Furthermore, the outcome of an auction would be perceived as 'fair', because the 'polluter pays' principle holds and auction revenues could be used for other purposes, including compensation to households or companies for increased electricity prices, funding research and development in energy-efficient technologies, reducing public debt, or lowering distorting taxes, thus improving the efficiency of the entire economy (double dividend). In the light of the small increase in auctioning, setting a minimum level rather than an EU-wide maximum level for the auction share may be more effective.[22]

Compared with phase I, some MS have managed to reduce the complexity of the allocation rules. This is especially true for Germany, where allocation in phase I was based on almost 60 different rules or combinations of rules. Several MS have also facilitated or abandoned special provisions for early action, process-related emissions or CHP installations. Likewise, the use of benchmarks together with standardized utilization rates for new projects also improves the transparency of allocation rules. However, these improvements can be observed almost exclusively in the EU-15 MS. In contrast, several new MS have introduced special allocation rules in phase II. When reviewing the NAPs, the EC will also have to assess whether the opt-in provisions for small entities (e.g. in Lithuania and Latvia) are attempts to further increase ET budgets and unduly favour domestic companies. In general, the allocation for JI set-asides in several new MS appears to suffer from double counting, which would lead to inflated ET budgets. Since the EU ETS Directive requires that companies not be unduly favoured (Annex III, criterion 5), the EC needs to ensure that MS do not unjustifiably over-allocate to their companies.

The decisions by the EC on the submitted NAPs will not only affect the effectiveness and economic efficiency of the NAPs included in this study and act as a signal to those MS who have not yet submitted their NAPs. Perhaps even more importantly, they will have repercussions for other carbon markets and investments and technology transfer through JI and CDM. Likewise, the Commission's assessment may boost or hamper other emissions trading schemes being set up around the world and will impact on post-2012 international climate policy negotiations. The implications of the Commission's decision on the first 10 NAPs published in late November 2006 for the macro level are briefly discussed in the Epilogue to this article.

Acknowledgements

Senior authorship is shared. The authors would like to thank two anonymous reviewers for their thoughtful comments and suggestions to further improve the article. Johanna Cludius, Jakob Rager, Manuel Strauch and Saskia Ziemann provided excellent research assistance. The usual disclaimer applies. Part of this research was completed while Joachim Schleich was a visiting professor at the Université Louis Pasteur, Strasbourg, France.

Epilogue

On 29 November 2006 the European Commission published its decisions on the NAPs of Germany, Greece, Ireland, Latvia, Lithuania, Luxembourg, Malta, Slovakia, Sweden and the UK. In this Epilogue we briefly present the main outcomes at the macro level and relate these to the findings of our article.

As a first overview, Figure 9 shows the demanded cuts in ETS budgets for phase II in absolute and relative terms. As can be seen, only the proposed cap of the UK was accepted by the Commission. The largest reduction in absolute terms is required of Germany, with almost 29 million EUA/a (compared with its NAP II budget of 482 million EUA/a), while the largest cut in relative terms applies to Latvia, with almost 58%. In total, the Commission reduced the phase-2 budgets of these 10 MS by 63.9 million EUA/a or 6.9%. Of these, 40.5 million EUA/a were requested of EU-15 MS (corresponding to a reduction of 4.7%), while 23.5 million EUA/a can be attributed to the new MS (representing a cut of 34.2%).

The Commission also evaluated the substantiation of the proposed governmental usage of KM. This resulted in a downsizing from 3.61 $MtCO_2e/a$ to 2.43 $MtCO_2e/a$ for Ireland. Ireland also needs to lower its proposed KM limit for companies from 50% to 21.9%, and Sweden its KM limit for EU ETS firms from 20% to 10% – the reasoning behind these cuts are supplementarity restrictions.

Table 2 shows the results of applying the four criteria used in this article to the new ETS budgets after the Commission's ruling on the first 10 NAPs. The updated calculations based on adjusted phase-II budgets show that the majority of MS now meet all the criteria. Due to high growth rates for the EU-10 MS, the only notable exception is the comparison of their permitted phase-II budgets with 2005 emissions.

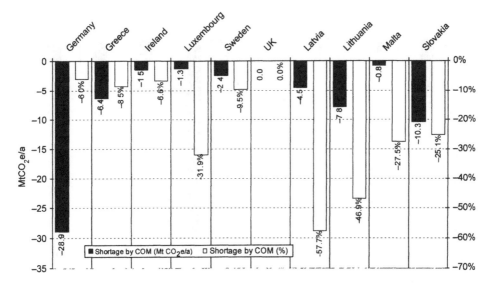

Figure 9. Reduction in phase II budgets required by the Commission (in $MtCO_2e/a$ and as a percentage of original ET budget).
Source: Fraunhofer ISI based on CEC (2006a, 2006c), UNFCCC (2006) and NAPs I+II of MS.

Table 2. Results for three criteria at aggregate level of 10 NAPs after COM decision

| | Approved ET-budget in phase II compared to | | | | | |
| | VET 2005 (criterion 1) | | ET budget in phase I (criterion 2) | | Emission projections for 2010 (criterion 3) | |
	in million EUA)	in % of VET 2005	in million EUA	in % of ET-budget phase I	in million EUA	in % of projected emissions
EU-15 (6)	−113.8	−14.6%	−75.6	−9.3%	−80.8	−9.9%
new MS (4)	2.3	5.7%	−6.5	−14.5%	−20.0	−44.3%
Total (10)	−110.7	−13.6%	−82.1	−9.5%	−100.8	−11.7%

Source: Fraunhofer ISI based on CEC (2006a, 2006c) and registry data (CITL as of 23 October 2006), EEA (2006), UNFCCC (2006) and NAPs I+II of MS.

Figures 10 and 11 show how the new phase-II budgets relate to the hypothetical allocation scenario (HAS), first in absolute, then in relative terms. This figure clearly differs due to the reductions in EU ETS budgets requested by the Commission: almost all MS are now requested to assign EU ETS budgets that are close to or even clearly below the HAS. The EU ETS sector would thus actually shoulder an over-proportional reduction burden compared to the rest of the economy, which – due to lower marginal abatement costs in the EU ETS sector – should reduce the overall abatement costs borne by society for meeting climate policy reduction targets.

Looking at these figures, it becomes clear that the European Commission's requested additional emission budget reductions for the first 10 national allocation plans is a significant and – as elaborated in this article – important step towards a more credible EU ETS.

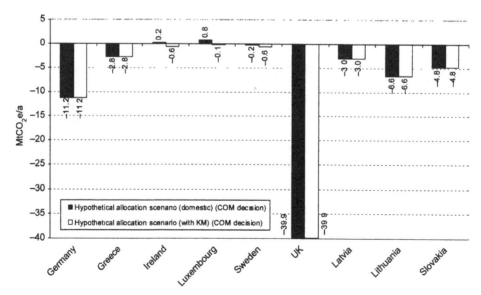

Figure 10. COM-approved ET budget for phase II compared with 'hypothetical allocation scenario' (in MtCO$_2$e/a).
Source: Fraunhofer ISI based on CEC (2006a, 2006c) and registry data (CITL as of 23 October 2006), UNFCCC (2006) and NAPs I+II of MS.

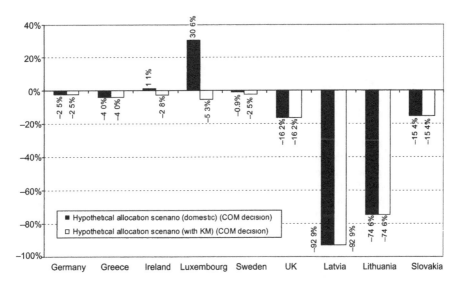

Figure 11. COM-approved ET budget for phase II compared with 'hypothetical allocation scenario' (as a percentage).
Source: Fraunhofer ISI based on CEC (2006a, 2006c) and registry data (CITL as of 23 October 2006), UNFCCC (2006) and NAPs I+II of MS.

Notes

1   Intended governmental use of Kyoto mechanisms: Belgium 7 $MtCO_2e/a$, Italy 20 $MtCO_2e/a$, Ireland 3.6 $MtCO_2e/a$, Luxembourg 4.7 $MtCO_2e/a$, the Netherlands 20 $MtCO_2e/a$, Spain 57 $MtCO_2e/a$ and Sweden 1.1 MtCO2e/a. Since Sweden is on a reduction path aiming at –4%, it is unlikely to use these credits in 2008–2012. When setting its ET budget, Sweden did not base its calculations on its purchase of Kyoto mechanisms.
2   Actual allocation excludes opt-outs, includes opt-ins and new entrants in 2005 (CITL data as of 23 October 2006).
3   The CITL data for Poland still only covers less than 60% of the cap set in Poland's first NAP because not all installations are connected to the registry. We therefore took the cap in phase 1 (excluding NER, 238.3 million EUA) as a proxy for the actual allocation in 2005, and estimated the actual emissions of all Polish installations covered by the EU ETS by applying the same percentage of surplus allocation as that of the installations already registered in CITL (140 million EUA actual allocation vs. 113 million EUA actual emissions in 2005, yielding a surplus allocation of 27 million EUA or some 19% (for 461 installations)). As a result, we estimate an over-allocation of approx. 46 million EUA in 2005.
4   Since the emission level in the absence of the EU ETS cannot be determined (it is counterfactual), the extent of possible over-allocation cannot be determined either. In fact, Buchner and Ellerman (2006) tentatively suggest that a substantial part of the surplus may also have been the consequence of abatement measures.
5   More specifically, the NAP guidance for phase II states that '...Member States should therefore in any case include also combustion processes involving crackers, carbon black, flaring, furnaces and integrated steelworks, typically carried out in larger installations causing considerable emissions' (CEC, 2005a, p. 9).
6   This figure is based on the following estimates provided in NAPs and supporting documents: Belgium 5.26 $MtCO_2e/a$, France 5 $MtCO_2e/a$, Germany 11 $MtCO_2e/a$, Ireland 0.4 $MtCO_2e/a$, Lithuania 0.06 $MtCO_2e/a$, the Netherlands 4.15 $MtCO_2e/a$, Slovakia 1.73 $MtCO_2e/a$, Spain 6.77 $MtCO_2e/a$, Sweden 2 $MtCO_2e/a$ and the UK 9.5 $MtCO_2e/a$. Some MS have not yet provided a proxy for the size of emissions or the allocation to additionally covered installations.
7   Opt-outs for the UK were approx. 30 $MtCO_2e/a$, and for the Netherlands about 7.8 $MtCO_2e/a$.
8   So far, three Member States plan to include additional installations with N_2O emissions from adipic and nitric acids, glyoxalic acid and glyoxal production. The intended number of allowances for N_2O emissions from these opt-ins is rather small: France 5.44 million EUA, Netherlands 1.43 million EUA, Wallonia in Belgium has not yet provided any details.
9   For Estonia, Germany and Poland, we multiplied the recently published emissions data from the EEA (2006) by the ratio of CO_2 emissions of the ET sector as of 2004/05.

10 It is beyond the scope and focus of this article to assess the accuracy of such projections, recognizing that MS may have an incentive to use biased (inflated) figures. For example, Neuhoff et al. (2006b) provide further insights on the use of projections in the NAPs.

11 The second scenario is not relevant for Sweden because – although it intends to purchase credits from Kyoto mechanisms – the decision on the actual use of these credits for 2008–2012 is still pending, and the amount intended to be purchased was not taken into account when setting Sweden's ETS cap for phase 2.

12 For overviews see, for example, Betz et al. (2004), Ecofys (2004), German Emissions Trading Authority (DEHSt) (2005) and Matthes (2005).

13 In some countries, the energy sector only includes power installations connected to the grid. In other MS, the energy sector also includes power installations in the industry sector (see the Appendix for an overview). For simplicity we usually do not make this distinction when presenting the general results.

14 Note that if the emission budget for a particular group of installations is fixed, then a BM allocation implies that the allocation to an installation is in proportion to the share of the activity level of that installation. In particular, the allocation to an installation is independent of the level of the benchmark.

15 The Netherlands, Flanders and Wallonia, where allocation is based on covenants or voluntary agreements, use BAT benchmarks for existing installations. However, as in phase I, they use benchmarks to calculate the efficiency factor (i.e. difference between BAT and actual efficiency) which is used in the allocation formula (see Appendix).

16 Since at the time of writing (October 2006) there was no NAP 2 available for Denmark, it could not be determined whether Denmark is continuing to use auctioning for phase II. The draft NAP for Hungary includes an auctioning share of 5%.

17 To prevent excess allocation, some MS (Austria, Germany) had included so-called *ex-post* adjustments of the allocation in phase I. Since *ex-post* adjustments are at odds with the logic of emissions trading (*ex-ante* principle of allocation), the EC has ruled against them.

18 An emergency or standby installation may be excluded from the aggregation if it is proven that it cannot be physically operated at the same time (UK NAP p. 48 and Flemish NAP p. 19).

19 At least at first glance, Slovakia's plan to introduce a separate scheme for small emitters is surprising, but cannot be assessed in more depth because there is no detailed information available as yet.

20 See AEA Technology Environment, Ecofys UK (2006) for an assessment of further inclusion of gases and sectors.

21 So far, the Commission's attempt to harmonize the inclusion and interpretation of Annex I (CEC, 2005a) has led to the inclusion of an estimated 45.9 $MtCO_2e/a$ in phase II compared with phase I (because of a lack of data, the figures for Italy are not included).

22 See also Hepburn et al. (2006) on auctioning within the EU ETS and on setting a price floor.

References

AEA Technology Environment, Ecofys UK, 2006. LETS Update: Scoping Phase report.

Åhman, M., Burtraw, D., Kruger, J., Zetterberg, L., 2007. A Ten-Year Rule to guide the allocation of EU emission allowances. Energy Policy 35(3), 1718–1730.

Åhman, M., Holmgren, K., 2006. New entrant allocation in the Nordic energy sectors: current principles and options for the EU ETS. Climate Policy 6(4), 423–440.

Betz, R., Ancev, T., 2006. Emission trading: how to determine the efficient coverage, In: IAEE Proceedings, 29th IAEE Conference 7–10 June 2006, Potsdam.

Betz, R., Eichhammer, W., Schleich, J., 2004. Designing national allocation plans for EU emissions trading: a first analysis of the outcomes. Energy and Environment 15(3), 375–425.

Böhringer, C., Lange, A., 2005. Mission impossible!? On the harmonization of national allocation plans under the EU Emission Trading Directive. Journal of Regulatory Economics 27(1), 81–94.

Böhringer, C., Hoffmann, T., Lange, A., Löschel, A., Moslener, U., 2005. Assessing emission regulation in Europe: an interactive simulation approach. Energy Journal 26(4), 1–22.

Böhringer, C., Hoffmann, T., Manrique de Lara-Penante, 2006. The efficiency costs of separating carbon markets under the EU emissions trading scheme: a quantitative assessment for Germany. Energy Economics 28(1), 44–61.

Buchner, B., Ellerman, A.D., 2006. Over-Allocation or Abatement? A Preliminary Analysis of the EU ETS Based on the 2005 Emissions Data. FEEM Working Paper 139.06. FEEM [available at http://ssrn.com/abstract=946091].

Buchner, B., Carraro, C., Ellerman, A.D., 2006. The allocation of European Union allowances: lessons, unifying themes and general principles. 116.06, FEEM Working Paper. Fondazione Eni Enrico Mattei, Venice, Italy.

CEC, 2003a. Directive 2003/87/EC of the European Parliament and the Council of 13 October 2003: Establishing a Scheme for Greenhouse Gas Emission Allowance Trading within the Community and Amending Council Directive 96/61/EC, 32–46.

CEC, 2003b. Non-paper on the Installation Coverage of the EU Emissions Trading Scheme and the Interpretation of Annex I, CEC, Brussels.

CEC, 2004a. Communication from the Commission on Guidance to Assist Member States in the Implementation of the Criteria listed in Annex III to Directive 2003/87/EC Establishing a Scheme for Greenhouse Gas Emission Allowance Trading within the Community and Amending Council Directive 96/61/EC, and on the circumstances under which force majeure is demonstrated. CEC, Brussels.

CEC, 2004b. Directive 2004/101/EC of the European Parliament and the Council of 27 October 2004 amending Directive 2003/ 87/EC Establishing a Scheme for Greenhouse Gas Emission Allowance Trading within the Community, in respect of the Kyoto Protocol's Project Mechanisms, pp. 18–23.

CEC, 2005a. Communication from the Commission on Further Guidance on Allocation Plans for the 2008 to 2012 Trading Period of the EU Emission Trading Scheme. CEC, Brussels.

CEC, 2005b. EU Action against Climate Change: EU Emissions Trading – An Open Scheme Promoting Global Innovation. CEC, Brussels.

CEC, 2006a. Communication from the Commission to the Council and to the European Parliament on the Assessment of National Allocation Plans for the Allocation of Greenhouse Gas Emission Allowances in the Second Period of the EU Emissions Trading Scheme accompanying Commission Decisions of 29 November 2006 on the National Allocation Plans of Germany, Greece, Ireland, Latvia, Lithuania, Luxembourg, Malta, Slovakia, Sweden and the UK in accordance with Directive 2003/87/EC. CEC, Brussels.

CEC, 2006b. Communication from the Commission to the Council, The European Parliament, the European Economic and Social Committee and the Committee of the Regions, on Building a Global Carbon Market: Report Pursuant to Article 30 of Directive 2003/87/EC. CEC, Brussels.

CEC, 2006c. Community Independent Transaction Log: National Reports on Verified Emission and Surrendered Allowances. CEC, Brussels.

CEC, 2006d. EU Emissions Trading Scheme Delivers First Verified Emissions Data for Installations, IP/06/XXX. CEC, Brussels.

Cramton, P., Kerr, S. 2002. Tradable carbon permit auctions: how and why to auction not grandfather. Energy Policy 30, 333–345.

Cremer, C., Schleich, J., 2006. Using benchmarking for the primary allocation of EU allowances in the German power sector. In: 29th IAEE International Conference 2006, Potsdam.

Criqui, P., Kitous, A., 2003. Kyoto Protocol Implementation (KPI): Technical Report: Impacts of Linking JI and CDM Credits to the European Emissions Allowance Trading Scheme. A Report for DG Environment, CNRS-IEPE and ENERDATA S.A.

del Río González, P., 2006. Harmonization versus decentralization in the EU ETS: an economic analysis. Climate Policy 6(4), 457–475.

Dinan, T., Rogers, D., 2002. Distributional effects of carbon allowance trading: how government decisions determine winners and losers. National Tax Journal 40(2), 199–222.

Ecofys, 2004. Analysis of the National Allocation Plans for the EU ETS. DEFRA (Ed.), London.

EEA, 2006. Greenhouse Gas Emission Trends and Projections in Europe, 9/2006. EEA Report. EEA, Copenhagen, Denmark.

Ehrhart, K.-M., Hoppe, C., Schleich, J., Seifert, S., 2005. The role of auctions and forward markets in the EU ETS: counterbalancing the cost-inefficiencies of combining generous allocation with a ban on banking. Climate Policy 5(1) 31–46.

Ellerman, A.D., Joskow, P.L., Harrison D., 2003. Emissions Trading in the US: Experience, Lessons, and Considerations for Greenhouse Gases. Pew Center on Global Climate Change, Arlington, VA, USA.

European Council, 1999. Council Conclusion on a Community Strategy on Climate Change. European Council, Brussels.

European Council, 2005. Presidency Conclusions 7619/1/05 Rev. European Council, Brussels.

Gagelmann, F., Frondel, M., 2005. The impact of emission trading on innovation: science fiction or reality? An Assessment of the Impact of Emissions Trading on Innovation. European Environment 15(4), 203–211.

German Emissions Trading Authority (DEHSt), 2005. Implementation of the Emissions Trading in the EU: National Allocation Plans of all EU States. UBA, Berlin.

Graichen, P., Requate, T., 2005. Der steinige Weg von der Theorie in die Praxis des Emissionshandels: Die EU-Richtlinie zum CO_2- Emissionshandel und ihre nationale Umsetzung. Perspektiven der Wirtschaftspolitik 6(1), 41–56.

Hepburn, C., Grubb, M., Neuhoff, K., Matthes, F., Tse, M., 2006. Auctioning of EU ETS phase II allowances: how and why. Climate Policy 6(1), 137–160.

Kruger, J., Pizer, W.A., 2004. The EU Emissions Trading Directive – Opportunities and Potential Pitfalls, 04-24. Resources for the Future Discussion Paper, RFF, Washington, DC.

Matthes, F., 2005. The Environmental Effectiveness and Economic Efficiency of the European Union Emissions Trading Scheme: Structural Aspects of Allocation. Report by Öko-Institut Berlin to WWF, Öko-Institut (Ed.), Berlin.

Misiolek, W.S., Elder, H.W., 1989. Exclusionary manipulation of markets for pollution rights. Journal of Environmental Economics and Management 16(2), 156–166.

Neuhoff, K., Åhman, M., Betz, R., Cludius, J., Ferrario, F., Holmgren, K., Pal, G., Grubb, M., Matthes, F., Rogge, K., Sato, M., Schleich, J., Sijm, J., Tuerk, A., Kettner, C., Walker, N., 2006a. Implications of announced phase II national allocation plans for the EU ETS. Climate Policy 6(4), 411–422.

Neuhoff, K., Ferrario, F., Grubb, M., Gabel, E., Keats, K., 2006b. Emission Projections 2008–2012 versus national allocation plans II. Climate Policy 6(4), 395–410.

Peterson, S., 2006. Efficient Abatement in Separated Carbon Markets: A Theoretical and Quantitative Analysis of the EU Emissions Trading Scheme. 1271, Kiel Working Paper, Kiel.

Pezzey, J., Park, T., 1998. Reflections on the double dividend debate. Environmental and Resource Economics 11(3–4), 539–555.

Radov, D., Harrison, D., Klevnas, P., 2005. EU Emissions Trading Scheme Benchmark Research for Phase II: Final Report. Entec UK Ltd. and NERA Economic Consulting (Ed.).

Schleich, J., Betz, R., 2005. Incentives for energy efficiency and innovation in the European emission trading system. European Council for an Energy-Efficient Economy (Paris): Proceedings of the 2005 ECEEE Summer Study. Energy Savings: What Works & Who Delivers? ECEEE, Mandelieu, Côte d'Azur, France.

Schmalensee, R., Joskow, P., Ellerman, D., Montero P., Baily, E., 1998. An interim evaluation of sulfur dioxide emissions trading. Journal of Economic Perspectives 12(3), 53–68.

Sijm, J.P., Neuhoff, K., Chen, Y., 2006. CO_2 cost pass-through and windfall profits in the power sector. Climate Policy 6(1), 49–72.

Spulber, D.F., 1985. Effluent regulation and long-run optimality. Journal of Environmental Economics and Management 12, 103–116.

Sterner, T., Muller, A., 2006. Output and Abatement Effects of Allocation Readjustment in Permit Trade. Resources for the Future Discussion Paper 06–49. RFF, Washington, DC.

UNFCCC, 2006. National Inventory Submissions. UNFCCC, Bonn.

Zetterberg, L., Nilsson, K., Åhman, M., Kumlin, A.-S., Birgersdotter, L., 2004. Analysis of National Allocation Plans for the EU ETS, IVL Report 1591. Stockholm, Sweden.

Appendix

Summary table of national allocation plans for phase II

	BE-B	BE-F	BE-W	DE	EE
Number of installations					
Phase II (phase I)	8(13)	178(178)	172 (114)	N.A. (1,849)	45(43)
Opt-in in phase II (I)	0(0)	0(0)	Tbd (0)	0(0)	0(0)
Additional gases or sectors (number of installations)			Yes, N$_2$O (N.A.)		
New Entrant Reserve					
Million EUAs p.a. (% of ET budget)	0.0143 (27.46%)	3.612 (10.18%)	1.375 (6.08%)	10 (2.4%)	1.7 (3%)
First come first served?	N.A.	N.A.	Yes	No	Yes
Replenished if empty?	No	Yes	No	Yes	No
Surplus management	Cancelled	Auctioned or banked	Cancelled or sold	Sold	Sold
Other reserves?	Special CHP	No	No	Plus special reserves: admin. costs for JI/CDM (2 Mt); replenishment NER phase 1 (5 Mt)	2 Mt reserves for JI projects with total of: 1.7 Mt
Auction					
Share of ET-budget incl. Reserve in Phase II (I)	0% (0%)	0.5% (0%)	0% (0%)	0% (0%)	0% (0%)
Use of auction revenue – restricted participation		Climate policy, e.g. Kyoto Mechanisms Tbd			
Sectoral differentiation					
B/w energy and non-energy? Energy budget as residual?	Yes, No	Yes, No	Yes, Yes	Yes, Yes	No
Allocation to existing installations Two steps/One step 1. step = sector budget (SB) 2. step = Individual allocation (IA)				*Two steps*	
a) Energy	a) IA = average emissions in 2002–2005 CF=1	a) IA = Installed capacity* technology-specific load factor* uniform BAT benchmark (0.359 t CO$_2$/MWh)	a) IA = Installed capacity* technology-specific load factor* uniform BAT benchmark (0.4 t CO$_2$/MWh)* CF (=0.839) (= value of 0.336 t CO$_2$/MWh)	*a) b) SB:IA:* Average emissions (2000–2005)* CF (=0.85)	*a) b)* IA = emissions 1995–2005 (district heating) or 2000–2005 (electricity and industry)* growth factor
b) Non-energy	b) IA = emissions 2005* growth factor* individual reduction potential* CHP potential factor	b) Installation part of covenant: IA = covenant agreement ("world top by 2012") – Installation not part of covenant: CF = 0.85 (diminished by 0.008 each year)	b) IA = emissions (1 yr. out of 1999–2002),* projected growth* efficiency factor (indiv. agreed or assessed) – CF=0.97, if (VET2005-allocation) > 10%, CF=1 otherwise	*b) IA = Average* emissions 2000–2005* CF (=0.9875)	(= 6.5% for electricity/3% for district heating and industry) – no CF
c) Special provisions CHP	c) No	c) CF=1	c) IA = average emissions 2000–2004 – CF=1	c) CF=0.9875	c) Increase of CHP rewarded as early action

Summary table of national allocation plans for phase II (Cont'd)

	ES(Draft)	FR	GR	IE	IT(Draft)	LT	LU
Number of installations							
Phase II (phase I)	N.A.(957)	1193(1,172)	150(139)	155(143)	995(1,240)	135(134)	15(15)
Opt-in in phase II (I)	18(0)	18(0)	0(0)	0(0)	0(0)	Yes, figure	0(0)
Additional gases or sectors (number of installations)	Yes, N_2O(18)	Yes, N_2O(18)			No	N.A. (34)	No (0)
New Entrant Reserve							
Million EUAs p.a. (% of	7.96	9	6.2	1.14	8	2	0.59
ET budget)	(5.2%)	(5.8%)	(8.2%)	(5%)	(4.12%)	(11.9%)	(14.9%)
First come first served?	Yes	N.A.	Yes	Yes	Yes	N.A.	No
Replenished if empty?	No	Maybe	No	No	No	Yes, from auction part	Yes
Surplus management	Sold	Tbd	Auctioned	Cancelled	Cancelled	Cancelled Reserve for JI and closure of Ignalia NPP[a]	Sold
Other reserves?	No	No	Special CHP reserve	No	No	No	No
Auction							
Share of ET-budget incl. Reserve in Phase II (I)	0% (0%)	0% (0%)	0% (0%)	0.5% (0.75%)	0% (0%)	2.7% (1.5%)	5% (0%)
Use of auction revenue – restricted participation				Admin. costs Unrestricted Tbd Tbd		Unrestricted Yearly	Purchase of Kyoto mech. domestic Tbd
Sectoral differentiation							
B/w energy and non-energy? Energy budget as residual?	Yes, No	No	No	Yes, No	Yes, Yes	No	No
Allocation to existing installations							
Two steps/One step 1. step = sector budget (SB) 2. step = Individual allocation (IA)	Two steps	Two steps	Two steps	Two steps	Two steps	Two steps	
a) Energy	a) IA = installation capacity* load factor* BAT benchmark (technology specific)* CF (=0.746)	Two steps a) b) SB = production (2004/2005)* growth rate* average benchmark (2004/2005)* reduction potential* IA: CF (=0.9729) – IA: installation's share of emissions in BP (varying: 1996–2005, sometimes one single year)	Two steps a) b) SB = projected emissions* CF (=0.89 for combustion/=1.0 for CHP and process emissions/=0.91 to 0.99 for industry) IA = average emissions 2000–2004 (without lowest year)* sector-specific CF	Two steps a) b) SB = [share of sector emissions 2003* CF (=0.9 for energy/=1 for industry)* 0.95 (auction factor)] – sector specific allocation for New Entrants	Two steps a) b) SB = average allocation 2005–07 (Energy, Steel, Refining additional reductions) a) IA=output 2005* fuel – & technology-specific BAT BM* trend factor* CF (=0.9897) Trend factor = energy policy e.g. renewables	Two steps a) b) SB = average emissions (2002–2005)* projected growth* efficiency factor (=0.9 for energy/=0.9 to 1.0 for industry) 0.95 (auction factor) Refinery: emissions increase due to legislation:1.153	a/b) IA= average emissions (3 yrs. from 2002–2005)* growth factor* CF(=0.991)
b) Non-energy	Two steps b) SB = projected output 2010* average benchmarks (2005)* efficiency factor IA = avg. specific emissions* output (2 yrs from 2000–2005)* install. specific CF		"Fuel coefficient" used for other combustion paper and cardboards, lime and ceramics Steel and Cement: special rules	a) b) IA = share of emissions (2003–2004)* total SB	b) IA = allocation 2007 (1 + 0.03* individual efficiency factor + 0.03* individual growth factor)* CF CF= vary	IA = Share of SB based on: 2* Fuel consumption in toe (2002–2005)* 0.5 t CO_2/toe + if applicable: process-related emissions + 2* early action bonus + 2* CHP bonus	
c) Special provisions CHP	c) Projected emissions (based on VET 2005)	c) No	c) CF=1	c) Electricity part: allowances from energy budget based on BAT gas CCGT- benchmark	c) CHP similar to a) but double benchmark-energy savings of 20%	c) CHP double benchmark	c) No

Summary table of national allocation plans for phase II (*Cont'd*)

	LV	NL	PL	SE	SK	UK
Number of installations						
Phase II (phase I)	95(91)	304(207)	N.A. (945)	735(700)	183(209)	1070(1057)
Opt-in in phase II (I)	26(20)	3(0)	0(0)	261(13)	0(0)	0(0)
Additional gases or sectors (number of installations)	No	Yes, N_2O (3)	N.A.		Plan ETS for small entities only	
New Entrant Reserve						
Million EUAs p.a. (% of ET budget)	3.5 (45%)	6.2 (6%)	9 (3.2%)	3 (12%)	1.8 (4%)	17.3 (7%)
First come first served?	N.A.	Yes	N.A.	Yes	Yes	Yes
Replenished if empty?	No	Tbd	N.A.	No	No	No
Surplus management	Maybe	Tbd		Tbd	Tbd	Special CHP reserved
Other reserves?	Auctioned Reserve for JI projects	Reserve for legal claims (0.5 MT/a)	Auctioned Reserve for JI projects Forestry reserve		No	Auctioned Contingency fund w/in NER (0.47) Mt
Auction						
Share of ET-budget incl. Reserve in Phase II (I)	0% (0%)	4% (0%)	1% (0%)	0% (0%)	0% (0%)	7% (0%)
Use of auction revenue – restricted participation		Compensate low–volume power user Tbd Tbd	Natl. Fund for environ. protection installations that were not allocated enough EUAw Tbd			Tbd Unrestricted Tbd
Sectoral differentiation						
B/w energy and non-energy? Energy budget as residual?	No	No	No	Yes, Yes	Yes, No	Yes, Yes
Allocation to existing installations Two steps/One step 1. step = sector budget (SB) 2 step = Individual allocation (IA)		*Two steps*	*Two steps*			*Two steps*
a) Energy	a) b) IA= average output in sector-specific BP (varies between 2001 and 2006)* (fuel-and product-specific benchmarks)* growth factor* CF (= 0.98)	a) IA= average emissions (3 yr. from 2000–2005)* growth factor* efficiency factor* CF(=0.73)* efficiency factor (based on covenant)-CF includes 0.15 cut for windfall profits	a) b) SB = output 2005* growth rate* sector average benchmarks (2005)* efficiency factor a) IA= projected output* fuel specific benchmarks, accounting for SO_2	a) IA= average emissions in (1998–2001)* CF (=0.3 to 0.4)	a) IA Thermal: average emissions in 1998–2003 (or 2005, if higher)* growth of apartment stock (=1.004) Electric and thermal: projected energy output* emissions/output (1998–2003)	a) SB= (total ET budget–industry allocation)* CF (=0.7) – IA= capacity* standardized load factor (2000–2003)* technology– and fuel-based benchmark[2]
b) Non-energy		b) IA= emissions (3 yrs. from 2000-2005)* growth factor (1.7)* efficiency factor* CF (=0.87 combustion emissions/=0.92 for process emissions)	b) IA= similar to SB and projected output agreed with associations + CHP and early action bonus	b) All, except BOF-steel[1]: IA= emissions in (1998–2001)* growth in process-related emissions* CF(=1); BOF-steel: projected output* EU average benchmark (2005)	b) Large emitters: negotiated Small emitters emissions: (1998–2005)* sector specific growth rates	b) SB = projected emissions incl. growth and reduction potential CF=IIA= installation's share emissions in 2000–2003, (–with year)
c) Special provisions CHP	c) Double benchmark	c) Efficiency benchmark No CF for small CHP	c) CHP bonus: double benchmark	c) CF=1	c) no	c) Separate "Good Quality CHP Sector"

Summary table of national allocation plans for phase II (Cont'd)

	BE-B	BE-F	BE-W	DE
Allocation to new installations a) Energy	Free allocation a) b) Based on projected emissions	Free allocation a) Based on Installed capacity* technology-specific load factor* uniform benchmark (0.359 t CO_2/MWh)	Free allocation a) IA = Installed capacity* technology-specific load factor* uniform BAT bench mark (0.4 t CO_2/ MWh)* CF (=0.839) (= value of 0.336 t CO_2/ MWh)	Free allocation a) Based on fuel specific BAT-BMs
b) Non-energy		b) Installation part of covenant: IA= covenant agreement ("world top by 2012") – Installation not part of covenant: CF=0.85 (diminished by 0.008 each year)	b) Allocation based on individual BAT and projected production	b) For homogenous products (e.g. cement, glass, tiles) standardized load factors and BAT-BMS (differentiated by sub-product groups or technologies); allocation for other industry installations based on BAT and standardized load factors–for all: no compliance factor for 14 years
c) Special provisions for *CHP*	c) Special CHP New Entrants Reserve		c) CF=1	c) Double benchmark
d) Definition of New entrant				
Closure rules Issuance of allowances for x years after closure Definition of closure: if permit is terminated? Transfer of allocation to new projects; Phase II (I)	0 N.A. No (no)	0 Yes Yes (no)	0 N.A. No (no)	0 No: average emissions in 2005–2006 < 20% of average emissions 2000–2004 Yes (yes), restricted to same activity
Combustion installations in industry treated same as industrial installation?	Yes	N.A.	N.A.	Same as energy sector
New special provisions for **early action** in phase II (I) Indirectly via base period/benchmark Directly via less strict CF	No (yes)	Indirectly via covenant (no)	Indirectly via efficiency factor, (indirectly via BM)	No (directly)
Special provisions for **process-related emissions**? At installation or sector level? Phase I (II)	No (no)	Installations level depending on covenant (both)	Installation-level depending on efficiency factor(no)	Sector-level via higher CF (installation level)
Special treatment of **small installations**? Definition of small installations	De minimis threshold to exclude <3 MW[4]	De minimis threshold to exclude <3 MW	De minimis threshold to exclude <3 MW[4]	CF of 1.0 if <25.000 t CO_2 p.a.

Summary table of national allocation plans for phase II (Cont'd)

	EE	ES (Draft)	FR	GR	IE	IT (Draft)	LT
Allocation to new installations a) *Energy*	Free allocation a) No information on allocation method b) Estonian BAT benchmarks	Free allocation a) Same rules as for existing installations b) BAT BM* projected output 2008–12	Free allocation a) b) Based onBAT gas benchmarks* projected output; list of benchmarks to be set up	Free allocation a)b) Capacity* load factor* specific emission factor* sector specific CF for existing installations (if specific emission factor is BAT, CF=1)	Free allocation a) b) Based on BAT (differentiated by fuel and technology-)* installation specific projected emissions capped at 88% of projected emissions	Free allocation a) Capacity* load factor* fuel and technology specific BM (same as for incumbents)	Free allocation a) b) Based on product-specific BM, and standardized load factors
b) *Non-energy*						b) output projections or capacity and expected use* AT benchmark More (to be defined)	
c) Special provisions for *CHP* d) Definition of New entrant	c)No	c) According to projected emissions	c)No d) To phase 2 New Entrants	c) CF=1 and special CHP NER	c) Specific reserve Double benchmark	c) Double benchmark and energy saving index	c) Double benchmark
Closure rules Issuance of allowances for x years after closure Definition of closure: if permit is terminated? Transfer of allocation to new projects; Phase II (I)	N.A.	0 N.A. No (no)	N.A.	0 Yes Yes, same product and same operator	Closing installation retain 75% allocation or a maximum of 25,000 EUAs/a Yes N.A.	0 Permanent suspension of production activity, total suspension for > 6 months, partial closure possible leads to partial allocation. N.A.	0 Yes No
Combustion installations in industry treated same as industrial installatiom?	No distinction in rules energy/industry	N.A.	Yes	No distinction in rules energy/industry	Yes	Same as energy with >20MW th which sell > 51% to grid	Yes
New special provisions for **early action** in phase II (I) Indirectly via base period/benchmark Directly via less strict CF	Yes directly (via EA bonus, just CHP) (yes)	Yes, (indirectly via BM) (no)	Indirectly via early base period (indirectly)	No (indirectly)	No (no)	Indirectly through benchmarks or efficiency factor (yes)	Early action bonus for reduced emissions between 1996–2005
Special provisions for **process-related emissions?** At installation or sector level? Phase I (II)	No (no)	Depends on efficiency factor and CF	Sector-level, indirect via reduction potential (yes)	Yes, CF=1 (")	Yes, CF=1 (no)	Sector-level (via efficiency factor) (")	Inst. level calculated separately (no)
Special treatment of **small installations?** Definition of small installations	No	No	No	No	No	Not mentioned	Yes, opt-in

Summary table of national allocation plans for phase II (*Cont'd*)

	LU	LV	NL	PL	SK	SE	UK
Allocation to new installations a) Energy	Free allocation a) b) Based on uniform BAT BM and standardized load factors	Free allocation a) b) Based on projected output* fuel- and product-specific BM* efficiency facto (for energy sector)	Free allocation a) b) Based on BAT BM (covenant)* projected output (capped at 90%)	Free allocation a) b) based on-BAT BM* projected output	Free allocation a) b) Based on projected emissions or BAT (fuel and technology specific but not specified any further in NAP)	Free allocation a) only to highly-efficient CHP-based on uniform average benchmark (from 464 Swedish installations 2000–2004) and installation-specific projected output	Free allocation a) Based on uniform benchmark (CCGT)* standardized load factor*CF (=0.7)
b) *Non-energy*						b) Free allocation based on BAT and installation-specific projected output	b) Based on uniform benchmark (gas–unless not applicable)*standardized load factor* CF (=0.9 for boilers and generators /= 0.95 all others)
c) Special provisions for *CHP*	c) Double BM	c) Double BM		c) Double BM	c) No	c) See a)	c) See a) CF=1
d) Definition of New entrant				d) Installations which fall under Directive, but are not included in NAP 2			
Closure rules Issuance of allowances for x years after closure	0	N.A.	0	0	0	0	0
Definition of closure: if permit is terminated?	No, if less than 10% of base year	N.A.	Yes	N.A.	N.A.	Yes	Installation ceased operating/capacity or activity level below those given in Annex I
Transfer of allocation to new ; projects Phase II (I)	Yes	Yes, same product, based on output	Yes, same product, based on output	Yes, if same product	No	No	Yes, but not for power (yes)
Combustion installations in industry treated same as industrial installation?	No distinction in rules energy/industry	Yes	Yes (no cut for windfall profits)	Yes	Yes	Yes	Yes
New special provisions for **early action** in phase II (I) Indirectly via base period/benchmark Directly via less strict CF	No (no) benchmark (yes)	Indirect via factor (")	Yes, via efficiency bonus (yes)	Yes, early action base period (")	Indirectly via base period (")	Indirectly via and rationalisation rule (")	Indirectly via base period
Special provisions for **process-related emissions**? At installation or sector level? Phase I (II)	No (inst. level)	No (no)	Installation –level (no)	Indirect via efficiency factor (")	Not specified (")	Via special growth rate (")	Sector-level (sector-level)
Special treatment of **small installations**? Definition of small installations	No	No	Yes, special interpretation of aggregation rule, opt-out in 1 phase	No	Allocation methods applied according to inst. size (see above)	No	Voluntary opt -out for instal. <3 MW

Note: Tbd = to be decided, N.A. = not available, NPP = nuclear power plant, (") = ...“...., CF = compliance factor, BOF = basic oxygen furnace 2) Coal: 0.91 t CO_2/MWh; Oil: 0.83 t CO_2/MWh; Gas: 0.4 t CO_2/MWh. 3) Special reserve for nuclear power plant of 4.8Mt/year was denied to be allocated ex-post. Lithuanian government will establish ex-ante procedure until 1st November 2006. 4) De minimis threshold only in Flemish NAP included, but other regions in Belgium seem to adopt it too. Energy typically corresponds to power installations, but some countries will also include combustion installations in general (e.g. steam generators). Million EUAs corresponding to Million t of CO_2 emissions.

Source: National allocation plans of various countries

www.climatepolicy.com

Emission projections 2008–2012 versus national allocation plans II

Karsten Neuhoff[1]*, Federico Ferrario[1], Michael Grubb[1], Etienne Gabel[2], Kim Keats[2]

[1]University of Cambridge, Faculty of Economics, Austin Robinson Building, Sidgwick Avenue, Cambridge, CB3 9DE, UK
[2] ICF International, Sardinia House, 52 Lincoln's Inn Fields, London WC2A 3LZ

Abstract

We compare the national allocation plans (NAPs), proposed and submitted by EU Member States as of October 2006, with our estimations for CO_2 emissions by the installations covered by these NAPs. The collective allocations proposed under phase II NAPs exceed the historic trend of emissions extrapolated forward. Using our projections we find, depending on uncertainty in fuel prices, economic growth rates, performance of the non-power sector and CDM/JI availability, a 15% chance of a 'dead market' with emissions below cap even at zero prices. With an expected inflow of committed CDM/JI credits of 100 $MtCO_2$/year, allowance supply will exceed demand in 50% of cases without any carbon price, and in 80% of our €20/tCO_2 scenarios. Banking of allowances towards post-2012 conditions could create additional demand, but this is difficult to anticipate and conditional on policy evolution. The proposed phase II NAPs would result in low prices and only small volumes of CDM/JI would enter the EU ETS. CDM/JI would almost exclusively be public-sector funded, placing the cost of Kyoto compliance entirely upon governments.

Keywords: Emissions trading; Allocation plan; Europe; Projections

1. Introduction

This article projects the balance of supply and demand of allowances to emit CO_2 under the European emissions trading scheme (EU ETS) for the period 2008–2012. This balance will determine the scarcity, and hence the allowance price, during this period. Our aim is therefore to assess the collective implications of the proposed plans for the operation of the EU ETS in phase II.

Installations covered by the scheme have to provide CO_2 allowances for every tonne of CO_2 they emit. This forms the demand for allowances under the scheme. The supply to the market follows from tradable allowances allocated to existing or new installations or auctioned by governments as defined in the national allocation plans. The linking directive allows for some additional allowance supply to the EU-ETS market from project credits under the clean development mechanism (CDM) or joint implementation (JI) projects. To the extent that allowances from the

* Corresponding author. Tel.: +44-1223-335290; fax: +44-1223-335299
E-mail address: karsten.neuhoff@econ.cam.ac.uk

period 2008–2012 are banked to future periods, this would create additional demand. It seems rather certain that no allowances from the period post-2012 can be borrowed to cover emissions in the period 2008–2012, so no additional supply from banking is expected.

In light of the NAPs that have been proposed by Member States for the second phase, this article aims to assess their aggregate impact on the market. We first collated the information in each plan – itself a complex exercise given some of the special provisions. Then we made different projections for the possible inflow of allowances from the CDM and JI project mechanisms. We start by comparing allocation against extrapolation of past trends. The main contribution of the article is a projection of the CO_2 emissions from installations covered by the European emission trading scheme. With the models we explore the implications of different price and growth scenarios.

In projecting these emissions we started from the verified emission data from the year 2005. For the non-power sectors we used two different modelling approaches to project the anticipated emissions in the period 2008–2012 on a sectoral level for each country. In the power sector, emissions are very sensitive to fuel and CO_2 prices. Therefore we applied a detailed power sector model developed by ICF International to project country-level emissions.

One inherent uncertainty in this field is caused by limited or restricted data availability. First, there is still some concern about the accuracy of monitoring of CO_2 allowances at the installation level – and future changes to the monitoring guidelines could alter the aggregate monitored emissions. Second, for three Member States, only limited information about verified emissions for our base year 2005 was available. If aggregate emissions of installations covered by ETS in these Member States were below our assumptions, then the gap between projected emissions and the cap could be bigger (and vice versa). In Section 6 we provide a more detailed discussion of the sensitivity of our modelling to various parameters and model choices.

We projected emissions and assessed the cap on a national level. We also verified our power sector model, the assumptions on the cap and the split between sectors on the national level. However, we did not have the resources to comprehensively compare our projections against all national projections.

2. Methodology and assumptions

To project future CO_2 emissions, we treat the power sector separately from other sectors covered by the ETS. For the power sector we examine emissions using the Integrated Planning Model (IPM) of ICF International, which simulates every European power station and investment decisions in new power stations. For the remaining sectors we use two approaches. First, we start from the verified emissions from 2005, adjust for the coverage of the ETS and then apply sector-specific growth rates from a recent DTI BAU study combined with country-specific CO_2 growth rates from OECD projections (OECD, 2006). The second approach to project emissions of the non-power sectors involves applying country- and sector-specific CO_2 growth rates as determined by the E3ME model of Cambridge Econometrics and calibrated for the Matisse FP6 project (Matisse, 2006), assuming CO_2 prices around €20/tCO_2. The detailed assumptions and our treatment of missing data are explained in Appendices 1 and 2.

To explore sensitivity to prices, we use four different fuel price assumptions from a recent UK Department of Trade and Industry study (DTI, 2006b) (see Appendix 3).

To determine the total cap, we use the publicly available data from NAPs, assuming that all New Entrant Reserves (NERs) will be issued. Some NAPs envisage that New Entrant Reserves will be

Table 1. Our estimations of CAP including inflows from
JI and CDM projects (MtCO$_2$/year)

CAP	2074
CAP with NER	2178
CAP with NER, high CDM/JI inflow	2378

cancelled if not issued to new entrants.[1] Without any new build in these countries, the total EU cap would be reduced by 20 MtCO$_2$/year.

We furthermore take into account the potential inflow of allowances into the EU ETS from CDM and JI projects. Following a more detailed discussion in Grubb and Neuhoff (2006), we assume a potential range of between 0 and 1,000 MtCO$_2$ international project credits and allowances to enter the ETS during the period 2008–2012. The upper level is one-third lower than the total projected availability of CDM and JI for Europe, assuming that at least some of the inflow would be taken by government inflow in all cases; it is also roughly consistent with the 'supplementarity' constraint that many Member States have built into their plans in line with Kyoto commitments, representing, even at this maximum level, an inflow of less than 10% of allocated allowances. Indeed the EU Commission insisted in their decision on the first 10 second-phase NAPs (Nov 2006) that some Member States tighten their supplementary condition. Table 1 gives the range that we assume for cap and inflow (Appendix 4).

3. Emission projections in relation to historic trends

To verify our emission projections, we first compared them to historic emissions from 1990–2004 using data from the European Community GHG Inventory (EEA, 2006) as shown in Figures 1 and 2.

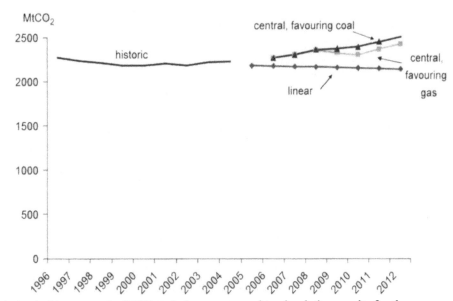

Figure 1. Linear trend of ETS emissions compared to simulation results for the case of zero CO$_2$ price and central fuel price assumptions.

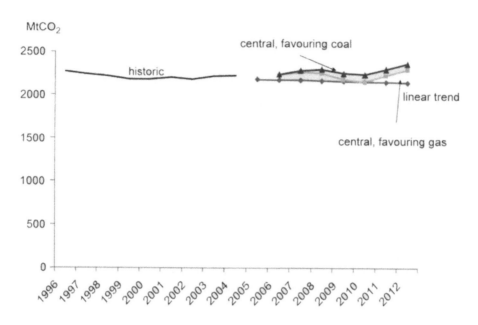

Figure 2. Linear trend of ETS emissions compared to simulation results for the case
of a €20/tCO$_2$ price and central fuel price assumptions.

As the Inventory only provides data on the total national greenhouse gas emissions, we follow
Georgopoulou et al. (2006) and assume that the share of emissions associated with ETS sectors
stays constant. Fitting a linear trend to this historic emission from 1990–2004 (later start for
accession countries), we then extrapolated the BAU development of emissions for 2005–2012
(Appendix 5).

Figures 1 and 2 illustrate that the emissions under this linear trend are lower than projected in
the two central fuel price scenarios as defined by the UK Department of Industry (DTI, 2006a).
The most likely reason for this, despite a decade of decline or stability, is that the model assumes
a slowdown in the rate of energy efficiency improvements and a slowdown in the historic shift
from coal towards natural gas, in the light of higher natural gas prices. We do, however, note a
general tendency that models have previously projected emissions growth that has not materialized.
As our model approach is also likely to underestimate emission reductions from unanticipated
technological, institutional and behavioural changes, our results may be conservative – the excess
allocation that we estimate for NAP IIs might in practice be even higher. To set this in the context
of phase II allocations, the total phase II cap with NER implied by the proposed NAPs is slightly
above the average emissions levels over the past 10 years.

Figure 2 illustrates that with a price of €20/tCO$_2$, emissions from the ETS sectors are projected
to be roughly stable at current levels, still slightly above the historic trend.

4. Numerical results from simulations under uncertainty

Figure 3 compares the total NAP II allocation (the horizontal line spanning 2008–2012) against
most recent emissions data (2005), the phase I cap, and a range of projections for emissions over
the period assuming €0/tCO$_2$. We assume four different fuel price scenarios, three different economic
growth rates, and apply two different models for the non-power sector. Thus the projection range

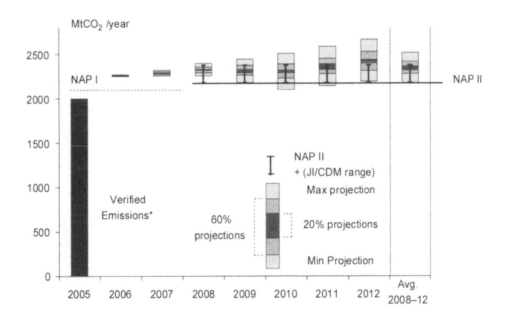

Figure 3. Projected CO_2 emissions versus cap for the BAU (assuming zero CO_2 price).

depicts the outcome of 24 different model scenarios. The vertical lines with T-endings show the range of potential inflow from JI and CDM credits into ETS.

Note that the phase I cap was significantly above the 2005 verified emissions, and the NAP II allocations in turn represent a significant increase over phase I. This suggests that Member States did not take on board the experience from the observed crash in CO_2 prices in May 2006 when proposing their NAPs for phase II.

Our model estimates of emissions for 2006 exceed the 2005 verified emissions, for four reasons. First, in the electricity modelling we do not reflect that some gas generation is operated, despite being more expensive than coal, because it is supplied under take-or-pay gas contracts. This would have decreased CO_2 emissions by 100 Mt. Second, the electricity model calculates aggregate CO_2 emissions for the year 2006 that exceed verified emissions in 2005 by 25 Mt. We decided against scaling the output to match the observed data, as the differences could equally be caused by slight variations in input prices and hydro availability. Third, with GDP growth, emissions from the non-power sector are expected to grow by 25 Mt. Fourth, 63.1 Mt of additional installations are covered under NAP II that either opted out of NAP I or where the coverage was extended.

The range of results for 2008–2012 illustrates that emission projections are subject to considerable uncertainty. Figure 3 shows the distribution in terms of five probability bands, with the central red illustrating the central 20% of scenario outcomes. The results show that, even with a zero carbon price (a 'no EU ETS' scenario):

– *Without any inflow of CDM and JI credits, allowance supply will exceed demand in 20% of our scenarios.* In other words, based on the proposed NAPs for the second phase and a range of other input assumptions, there is a one-in-five risk that the EU ETS would be unable to sustain any carbon market or incentive to abate, at home or abroad. We could only expect a positive price if banking moves a significant share of the allowances towards the post-2012 period.

– *If inflows from JI and CDM projects are high (200 MtCO$_2$/year), 80% of the projections result in excess supply.* Obviously, there is a certain paradox in a combination of high emission credit imports with an overall surplus market, but it illustrates that current phase II allocations are extremely unlikely to support private purchase of emission credits on the scale that suppliers may be hoping for, even at very low carbon prices.

Figure 4 illustrates the equivalent results if the power sector adjusts investment and operational decisions to reflect a carbon price of €20/tCO$_2$. Obviously, this reduces the total emissions in our 24 model scenarios, as depicted.

Figure 4 shows that:

– in 50% of the scenarios assuming an allowance price of €20/tCO$_2$, emissions would fall below the European cap even without any inflows of JI and CDM credits into the EU ETS;
– at the high level of credit inflow, the probability of sustaining a €20/tCO$_2$ price is very small, and even in our central case (100 MtCO$_2$/year), there is only a 20% chance of the market sustaining a price of €20/tCO$_2$.

This suggests that the currently published allocation levels of NAPs II are simply not consistent with sustaining CO$_2$ prices at significant levels.

The level of the CO$_2$ emissions in this projection suggests that if the European countries want to ensure CO$_2$ prices close to €20/tCO$_2$ then allocation has to be cut back significantly to reduce the aggregated EU cap. The implication based on our projections is that if a 200 Mt tightening were associated with a similar level of JI/CDM imports (200 Mt/year), there would then be roughly a 50% chance of the market sustaining a price of around €20/tCO$_2$ – before taking account of

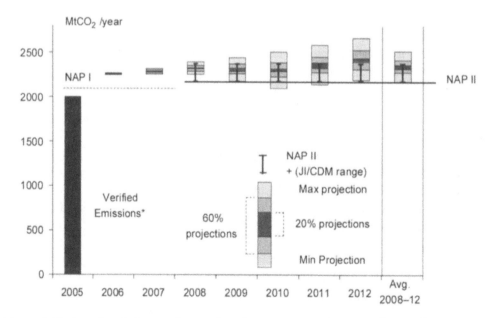

Figure 4. Projected emissions and cap, when the power sector is exposed to a price of €20/tCO$_2$.

responses outside the power sector. Subsequent to the initial publication of this article, the EU Commission has announced their decision on the first 10 NAPs. If the commission will apply the same methodology across all Member States, then this will, according to our calculations, result in a cut of 200 Mt/year.

5. Discussion

5.1. Implications for the NAP approval process

Comparing the projections for CO_2 emissions presented in this article to the proposed NAPs (before the Commission's decision), we concluded that they are unlikely to support a viable CO_2 market. These conclusions are consistent with those of Betz et al. (2006, this issue) and put a spotlight on the European Commission's NAP approval process. The Commission has to evaluate each NAP on its own merits, in relation to the criteria laid out in the Directive. Nevertheless, given the relative ambition of some of the NAPs (e.g. Spain, Italy, the UK) our collective result must imply that many other NAPs contain over-allocation based on emission projections which, at least when considered collectively, are implausible. This would contravene the relevant terms of the Directive.

A further basis on which the Commission might critically assess the national allocation plans are State Aid considerations. Johnston (2006) argues that free allowance allocation does constitute State Aid, which has to be notified according to the Directive. One relevant provision for the assessment of such State Aid could be the proportionality principle – the benefits from the free allocation should be proportional to the transition costs for companies from the introduction of emission trading.

Moreover, the weak allocations raise questions about the consistency of plans with national Kyoto targets, which is another criterion relevant to Commission assessment. In principle, countries could 'fill the gap' with purchases of JI/CDM, to which we now turn.

5.2. Implications for CDM/JI credits and government purchase

Weak allocations in the EU ETS do not necessarily imply a weak market for CDM/JI credits. As long as countries comply with Kyoto, the total demand for CDM/JI (or equivalent transfers of AAUs under Green Investment Schemes – an option not open to ETS private-sector participants) is set by the difference between national emissions and Kyoto targets over the period 2008–2012. The real implication of weak EU ETS allocations is on the cost of compliance to governments, specifically finance ministries and taxpayers, through three factors:

- *Substitution*: more allocations to ETS sectors mean that the private sector will have less need to purchase CDM/JI credits that would contribute to national compliance; governments must pay for these directly.
- *Increased total need*: a weak EU ETS price means that EU ETS sectors undertake less abatement, resulting in higher national emissions, and in aggregate a greater total need for CDM/JI credits. National governments could also decide to acquire additional credits (AAUs) from countries such as Russia and the Ukraine.
- *Price escalation*: the greater aggregate demand for CDM/JI credits might reasonably be assumed to have some impact on the overall CDM/JI market, increasing the price.

In short, the excessive allocations under the proposed national allocation plans mean that governments have to take up the slack, and substitute for less domestic abatement by funding additional abatement abroad at a higher unit cost to the taxpayer. This would imply that the Kyoto credits market will become a largely public-sector funded operation, rather than leveraging the private investment that many had originally envisaged.

The excessive EU ETS allocation would thus conflict with a desirable emissions pathway. It is also inconsistent with the principle that ETS sectors' share of the national emission budget should decline given large mitigation potentials, especially in the power sector.

5.3. Implications for auctioning and other mechanisms

This article has argued that the continuation of the EU ETS as an effective market during the Kyoto period requires that the currently proposed volume of total free allocations is reduced, probably by a couple of hundred $MtCO_2$ per year. However, our analysis has emphasized the high levels of uncertainty prevalent in emission projections. This suggests that Member States should consider carefully measures to increase price stability and thus improve investment certainty.

One option would be the increased use of auctions. Auctions in themselves could, in principle, provide a source of revenue for government purchases of Kyoto credits. In addition, if all Member States were to auction allowances within the 10% limit of the Directive (200 Mt/year) and the auctions were implemented with a price floor, then this would cover the range of uncertainty in the projections (Hepburn et al., 2006). This could ensure that, in the case of low emissions, a reduced inflow from the auctions would maintain prices, without distorting the demand/supply balance in the case of higher demand.

Banking of allowances to the period post-2012 could also help to support the price, if participants believe that the future allowance price will be higher. Banking has worked effectively in SO_2 and NO_x programmes in the USA (Ellerman, 2006). However, the same mechanism in the EU ETS would be subject to a high degree of uncertainty due to its iterative allocation approach and the complexity of post-2012 negotiations. These added uncertainties could subject the EU ETS to greater price volatility, and may thus reduce the effectiveness of banking as a mechanism to reduce investment risk.[2]

6. Caveats and sensitivities

It is important to note that this study does not calculate the impact of CO_2 prices on the CO_2 emissions of the non-power sector. It relies on (a) a DTI study (DTI/OEF, 2006), which assumes CO_2 emissions under a zero CO_2 price and then gives aggregate figures on the price response of the covered sector to allowance prices, and (b) the E3ME study (Matisse, 2006), which assumes a positive allowance price (increasing from €18 to €25/tCO_2 during phase II). Using data from the E3ME study, our emission projections for the non-power ETS sectors decrease by 75 Mt relative to our simulations based on DTI data. As both approaches differ in various dimensions, it is not clear to what extent this difference can be attributed to the emission reductions or are due to CO_2 prices. Therefore we did not differentiate between the two approaches, and depicted the results both for the €0 and €20/tCO_2 case as a component of the prediction uncertainty.

Table 2 illustrates how different assumptions affect the projected CO_2 emissions from the EU ETS sectors. As a basis for Figures 3 and 4 we calculated the impact of combining all these scenarios.

Table 2. Sensitivity of projected CO_2 emissions to model parameters

(Average 2008–2012)	Zero CO_2 price		€20/tCO_2	
	MtCO$_2$/year	Change	MtCO$_2$/year	Change
Central fuel price favouring gas, DTI	2352		2218	
Matisse study with E3ME for non power	2277	–3.2%	2143	–3.4%
Fuel price scenario, central favouring coal	2416	2.7%	2289	3.2%
Fuel price scenario, low fuel price	2316	–1.5%	2160	–2.6%
Fuel price scenario, high fuel price	2444	3.9%	2407	8.5%
GDP growth 0.75% higher/a (= CO_2 growth)	2424	3.1%	2286	3.0%
GDP growth 0.75% lower/a (= CO_2 growth)	2282	–3.0%	2152	–3.0%

7. Conclusions

We compared the volumes of EUA supply proposed in the NAPs to a range of emission projections to assess whether there will be scarcity and a thus a viable emissions trading market. For this purpose, we combined a detailed power sector model for all European countries with two approaches to project emissions of the non-power emissions covered by ETS, and simulated CO_2 emissions until 2012. We used the data from currently available national allocation plans and extrapolated to the outstanding plans to determine the currently envisaged emission cap under ETS for the period 2008–2012. We also made assumptions about the possible inflows of JI and CDM project credits into the ETS.

The results suggest that it is possible that emissions will be lower than the volume of issued allowances in the scheme in a scenario where we assumed zero CO_2 prices and it is very likely that emissions will fall short of allowances in the scheme in a scenario with €20 t/CO_2. Thus, very low CO_2 prices are likely to result from the currently proposed second-phase NAPs. In the current arrangement only extensive banking into the period post-2012 could ensure a significant positive CO_2 price. However, given the uncertainty about post-2012 arrangements, such banking is unlikely to attribute very high values to allowances, and given the complexity of political negotiations, such banking is likely to introduce large volatilities in the prices of ETS allowances throughout the period 2008–2012. Hence the future of EU ETS risks being heavily undermined by second-phase NAPs submitted to the European Commission, unless decisions are made to amend proposals in line with a tighter overall volume of allowance allocation. Since the initial publication of the study, the Commission has decided on the first 10 national allocation plans, and has requested that nine countries reduce the total volume of allocated allowances. The range of CO_2 emissions simulated for the year 2008–2012 illustrates how sensitive emissions can be to changing GDP growth rates, fuel prices and to energy intensity and technology development in all sectors. To increase the predictability of CO_2 prices in the light of this uncertainty, one might consider using the flexibility of the EU Directive and lessen free allocation to sectors that are not exposed to competition outside of the EU (e.g. the power sector). The allowances not issued for free could then be auctioned, e.g. 10% of the allowances issued per country. If a harmonized European price floor were to be used in these auctions, then this could help to manage the volatility inherent in any system in which cutbacks are modest compared with the intrinsic uncertainties in emission trends, and create confidence that the price will not drop below the price floor. This would facilitate investment in low-carbon technologies and energy efficiency.

Acknowledgements

This article was sponsored by Climate Strategies (www.climate-strategies.org), with the Carbon Trust as lead investor. The opinions expressed in this article are those of the authors and do not express the views of the Carbon Trust. We are grateful for detailed input data on sectoral emission growth rates from Terry Barker (4CMR, Cambridge University), for detailed analysis of verified emission data from Stephan Schleicher (WIFO, Austria), and detailed comments from colleagues belonging to the Climate Strategies research network: Felix Matthes (Öko Institute, Germany), Luis Olmos (IIT, University Comillas, Spain), Jos Sijm (ECN, Netherlands), Michal Sobotka (University of Cambridge) and Misato Sato (University of Cambridge).

Notes

1 The NAPs specify that Cyprus, Denmark, Lithuania, Latvia, Malta and Portugal should not sell the excess NER back to the market. In the French NAP it has not been decided whether to cancel the excess NER or auction it, but for the purpose of calculating the maximum possible reduction of the cap, we assume that it will be cancelled.
2 Note also that, in the longer term, governments could issue option contracts for CO_2, also ensuring a price floor (Ismer and Neuhoff, 2006). European governments could thus guarantee buying back allowances until the scarcity of allowances is increased to the strike price of the option contracts.

References

Betz, R., Rogge, K., Schleich, J., 2006. EU emissions trading: an early analysis of national allocation plans for 2008–2012. Climate Policy 6(4), 361–394.
DTI, 2006a. UK Energy and CO_2 Emissions Predictions: Updated Projections to 2020. Department of Trade and Industry, February 2006 [available at http://reporting.dti.gov.uk/cgi-bin/rr.cgi/http://www.dti.gov.uk/files/file26363.pdf].
DTI, 2006b. UK Energy and CO_2 Emissions Predictions: Updated Projections to 2020. Department of Trade and Industry, July 2006 [available at http://reporting.dti.gov.uk/cgi-bin/rr.cgi/http://www.dti.gov.uk/files/file31861.pdf].
DTI/OEF, 2006. Research on Output Growth Rates and Carbon Dioxide Emissions of the Industrial Sectors of the EU ETS. Department of Trade and Industry, Oxford Economic Forecast, February 2006 [available at http://reporting.dti.gov.uk/cgi-bin/rr.cgi/http://www.dti.gov.uk/files/file26365.pdf].
EEA, 2006. Annual European Community Greenhouse Gas Inventory 1990–2004 and Inventory Report 2006. Submission to the UNFCCC Secretariat, EEA Technical Report No. 6/2006, June 2006.
Ellerman, A.D., 2006. The US SO2 cap-and-trade programme. In: OECD, Tradeable Permits – Policy Evaluation, Design and Reform. Organization for Economic Cooperation and Development, Paris, pp. 71–98.
Entec, 2006. Analysis of the EU ETS News Flows for an Investor Audience, Final Report for The Carbon Trust, June 2006.
EU Commission, 2006a. Community Independent Transaction Log [available at http://ec.europa.eu/environment/ets/].
EU Commission, 2006b. Allocation Plans and Decisions for 2008 to 2012, European Commission, DG Environment [available at http://ec.europa.eu/environment/climat/2nd_phase_ep.htm].
Eurostat, 2006. Real GDP Growth Rate, Economy and Finance – Main Structural Indicators [available at http://epp.eurostat.ec.europa.eu/portal/page?_pageid=1996,39140985&_dad=portal&_schema=PORTAL&screen=detailref&language=en&product=SDI_MAIN&root=SDI_MAIN/sdi/sdi_ed/sdi_ed_inv/sdi_ed1110].
Georgopoulou, E., Sarafidis, Y., Mirasgedis, S., Lalas, D.P., 2006. Next allocation phase of the EU emissions trading scheme: how tough will the future be? Energy Policy 34(18), 4002–4023.
Grubb, M., Neuhoff, K., 2006. Allocation and competitiveness in the EU emissions trading scheme: policy overview. Climate Policy 6(1), 7–30.
Hepburn, C., Grubb, M., Neuhoff, K., Matthes, F., Tse, M., 2006. Auctioning of EU ETS phase II allowances: how and why? Climate Policy 6(1), 137–160.
IMF, 2006. World Economic Outlook. International Monetary Fund, Washington, DC.

Ismer, R., Neuhoff, K., 2006. Commitments through Financial Options: A Way to Facilitate Compliance with Climate Change Obligations. Electricity Policy Research Group Working Paper. EPRG 06/25 [available at http://www.electricitypolicy.org.uk/pubs/wp/eprg0625.pdf].

Johnston, A., 2006. Free allocation of allowances under the EU emissions trading scheme: legal issues. Climate Policy 6(1), 115–136.

Matisse, 2006. Project supported by the Sixth Framework Programme of the European Union [information available at http://www.matisse-project.net/projectcomm].

OECD, 2006. OECD Economic Outlook No. 79. Organization for Economic Cooperation and Development, Paris.

UCTE [Union for the Co-ordination of Transmission of Electricity] [available at http://www.ucte.org].

WIFO, 2006. EU Emissions Trading Scheme: The 2005 Evidence. Austrian Institute for Economic Research, Vienna.

Appendix 1: Verified emissions

We started with verified emission data (EU Commission, 2006a, 27 September 2006) differentiated into iron and steel, cement, lime, glass, pulp and paper, ceramics, others, and primary aluminium. Based on WIFO (2006), we separated the classification combustion installations into power- and non-power-related combustion installations. Since we could not allocate the non-power combustion installations to specific sectors, we included them in the category 'others'.

For Poland, data on only 331 installations were available as of 27 September 2006, representing allocated allowances for 115.2 $MtCO_2$ out of a total NAP I of 239.1 $MtCO_2$. We assumed that the installations not reported in the CITL will have the same ratio to allocated emissions as the installations for which already reported data are available. Thus we assumed 189.0 $MtCO_2$ emissions for Polish installations covered by ETS in 2005 (implying a total national surplus of 50.1 $MtCO_2$). In our simulations of the European power sector, we calculated 132 $MtCO_2$ emissions for Polish power installations covered by ETS, and used this figure to separate between power- and non-power-related emissions.

For Cyprus and Malta no data were available and we assumed that they had the same ratio between verified emissions and NAP I allocation as the Member States for which full data were available. We did not have data available that allowed us to differentiate between power and non-power installations and thus applied a general emission growth trend to all emissions.

We added to these verified emissions the volume of new installations covered under NAP II that either opted out or were not covered under NAP I (5.3 $MtCO_2$ in Belgium, 11 Mt in Germany, 32 Mt in the UK, 6.6 $MtCO_2$ in the Netherlands, 5.5 in France, 0.7 in Portugal, 2 in Sweden).

Appendix 2: Projections for the non-power sector

To project the CO_2 emissions for the non-power sector, we first used an approach based on a recent DTI study (DTI, 2006a, 2000b) and then an approach based on a European model developed by Cambridge Econometrics.

For the first approach, we applied to the verified emissions per sector and country the sector-specific emission growth rates used by the UK DTI (DTI, 2006a; DTI/OEF, 2006), scaled by the differences in the expected national growth rates (Table 3). For example, the Spanish GDP is expected to grow 0.6% faster in 2006 than the UK GDP; thus we also assumed that emissions across the sectors increase 0.6% faster in Spain than in the UK. GDP growth projections for the period 2006–2007 are based on Eurostat (2006) and for the period 2008–2012 are based on OECD (2006) and IMF (2006).

Table 3. Assumed GDP growth rates

	2006	2007	2008–2012
AT	2.5%	2.2%	2.4%
BE	2.3%	2.1%	1.9%
CY	3.8%	3.8%	2.8%
CZ	5.3%	4.7%	3.8%
DE	1.7%	1.0%	2.0%
DK	3.2%	2.3%	1.1%
EE	8.9%	7.9%	4.6%
ES	3.1%	2.8%	2.5%
FI	3.6%	2.9%	1.5%
FR	1.9%	2.0%	2.1%
GR	3.5%	3.4%	3.1%
HU	4.6%	4.2%	3.0%
IE	4.9%	5.1%	3.6%
IT	1.3%	1.2%	1.4%
LT	6.5%	6.2%	4.6%
LU	4.4%	4.5%	4.0%
LV	8.5%	7.6%	4.6%
MT	1.7%	1.9%	4.6%
NL	2.6%	2.6%	2.1%
PL	4.5%	4.6%	4.5%
PT	0.9%	1.1%	2.0%
SE	3.4%	3.0%	1.8%
SI	4.3%	4.1%	4.6%
SK	6.1%	6.5%	5.5%
UK	2.4%	2.8%	2.5%

Sources: 2006–2007 data from Eurostat (2006)
2008–2012 data from OECD (2006), except for CY, EE, LT, LV, MT and SI
(IMF, 2006).

The application of the DTI model outside of the UK makes the implicit assumption that the technological mix within a sector is roughly comparable across Europe. This is certainly a bold assumption, but we have no data available that allow us to assess what type of bias it introduces. By correcting for the relative size of different sectors, we intend to address the main concern of any such transfer – a different sectoral composition between countries.

The second approach uses sector- and country-specific growth rates computed from Cambridge Econometrics modelling. They represent those of the baseline scenario for the FP6 project Matisse using the E3ME model, covering the 2005–2010 period (Matisse, 2006). For the purposes of this article, we assume that the sector-specific growth rates are constant in 2011 and 2012. As the definitions of sectors under E3ME did not exactly match the classifications of verified emissions, we matched these sectors as described in Table 4.

Table 4. Mapping of E3ME model results to classification used for verified emissions

CITL	Matisse/E3ME
Refineries	2 – Other energy own use and transformation
Cement and lime	6 – Non metallic NES
Ceramics	6 – Non metallic NES
Glass	6 – Non metallic NES
Pulp and paper	10 – Pulp and paper
Iron and steel	3 – Iron and steel
Other	12 – Other industry

Note: NES = not elsewhere specified.

Table 5. Fossil fuel price assumptions from DTI (2006b)

	Central – Favouring GAS			Central – Favouring COAL		
	Oil ($/bbl)	Gas (p/therm)	Coal (£/t)	Oil ($/bbl)	Gas (p/therm)	Coal (£/t)
2005	55	41	33.6	55	41	33.6
2010	40	25.8	27.2	40	33.5	27.2
2015	42.5	27.3	26.1	42.5	35	26.1
2020	45	28.8	25	45	36.5	25
	High prices			Low prices		
	Oil ($/bbl)	Gas (p/therm)	Coal (£/t)	Oil ($/bbl)	Gas (p/therm)	Coal (£/t)
2005	55	41	33.6	55	41	33.6
2010	67	49.9	36.5	20	18	19
2015	69.5	51.4	36.5	20	9.5	16.8
2020	72	53	36.5	20	21	14.6

Appendix 3: Projections for the power sector

For our analysis of the European power sector, we use the Integrated Planning Model (IPM) developed by ICF International. The IPM is a linear programming model that selects generating and investment options to meet overall electricity demand today and on an ongoing and forward-looking basis over the chosen planning horizon at minimum cost. Further details about the model are available from the EPA website (http://www.epa.gov/airmarkets/epa-ipm/).

Table 5 gives the fuel price assumptions for which we followed the July study of the Department of Trade and Industry in the UK (DTI, 2006b). These prices were also applied to other European countries, correcting for location/transport costs and adjusting the differing intra annual price profile for gas between the UK and continental Europe. Demand projections are based on the UCTE forecasts for all Member States except the UK (based on DTI projections).

We assumed that the EU renewables target is satisfied. The model calculates the emissions for all power stations. For one central fuel price scenario, we determined the volume of emissions that results from installations with less than 20 MW thermal capacity (56.4 MtCO$_2$/year). As these installations are mainly heat-driven, we assumed the emissions to stay constant across the time frame considered and across fuel price scenarios.

For the simulations, we constrained new-build CCGT and coal plants to those already commissioned until 2013. The only plants coming on before 2013 are firm builds, unplanned CT units and unplanned wind installations (this reflects the idea that for a CCGT or coal plant to become operational by 2012 it will already have to be commissioned today). This might understate the potential for emissions reductions from a more rapid shift to gas through additional investment in gas generation. However, given that we already observe an increase in gas demand for power generation in Europe in the low fuel price scenario with ETS price (from 6,700 TBtu to 11,300 TBtu coverage exceeding ETS), it is reasonable to assume caution with additional shifts to gas generation.

Table 6 presents the aggregate CO_2 emissions for European emissions, using the DTI-based projection on emissions from the non-power sector.

When comparing the model results in 2006 with the 2005 verified power sector emissions, we observed that we exceeded these emissions. This is what we expected, as many gas power stations have long-term take-or-pay contracts and were thus operating despite the high 2005 gas prices. To test our model, we implemented a minimum run requirement on gas. On a country-by-country basis, the same amount of gas had to be used in the power sector in the 2006 as observed in 2003. Using this constraint, our 2006 simulated data for all countries excluding Poland, Malta and Cyprus exceeded the verified emissions data for the power sector of these countries by only 2%. Most deviations on a per-country basis could be explained by the specific climatic conditions in the year 2005. Therefore we were content to use the model for emission projections.

For our long-term projections, we did not apply the minimum gas consumption constraint. We assume that the take-or-pay contracts for gas that we reflected in this constraint will be resolved as part of the European liberalization or that new gas-powered stations will be exposed to the market price for gas.

Appendix 4: NAPs II

We used information on the second-phase cap from the national allocation plans submitted to the EU Commission (2006b), and from the NAP II drafts published for public debate by those countries that had not officially approved them yet, as they represent the most up-to-date data available.

Table 6. EU emission projections for power sector using IPM model (MtCO$_2$) and based on DTI sector projections for non-power sector

CO$_2$ price	Fossil-fuel price scenario	2006	2007	2008	2009	2010	2011	2012
€0/tCO$_2$	Central – Fav GAS	2268	2299	2351	2322	2301	2363	2423
	Central – Fav COAL	2268	2303	2361	2373	2392	2448	2505
	High Prices	2268	2301	2355	2389	2433	2493	2549
	Low Prices	2269	2302	2352	2286	2240	2314	2388
€20/tCO$_2$	Central – Fav GAS	2228	2269	2255	2177	2149	2220	2289
	Central – Fav COAL	2239	2283	2299	2251	2236	2298	2362
	High Prices	2251	2290	2325	2342	2394	2459	2515
	Low Prices	2225	2263	2216	2140	2064	2147	2232
€20/tCO$_2$	Central – Fav gas, minimum gas constraint	2128						

As the NAPs for DK and HU have not been published (as of 24 September 2006) we assumed the same ratio between their cap 2005–2007 and 2008–2012 as applicable to the average of the other Member States.

We included the entire New Entrant Reserve in the cap and also included the emissions that are currently envisaged for auctions (7% UK, 0.29% Belgium, 3.9 $MtCO_2$ Netherlands, 2.6 $MtCO_2$ Poland, 0.48 $MtCO_2$ Lithuania, 0.11 $MtCO_2$ Ireland, 0.4 $MtCO_2$ Austria, 0.19 $MtCO_2$ Luxembourg).

We assume that total available CDM and JI credits for the period 2008–2012 are between 800 and 2,200 $MtCO_2$, while Japanese demand could range between 250 and 1,000 $MtCO_2$ (Grubb and Neuhoff, 2006). Very high availability is unlikely to coincide with very low Japanese demand and vice versa. We also have to allow for demand from governments to cover excess emissions in the non-covered sector. Thus we assume that inflows into ETS in the period 2008–2012 could range between 0 and 1,000 $MtCO_2$. Table 1 summarizes our assumptions about the cap.

Appendix 5: Historical emissions and linear trends

We used data on the total per-country greenhouse gas emissions for the period 1990–2004 from the annual European Community GHG Inventory (EEA, 2006).

Projections for 2005–2012 have been obtained by linear regression of the available sample of total GHG emissions for each country. The initial analysis on a country-by-country basis pointed to the well-known strong decline in emissions in accession countries during their early transformation in the 1990s, and therefore we subsequently excluded data for the Czech Republic, Estonia, Hungary, Lithuania, Latvia and Slovakia for the years until 1992, 1993, 1992, 1998, 1995 and 1993 for the estimation of the linear trend.

We then used data on the ETS share of CO_2 emissions relative to the total GHG emissions from Georgopoulou et al. (2006) based on 2003 data, and thus were able to derive the linear trend for EU ETS BaU emissions projections.

By adopting this procedure the implicit assumption was made that the proportion of greenhouse gases from 'trading' and 'non-trading' sectors would remain unchanged. As emissions from some of the non-trading sectors, such as transport, are in fact expected to increase significantly, it is likely that our approach overstates the extrapolated CO_2 emissions of the covered sector. This indicates that our estimations of CO_2 emission reductions in the covered sector are conservative and might potentially be higher, e.g. even more stringent caps would be required to ensure a strong CO_2 price.

Appendix 6: CITL classifications

An analysis of the CITL raw data performed by Entec highlighted the existence of 'some fundamental errors with regard to classification in the EC database of sites by sector/activity', although the cause is 'not yet known' (Entec, 2006, p. 4). Some of the problems of misclassification are addressed in our projections:

- An analysis of the CITL classification compared to that of NAP I for Spain, Italy and the UK illustrates some differences, which are, however, not persistent across countries and sectors. For Italy, the discrepancy is minimal (with the maximum around 2%), while although it is more relevant for the UK and Spain, it is not in the same sectors. Therefore, on aggregate, they might to some extent average out.

– Thanks to more accurate aggregate country data for the power sector (including CHP) provided by WIFO, it has been possible to correctly distinguish non-power verified emissions from the CITL 'combustion' class, thus substantially reducing the possible distortion scope to only 44% of the total cap in terms of allocations.

– If remaining errors are in the order of 5% and imply misspecification between sectors that have different projected CO_2 growth rates of 2%, then the aggregate error (1.02^7 after 7 years, e.g. 15%) is 0.3%.

Appendix 7: Analysis – allocated versus verified

Based on the data available in the Community Independent Transaction Log we were able to compare for every installation the verified emissions with the allocated allowances for the year 2005 (EU Commission, 2006a). We grouped all installations where over/under-allocation fell within ranges of ±2.5% under/over allocation. The intervals were then labelled according to the middle value of the interval. The remaining installations were summarized in the +100% and –100% categories.

Figure 5 shows the distribution of total emission permits according to the extent of under/over-allocation at the installation level as a fraction of the allocation received. The distribution is bell-shaped with a mean higher than zero, reflecting the overall long position of the EU ETS. According to the CITL classification, non-combustion installations, in general, received more allowances compared to their needs than combustion installations, although the latter includes both power and non-power sector installations, thus distorting the analysis by adding over-allocated installations to the category.

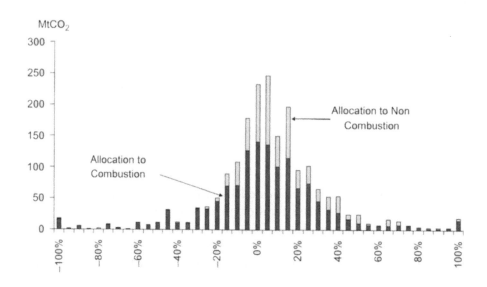

Neuhoff, Ferrario, Grubb, Gabel, Keats (Sept 2006)

Figure 5. Relationship between verified emissions and allowances allocated to installations in 2005.

Implications of announced phase II national allocation plans for the EU ETS

Karsten Neuhoff[1]*, Markus Åhman[2], Regina Betz[3], Johanna Cludius[3], Federico Ferrario[1], Kristina Holmgren[2], Gabriella Pal[4], Michael Grubb[1], Felix Matthes[5], Karoline Rogge[6], Misato Sato[1], Joachim Schleich[6], Jos Sijm[7], Andreas Tuerk[8,9], Claudia Kettner[8], Neil Walker[10]

[1] *University of Cambridge, Faculty of Economics, Austin Robinson Building, Sidgwick Avenue, Cambridge, CB3 9DE, UK*
[2] *IVL Swedish Environmental Research Institute, Box 210 60, SE 100 31, Stockholm, Sweden*
[3] *Centre for Energy and Environmental Markets (CEEM), Lecturer School of Economics, University of NSW, Sydney 2052, Australia*
[4] *Regional Center for Energy Policy Research (REKK), 1093 Budapest, Fövám tér 8, Corvinus University, Budapest, Hungary*
[5] *Öko-Institut (Institute for Applied Ecology), Büro Berlin, Novalisstr. 10, D-10115, Berlin, Germany*
[6] *Fraunhofer Institute for Systems and Innovation Research, Breslauer Strasse 48, 76139 Karlsruhe, Germany*
[7] *Energy Research Centre of the Netherlands (ECN), PO Box 37154, 1030 AD Amsterdam, The Netherlands*
[8] *Wegener Center for Climate and Global Change, Economics Department, University of Graz, Universitaetsstrasse 15/F4, A-8010 Graz, Austria*
[9] *Joanneum Research, Steyrergasse 17–19, 25a, 8010 Graz, Austria*
[10] *University College Dublin, Belfield, Dublin 4, Ireland*

Abstract

We quantified the volume of free allowances that different national allocation plans proposed to allocate to existing and new installations, with specific reference to the power sector. Most countries continue to allocate based on historic emissions, contrary to hopes for improved allocation methods, with allocations to installations frequently based on 2005 emission data; this may strengthen the belief in the private sector that emissions in the coming years will influence their subsequent allowance allocation. Allocations to new installations provide high and frequently fuel-differentiated subsidies, risking significant distortions to investment choices. Thus, in addition to supplying a long market in aggregate, proposed allocation plans reveal continuing diverse problems, including perverse incentives. To ensure the effectiveness of the EU ETS in the future, the private sector will need to be shown credible evidence that free allowance allocation will be drastically reduced post-2012, or that these problems will be addressed in some other way.

Keywords: Emissions trading; National allocation plans; Comparison; European Member States

* Corresponding author. Tel.: +44-1223-335290; fax: +44-1223-335299
E-mail address: karsten.neuhoff@econ.cam.ac.uk

1. Introduction

The EU Emissions Trading Scheme is designed to cap emissions of energy-intensive industry in Europe. Under the European Directive on Emissions Trading, each Member State is required to state within the proposed national allocation plan (NAP), both the allocation volume of emissions allowances to the covered sectors and the allocation methodology.

Sensible decisions on the allocation volume or 'cap' level by Member States are crucial. Stringent caps create scarcity, which holds the key to both the environmental efficacy of the scheme and good functioning of the CO_2 market. Yet, Neuhoff et al. (2006a, this issue) argue that the volume of allowances allocated under the currently proposed NAPs for phase II is too high, by comparing the NAPs with CO_2 emissions projection scenarios and the historic trend of emissions extrapolated forward. The analysis by Betz et al. (2006, this issue) also shows that, in many Member States, allocation for phase II is excessive relative to 2005 emissions, historic trends and country-level projections.

The national allocation plans also have to specify how the allowances are distributed among existing installations, new installations and auctions. Betz et al. (2006, this issue) analyse how the different approaches selected by Member States increase complexity and reduce transparency of the overall system. Much of this complexity arises from industry interests and aims to address distributional concerns. However, the complexity not only complicates participation by industry, but also complicates the role of NGOs and less-informed industrial sectors in controlling the outcome of the political process. Thus the need for harmonization in the methodology used across the Member States has been widely emphasized (e.g. del Rio González, 2006, this issue).

Economic theory and anecdotal evidence also suggest that the methodology chosen for the allowance allocation can directly influence decisions on investment, retrofitting and plant operation.

Fischer (2001) looks at the effects of output-based allocation, Harrison and Radov (2002) provide a policy-oriented description of allocation options, Palmer and Burtraw (2004) focus on distribution effects, Böhringer and Lange (2005) assess macro implications of increased allowance imports from inefficient emission-based allocation, Burtraw et al. (2005) assess the impacts of partial coverage by emissions trading schemes, Entec and NERA (2005) discuss benchmarks, and Matthes et al. (2005) assess distortions in phase I allocation plans, Åhman et al. (2007) argue for longer allocation periods and Bartels and Müsgens (2006) simulate the impact of the German allocation plans on investment decisions. A theoretical framework for the distortions from allocation procedures is provided by Neuhoff et al. (2005) and Sterner and Muller (2006).

This article compares the allocation methodologies envisaged in the different national allocation plans for the period 2008–2012 that have been submitted to the Commission or alternatively which were available in draft format at the end of December 2006.

Taking the power sector as an example, in this study we quantify the differences in free allowance allocation across Member States and across generation technologies.

– For new installations, investment incentives are distorted towards fossil-fuel generation and in many Member States even more towards CO_2-intensive fuel types. This reduces the effectiveness of EU ETS in reducing CO_2 emissions and compliance costs. Free allocation also represents output subsidies and might thus undermine substitution effects to less CO_2-intensive products.

The free allocation of allowances to new installations, with all its negative implications, is unique to the EU ETS, except for a few 'set asides' in the US NO_x programme.

- For existing installations, the heterogeneous allocation can distort the merit order choice, incentives for energy efficiency improvements and closure decisions, again detrimental for the cost-efficiency of the EU ETS in reducing CO_2 emissions. This effect is even stronger if *ex-post* adjustment is allowed. This is under legal dispute between Germany and the European Commission and is still demanded by some Member States. The large differences across countries again illustrate that significant reductions in free allowance allocation are not only economically, but also politically, possible.

A reduction in free allowance allocation in the period 2008–2012 could be used both to reduce the overall level of free allocation to the covered sector and also to increase the share of auctions. In its approval of the first 10 national allocation plans, the EU Commission made auctioning the one area of discretionary flexibility within its decision and where the deadline of 31 December 2006 does not apply. 'Without prior acceptance by the Commission', Member States can increase the share of auctioning up to 10%.

Distortions from the free allocation to existing facilities mainly occur because without credible government commitments about future allocation, owners and operators expect that the future allocation will be similar to the current approach. For example, allocation in many Member States factors installation-level emissions data from 2005 into allocation for 2008–2012. Thus, market participants expect future allocations to be similarly 'updated' over time – large emissions today will be rewarded by large volumes of free allocation in the future. This will distort their investment and operational choices (early action problem) and lead to a less cost-efficient outcome with higher costs to society.

A movement towards less distorting allocation methods increases confidence in non-distorting future allocation methods. The use of auctions and the initial use of benchmarks in some sectors and countries represent a promising start. A strong commitment to rapid phasing-out of free allowance allocation post-2012 could avoid most distortions. A thorough assessment of the free allocation under EC Law State Aid criteria could conclude that the continued allocation post-2012 would offer a disproportionate benefit relative to the cost of the environmental regulation (Johnston, 2006). This could provide a credible commitment towards phasing-out free allocation and thus address the early action problem.

This article does not address closure conditions. The expectation of receiving future allowances within the commitment period or in the next commitment period only with the continued availability or operation of a power station creates an incentive to postpone the retirement of power stations or to invest in the retrofit of power plants rather than closing the power station (Spulber, 1985; Neuhoff et al., 2006b). This distortion is only partially compensated for by transfer provisions (Gagelmann, 2006). Åhman and Holmgren (2006) and Betz et al. (2006, this issue) compare such closure and transfer provisions across Member States.

We summarize the information contained in the currently proposed (28 December 2006) national allocation plans for the period 2008–2012 and present it for general scrutiny in an Excel database.[1] Our first findings regarding the economic effects that might follow from these plans are summarized below. Please note that some national allocation plans still require approval by the Commission, while most of the national allocation plans assessed required some adjustments which are discussed within the Member States.

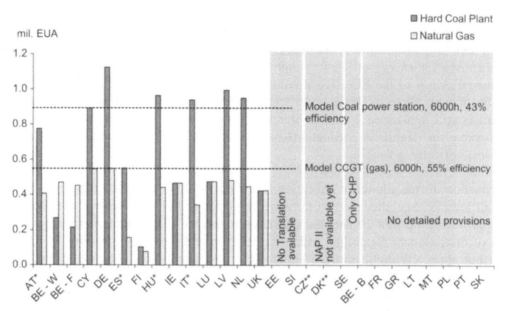

Figure 1. Comparison of new entrant allocation. * Draft NAP, ** NAP not available. In all Figures and Tables the regions of Belgium are identified as BE-F – Flemish, BE-W – Walloon, BE-B – Brussels. A different load factor is used for the UK (5,812 h for both coal and gas), as indicated in NAP II. In Germany (DE) a standardized load factor of 7,500 h is applied to all power plants.

2. Quantity of free allocation to installations – using the power sector as an example

To illustrate the distortions of free allocation to new investment, we calculate the subsidy that it constitutes for new-build coal and gas power stations[2] across the Member States.[3] To facilitate the comparison we assumed that a model power station runs for 6,000 h per year. Figure 1 illustrates that in all Member States, fossil-fuel generators receive high subsidies in terms of free new entrant allocation. In many countries, a new entrant allocation covers the emissions of CCGT gas plants, and in some countries it even covers all the emissions that a coal power station is expected to produce. While it is sometimes argued that new power stations should receive the allowances that they require for covering their emissions, this is not in accordance with economic principles. In liberalized electricity markets, power generators pass the opportunity costs of CO_2 allowances into the electricity price (Burtraw et al., 2002; Neuhoff and Keats-Martinez, 2005) and thus do not require any free allocation. This is desirable in order to achieve substitution effects, and is only avoided where electricity price regulation covers just real costs and not opportunity costs (Burtraw et al., 2005).

Any free allocation represents a subsidy – and where only fossil-fuel generation is subsidized, this distorts investment choices in favour of fossil-fuel generation. Where coal receives a higher allocation than gas, the investment choice is, in addition, distorted towards coal. The level of such subsidies under proposed second-phase NAP is so high that the construction of coal power stations is more profitable under the ETS with such distorting allocation decisions than in the absence of the ETS (Åhman and Holmgren, 2006; Matthes et al., 2006; Neuhoff et al., 2006a, this issue). The long-run consequences of these distortions can be significant since, once built, plants will stay on the system for many decades, significantly increasing the cost of shifting towards a low-carbon economy in the future (Bartels and Müsgens, 2006; Neuhoff et al., 2006b).

The German National Allocation Plan notified to the Commission not only provided the highest allocation for new coal generation in general, but the draft Allocation Law also contained a provision allowing an even higher free allocation for new lignite-fired installations. In addition, the current NAP guarantees the continuation of free fuel-specific allocation for 14 years. This would undermine investments in low-carbon technologies and has not been accepted by the EU Commission in its decision on the German NAP. Fixing the free allocation beyond the commitment period 2008–2012 would also reduce the flexibility to evolve climate policy in a national, European and global context in the coming decade and might pre-empt negotiations about future burden sharing between sectors or among European Member States. Since Germany has announced its intention to put climate change on the agenda of its Presidencies of the EU and the G8 in 2007, accepting changes on these long-term provisions would strengthen the German government's credibility for requesting more stringent emission targets from other countries.

Figure 2 illustrates the allocations per Member State to two standard types of existing power stations of 200 MW, assuming that they operate on average for 6,000 h/year. Once again, the large discrepancies between different EU Member States are striking. Also striking is how some countries can still justify large free allocation when others manage to negotiate with their industry a significantly lower level of free allowance allocation.

The high degree of free allocation to the power sector could easily be reduced without reducing power sector profits below pre-ETS levels (Pál and Bartek-Lesi, 2006). As these large demands by individual installations inflate the aggregate national and therefore the EU allowance budgets, such reductions are required in order to achieve a reduction of the EU ETS cap and thus to achieve the Kyoto emission target with sufficient scarcity for a strong price signal.

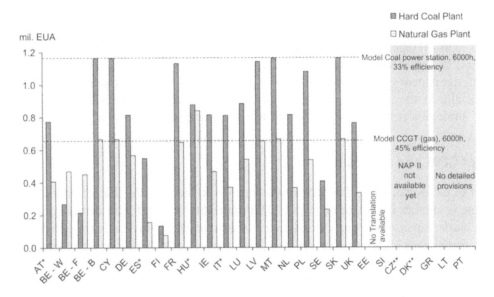

Figure 2. Comparison of allocations to existing facilities. * Draft NAP, ** NAP not available. Different load factors are used for BE-F (3,000 h for coal, 6,300 h for gas), ES (4,167 h for coal). PL – low SO_2-emitting installations. SE – adjustment factor assumed to be equal to 0.35.

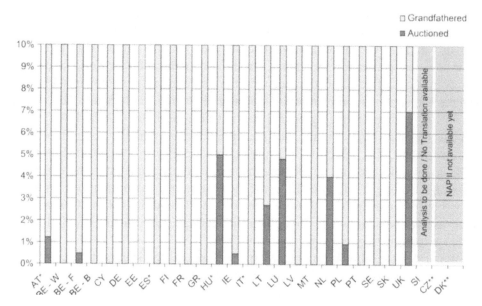

Figure 3. Comparison of the potential to extend the use of auctions between countries. * Draft NAP, ** NAP not available.

3. The use of auctioning

The EU Directive allows Member States to auction up to 10% of the allowances available. Figure 3 illustrates that all Member States can still make more use of this option. Making use of the 10% auction allowance in this phase would not only reduce distortions from the free allocation, but would also allow all parties involved to become comfortable with allowance auctions. Additionally, a minimum price auction could, by ensuring a price floor, further facilitate investment in low-carbon technologies (Hepburn et al., 2006). Auction revenues could be recycled to support industrial competitiveness and development and the initial deployment of suitable technologies. Furthermore, auctioning of significant amounts of allowances could support the transparency of the allowances market, especially in the settlement period, and avoid price volatilities resulting from asymmetric risk-hedging strategies between sectors which are short and sectors which hold long positions.

4. The use of CDM and JI credits

In the context of the overall Kyoto Protocol implementation framework, the linkage with the international trading scheme is another important dimension. With uncertainty over future demand for JI and CDM credits from Canada, Japan, other Annex I countries, and governments of the EU Member States themselves, some market participants anticipate that the European market could be flooded by these allowances to such an extent that the EU allowance price would plummet. Such uncertainty undermines investment certainty for low-carbon options and also poses obstacles to implementing a price floor using auctions.

Article 30(3) of the EU Directive on Emissions Trading requires that the use of JI and CDM credits is supplementary to domestic action. Figure 4 compares the maximum fraction of total allocation that can be covered by individual installations using JI and CDM credits under the currently proposed NAPs. As all installations can freely trade allowances, the only binding limit is the resulting

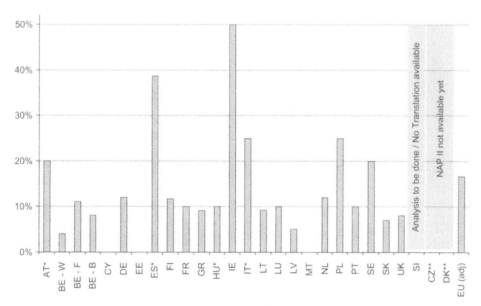

Figure 4. National limits of using JI/CDM credits for EU ETS compliance as a percentage of emissions allocations at installation level ('EU adj' excludes CZ, DK, SI; weighted average for ES). * Draft NAP, ** NAP not available. Limits on the use of Kyoto Credits of 70% of the overall phase-II allocation for the sector 'Electricity production for public service' and 20% for the others, at installation level.

overall import volume from JI and CDM credits. Extrapolating from the currently available NAPs for phase II, a maximum of 16.6% of the emissions of the eligible installations in the EU, or 315.1 $MtCO_2$, may be covered by JI and CDM credits. Whether this upper limit will be reached will depend on prices for EUAs and ERUs or CERs, which in turn depend on demand and supply. The upper limit could for example be reached if Japanese demand, which is estimated to account for about half of total demand for JI and CDM credits (Grubb and Neuhoff, 2006), were to fall.

Article 30(3) requires that the eligible installations across the EU also directly implement measures to reduce emissions by at least the same volume. However, current projections (Neuhoff et al., 2006a, this issue) do not support this hypothesis. Compliance with the Directive would thus require the reduction of the overall budget allocated and/or the volume of JI and CDM credits that can be imported into the EU ETS.

The EU Commission addresses this issue in its decisions on the NAPs. For example, in the Irish NAP the maximum amount of JI and CDM credits that can be used per installation to cover its emissions was declared to be 'inconsistent with Ireland's supplementarity obligations under the Kyoto Protocol and decisions adopted pursuant to the UNFCCC or the Kyoto Protocol, to the extent that it exceeds 21.914%'(EU Commission, 2006).

5. The basis for free allocation

The successful cap-and-trade programmes for SO_2 and NO_x in the USA allocate emission allowances to existing facilities typically based on emissions in a fixed historic base period, and then auction the remaining allowances. Only few US states have set aside allowances of their NO_x programmes for new sources. Thus, in most cases the free allowance allocation to existing installations constitutes a lump-sum transfer which does not create distortions for the effectiveness of the scheme.

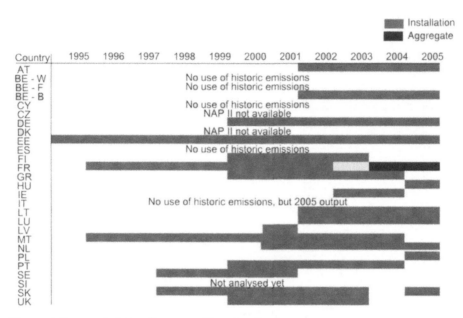

Figure 5. Base period for allowance allocation for the power sector.

In the European context, the limited availability of data, unknown mid- and long-term emissions reduction targets, and distributional considerations (regarding the allocation of allowances valued at around €30 billion) have prevented such a one-off allocation using one historic base period. Figure 5 shows that the 'historic' base period for allowance allocation for the period 2008–2012 has shifted to take account of the most recent data (including the year 2005) in many Member States.

If allowances are not allocated using a fixed historic base line or an auction, then Table 1 illustrates the different categories that can describe alternative allocation approaches (Grubb and Neuhoff, 2006). In Table 1, X indicates the types of distortions that result from the allocation process. The pyramid shape illustrates the increasing number of distortions that occur as we move down the Table from allocation based on auctions or a one-off allocation using a historic base line, to uniform benchmarks, then to fuel-specific benchmarks, and finally to emission-based allocation. Within each of these categories, in principle, allocation based on installed capacity is preferable to allocation based on projected output, which in turn is preferable to allocation based on historic output. The distortions only apply directly to existing facilities. If, however, investors in new installations expect that they will in the future be covered by similar provisions, then the provisions also result in distortions of investment decisions for new installations.

Following these classifications, we have assessed the performance of the allocation plans of different Member States. In Figure 6 we depict the methodology used to determine the allocation to existing facilities in the power (P) and other (O) sectors.

Distortions from allocation today are largely due to expectations about allocation in the future. For private-sector decision-makers, estimates of future allocation are inevitably based on allocation under the status quo. If emission levels in 2000–2005 are made the basis for the allocations in the period 2008–2012, then plant operators may expect that emissions in the period 2005–2010 will be the basis for the allocation post-2012. This creates a typical early action issue: that is to say,

Table 1. Effect of allocation methods to existing installations in the power sector

Allowance allocation method		**Impacts** More expenditure on extending plant life (and potential minimum-run) relative to new build	Increase operation of (higher) emitting plants		Less efficiency improvements
		Distortions Discourage plant closure	Discourage closure of higher emitting plants	CO_2-inefficient fuel choice and plant operation	Reduce incentives for efficiency improvements
	Auction				
Uniform benchmark	Installed capacity	X			
	Output projection	X	X		
	Historic output	X	X	$(X)^a$	
Technology/fuel-specific benchmark	Installed capacity	X	X		
	Output projection	X	X		
	Historic output	X	X	X	
Emissions-based	Emissions projection	X	X		X
	Historic emissions	X	X	X	X

[a] To avoid distortions between generation technologies, non-fossil-fuel stations would also have to receive free allowances. This would avoid internalization of CO_2 costs in the electricity price, and thus distort choices of input factors and consumption for electricity consumers.

allocation undermines the incentives to invest in emission reductions because such investment may be 'punished' during future allowance allocation. As allocation plans for phase II continue to allocate most allowances to existing facilities based on historic emissions, the early action problem remains to be addressed. Some countries experiment with benchmark approaches – and thus could possibly increase the confidence of private-sector investors that future allowance allocation methodology will improve in terms of economic efficiency and environmental effectiveness.

Figure 7 provides the same analysis for the allocation methodology to new entrants, again separately for the power sector (P) and other sectors (O). It illustrates the variety of approaches selected by different Member States. The big challenge, again, comes from the distortions that follow from private-sector expectations regarding the allocation methodologies in subsequent periods. Thus the assessment of the allocation for the existing installations also carries significance for investment decisions for new facilities.

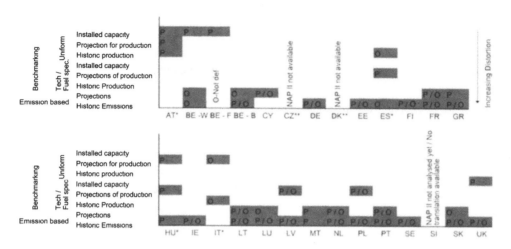

Figure 6. Pyramid of distortions applied to existing installations, power (P) and others (O).

6. Conclusions

We have quantified the volume of free allowances that different national allocation plans envisage to allocate to the power sector. This varies widely across Member States and technologies and can create strong distortions of investment decisions. The level of free allocation seems rather high, given that in most EU countries the electricity market is liberalized and electricity generators are therefore in a position to pass through the opportunity costs of CO_2 allowances. Thus, a significant reduction in free allowance allocation to the power sector seems viable for phase II of the NAPs. As the aggregate demand of individual installations inflates national, and therefore EU, allowance budgets, any such reduction could facilitate a reduction in the EU ETS cap as proposed by the EU Commission in its decision on the first 10 NAPs announced on 29 November 2006. This in turn can ensure sufficient scarcity of CO_2 allowances and a viable emissions market that drives low-carbon investment decisions.

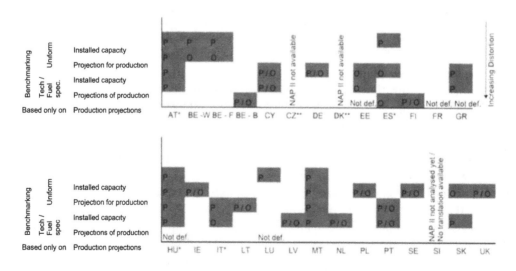

Figure 7. Pyramid of distortions applied to new installations, power (P), others (O).

A reduction in free allowance allocation, mainly to the power sector, could in addition allow for an increased use of the auctioning of CO_2 allowances. Auction volumes vary significantly across Member States. In all Member States, the potential for an increase to 10% envisaged by the Directive remains. The Commission made auctioning the one area of discretionary flexibility within its decision on the first 10 NAPs, 'without prior acceptance by the Commission', and even after the deadline of 31 December 2006. If a tighter cap, stringent limits on CDM and JI inflows, and 10% auctions were implemented, then a price floor in the auction – agreed between EU Member States – could also establish a price floor for EU allowances and thus facilitate low-carbon investments.

A comparison of the volume of CDM and JI credits that individual installations are allowed to use to cover their CO_2 emissions shows large discrepancies between Member States. A more stringent approach seems required in order to satisfy the supplementarity criteria of the Directive and also to avoid too much exposure of the EU ETS market to the uncertainties regarding Japanese and Canadian demands for JI and CDM credits. The Commission decided to disallow the higher limits envisaged in the Irish NAP.

Most allowances are still allocated relative to historic emissions. If the private sector takes this as an indicator for future allowance allocation, then we may face a serious early action problem. Some Member States have started to explore different benchmarking approaches, mainly for the power sector. This has the potential to reduce, but not eliminate, the economic distortions from free allowance allocation. Thus, to ensure the effectiveness of EU ETS in the coming years, it is important to provide credible evidence to the private sector that free allowance allocation will be drastically reduced post-2012. By disallowing the German provision to commit to free allowance allocation post-2012, the Commission has ensured that we retain the flexibility for such changes.

Finally, the EU Directive on Emissions Trading requires that Member States notify their national allocation plans to the Commission to be assessed in relation to State Aid criteria. There are some concerns that the excessive allocation to sectors that both pass on opportunity costs and receive free allowance allocation cannot be aligned with EC Law State Aid criteria (Johnston, 2006). One solution might be to treat the resulting benefits as a transitional payment to compensate for the transition costs of the environmental regulation. This would, however, require a strong commitment to phasing-out free allocation post-2012 – and would thus also address the early action problem.

Acknowledgements

This article was sponsored by Climate Strategies (www.climate–strategies.org), with the Carbon Trust as lead investor. The opinions expressed in this article are those of the authors and do not express the views of the Carbon Trust.

Financial support from the UK Research Council, Project TSEC, is gratefully acknowledged.

Notes

1 The database, which can be found at http://www.econ.cam.ac.uk/research/tsec/euets/, covers volume of the allocation, verified and projected emissions, allocation methodologies for power and non-power sectors, auctioning, general features, and evaluation of the allocation that a standard power plant would receive in each Member State according to the proposed rules.

2 We assume a 200 MW coal power station and combined cycle gas turbine with efficiencies of 33% (existing coal), 45% (existing CCGT gas), 43% (new coal) and 55% (existing CCGT gas).

3 BE-W Belgium Walloon, CY Cyprus, DE Germany, ES Spain, FI Finland, HU Hungary, IE Ireland, IT Italy, LV Latvia, NL Netherlands, UK, BE-F Belgium Flemish, EE Estonia, LU Luxembourg, SI Slovenia, AT Austria, CZ Czech Republic, DK Denmark, SE Sweden, BE-B Belgium Brussels, FR France, GR Greece, LT Lithuania, MT Malta, PL Poland, PT Portugal, SK Slovakia.

References

Åhman, M., Holmgren, K., 2006. Harmonising New Entrant Allocation in the Nordic Energy Sectors: Current Principles and Options for EU ETS Phase II. IVL Swedish Environmental Research Institute, Stockholm, Sweden.

Åhman, M., Burtraw, D., Kruger, J., Zetterberg, L., 2007. A Ten-Year Rule to guide the allocation of EU emission allowances. Energy Policy 35(3), 1718–1730.

Bartels, M., Müsgens, F., 2006. Do technology specific CO_2 allocations distort investments? In: Securing Energy in Insecure Times. International Association of Energy Economics, Potsdam, Germany.

Betz, R., Rogge, K., Schleich, J. 2006. EU emissions trading: an early analysis of national allocation plans for 2008–2012. Climate Policy 6(4), 361–394.

Böhringer, C., Lange, A., 2005. Mission impossible!? On the harmonization of national allocation plans under the EU Emissions Trading Directive. Downloadable Appendix: CGE model description. Journal of Regulatory Economics 27(1). 81–94.

Burtraw, D., Palmer, K., Bharvirkar, R., Paul, A., 2002. The effect on asset values of the allocation of carbon dioxide emissions allowance. Electricity Journal 15(5), 51–62.

Burtraw, D., Palmer, K., Kahn, D., 2005. Allocation of CO_2 Emissions Allowances in the Regional Greenhouse Gas Cap-and-Trade Program. RFF Discussion Paper 05-25. Resources for the Future, Washington, DC.

del Rio González, P., 2006. Harmonization versus decentralization in the EU ETS: an economic analysis. Climate Policy 6(4), 457–475.

Entec and NERA (2005). EU Emissions Trading Scheme Benchmark Research for Phase II. Final Report. DTI.

EU Commission, 2006. Decision on Irish NAP, 29 November [available at http://ec.europa.eu/environment/climat/2nd_phase_ep.htm].

Fischer, C., 2001. Rebating Environmental Policy Revenues: Output-Based Allocations and Tradable Performance Standards. RFF Discussion Paper 01-22. Resources for the Future, Washington, DC.

Gagelmann, F., 2006. Innovation Effects of Tradable Emission Allowance Schemes: The Treatment of New Entrants and Shutdowns. UFZ (Centre For Environmental Research), Department of Economics, Discussion Paper 4/2006.

Grubb, M., Neuhoff, K., 2006. Allocation and competitiveness in the EU emissions trading scheme: policy overview. Climate Policy 6(1), 7–30.

Harrison, D.J., Radov, D.B., 2002. Evaluation of Alternative Initial Allocation Mechanisms in a European Union Greenhouse Gas Emissions Allowance Trading Schemes. NERA Report to DG Environment, European Commission, NERA.

Hepburn, C., Grubb, M., Neuhoff, K., Matthes, F., Tse, M., 2006. Auctioning of EU ETS phase II allowances: how and why? Climate Policy 6(1), 137–160.

Johnston, A., 2006. Free allocation of allowances under the EU emissions trading scheme: legal issues. Climate Policy 6(1), 115–136.

Matthes, F., Graichen, V., Harthan, R.O., Repenning, J., 2006. Auswirkung verschiedener Allokationsregeln auf Investitionen im Strommarkt, www.oeko.de.

Matthes, F., Graichen, V., Repenning, J., Doble, C., Macadam, J., Taylor, S., Zanoni, D., Chodor, M., 2005. The Environmental Effectiveness and Economic Efficiency of the European Union Emissions Trading Scheme: Structural Aspects of Allocation. WWF, Öko Institute.

Neuhoff, K., Keats-Martinez, K., 2005. Allocation of carbon emission certificates in the power sector: how generators profit from grandfathered rights. Climate Policy 5(1), 61–78.

Neuhoff, K., Grubb, M., Keats, K., 2005. Impact of the Allowance Allocation on Prices and Efficiency. Electricity Policy Research Group, Judge Institute of Management, University of Cambridge, Cambridge, UK.

Neuhoff, K., Ferrario, F., Grubb, M., Gabel, E., Keats, K., 2006a. Emission projections 2008–2012 versus national allocation plans II. Climate Policy 6(4), 395–410.

Neuhoff, K., Keats Martinez, K., Sato, M., 2006b. Allocation, incentives and distortions: the impact of EU ETS emissions allowance allocations to the electricity sector. Climate Policy 6(1), 73–91.

Pál, G., Bartek-Lesi, M., 2006. The Polluter Profits Principle: A Note on the Grandfathering of CO_2 Emissions Rights in Lax-Cap Trading Regimes. REKK (Regional Centre for Energy Policy Research) Working Paper 2006-1.

Palmer, K., Burtraw, D., 2004. Distribution and Efficiency Consequences of Different Approaches to Allocating Tradable Emission Allowances for Sulfur Dioxide, Nitrogen Oxides and Mercury. RFF Discussion Paper. Resources for the Future, Washington, DC.

Spulber, D.F., 1985. Effluent regulation and long-run optimality. Journal of Environmental Economics and Management 12(2), 103–116.

Sterner, T., Muller, A., 2006. Output and Abatement Effects of Allocation Readjustment in Permit Trade. RFF Discussion Paper 06-49. Resources for the Future, Washington, DC.

New entrant allocation in the Nordic energy sectors: incentives and options in the EU ETS

Markus Åhman[1,2]*, Kristina Holmgren[1]

[1]IVL Swedish Environmental Research Institute, Box 210 60, SE 100 31 Stockholm, Sweden
[2]Department of Earth Sciences, Göteborg University, Sweden

Abstract

In the EU emission trading scheme (EU ETS), the treatment of new entrants has proved to be one of the most contentious issues. This article analyses the impact of allocation to new entrants in the energy sector, and identifies options for improved regulation in this field. The point of departure for the discussion is a comparative analysis of the allocation in phase I and phase II of the EU ETS to two hypothetical energy installations located in different EU Member States. The study focuses on the Nordic countries due to their integrated energy market. The quantitative analysis was complemented by interviews with policy-makers and industry representatives. The results suggest that current allocation rules can significantly distort competition. The annual value of the allocation is comparable to the fixed investment costs for a new installation and is not insignificant compared to expected revenues from sales of electricity from the installation. The study finds that the preferred option would be that Nordic countries should not allocate free allowances to new entrants in the energy sector. This should be combined with adjusted rules on allocation to existing installations and closures in order to avoid putting new installations at a disadvantage. A second, less-preferred choice would involve harmonized benchmarks across the Nordic countries.

Keywords: Emissions trading; Allocation; New entrants; Competitiveness

1. Introduction

In the EU emission trading scheme (EU ETS), the treatment of new entrants to the scheme has proved to be one of the most contentious issues. In the first set of national allocation plans (NAPs) this is also one of the areas where policies among Member States differ most. Clearly, given that all 25 Member States have set up provisions to give allowances to new installations free of charge, allocation to new entrants is a political priority. Decisions about allocations to new entrants involve considerations about investment incentives, perceived fairness, economic efficiency and competitiveness.

From a political point of view, it is difficult to introduce policies that would make new investments less attractive and closures of installations more favourable in one's own country than it is in

---

* Corresponding author. Tel.: +46-8-598-563-21; fax: +46-8-598-563-90
E-mail address: markus.ahman@ivl.se

neighbouring Member States. The government of a Member State may be tempted to introduce incentives that compromise the efficiency of the trading programme as a whole. The possibility that Member States could obtain a better outcome by individual action that undermines the outcome for the broader ETS constitutes the well-known 'prisoner's dilemma'. Thus, the extent to which national competitiveness may be affected by the allocation is a highly relevant question.

Although it is still too early to pass final judgement on the effects and efficiency of the EU ETS, it is clear that the design of some allocation methodologies has created distortions in competitiveness, and that the effectiveness of the system in guiding investments to low-carbon technology can be improved. However, there are good reasons to structure the discussion on competitiveness, as, in simplified terms, the EU ETS affects at least three distinct aspects of the issue:

- the competitiveness of Member States
- the competitiveness of new compared with existing installations
- the competitiveness of European companies active in a global market.

This article aims to examine the incentives created by the treatment of new entrants in the energy sectors of some northern European countries in the first two phases of the EU ETS. The article analyses potential effects of this regulation and identifies options for harmonization and improvements in future phases of the EU ETS. At the time of writing (December 2006), not all of the Member States had notified their NAPs for 2008–2012. Furthermore, some NAPs contained too little information on the treatment of new entrants to allow a complete assessment; however, for the purposes of this article, we believe that the available material is sufficient.

The analysis primarily covers the first two of the three aspects of competitiveness mentioned above. The first aspect, the competitiveness of Member States, is affected by differences in regulation between Member States. If the objective is only to create a level playing field within the EU, harmonization of the rules across Member States in such a way that the incentives provided to the operators by the allocation are equal is more important than the actual details of the regulation. Given that the treatment of new entrants can affect the efficiency of the entire trading scheme (Åhman et al., 2006), one could argue that the best solution would be to regulate at the EU level, although this would require a change in the EU Directive governing the EU ETS (European Union, 2003). Harmonizing the rules in the Nordic counties would be an important step in this direction. Given the structure of the Nordic energy market, with limited transmission capacity to the rest of the EU, a Nordic harmonization may suffice to avoid the most serious distortions of competition for companies within those countries. In the longer term, in particular considering the EU objective to reach an integrated European energy market, harmonization across the EU would carry further advantages.

The second aspect – competitiveness of new versus existing installations – should be analysed in the light of the close link between treatment of new entrants and rules on closures. As discussed in this article and shown previously (Åhman et al., 2006; Bode et al., 2005; Schleich and Betz, 2005) the policy on closures that dominates in the NAPs in the first two phases in the EU ETS, i.e. to withdraw the allocation to installations that close, constitutes an implicit subsidy of existing installations, as it provides incentives to not close down old plants. This puts new entrants at a disadvantage if the allocation to new installations is not generous enough to compensate for the subsidy of incumbents. Hence, the rules on new entrants in combination with those on closures may have important consequences for the incentives for new investments, to what technologies those investments are directed, and the competitiveness of new versus existing installations.

The third aspect, competitiveness of European companies active in a global market, is mainly driven by the differences in climate policy between EU and the rest of the world. In the context of emissions trading, the most important factor is the difference in the price of carbon between the EU and the rest of the world. Although the general competitiveness of European industry is important and could indeed be affected by European climate policy, it is not as relevant when discussing allocation methodologies. The first priority in order for the EU to be able to pursue a progressive climate policy without risking the competitiveness of industry would be to continue the efforts to achieve a broader, preferably a global, climate regime.

The starting point for the analysis is a comparison of the hypothetical allocation to two new standard energy installations to be localized in Denmark, Finland, Sweden, Germany, Poland, Estonia, Latvia or Lithuania, in phase I and phase II of the EU ETS, respectively. In order to understand the importance of the allocation, and the extent to which differences in allocation methodology can affect where investments in new capacity are made, the value of the allocation is compared to the fixed costs and annual revenues of the standard installations.

The discussion is focused on the Nordic countries and Germany, Poland and the Baltic States. The Nordic electricity market is almost completely integrated, with increasing transmission capacity to the other countries studied. Thus, all of the chosen countries affect each other to various degrees and the chosen region is well suited to study how differences in allocation methodology can affect an integrated or semi-integrated energy system.

2. Are new entrants discriminated against compared with existing installations?

There is an ongoing debate on how allocation to new entrants should be made, and to what extent allocation affects company behaviour and decisions (e.g. Åhman and Holmgren, 2006; Sterner and Muller, 2006). A basic question is whether new entrants should receive free allowances at all. A second question concerns the extent to which free allocation actually affects the investment decisions of operators.

Some observers claim that the denial of free allowances would discriminate against new entrants compared with existing installations, thus inhibiting new investments. Opponents of this view (e.g. Åhman and Zetterberg, 2005; Haites and Hornung, 1999; Harrison and Radov, 2002) point out that the main argument for free allocation to existing installations is to compensate them for sunk costs, i.e. costs for investments that were made before the ETS was constructed and that are now less profitable due to the carbon price. Since new entrants have no such sunk costs and operate with full knowledge of the ETS, this justification for free allocation to new entrants is not valid.

In our view there are two significant arguments that could justify free allocation to new entrants.

First, capital markets discriminate in the price they charge a firm for acquiring new capital in response to observable accounting measures such as debt, liquidity, and cash flow, and also due to uncertainties such as exposure to price volatility in factor inputs, including emission allowances. Since the firm is capital constrained, and the cost of capital varies with the amount of capital needed, free allocation reduces the need of the firm to borrow money. The lower requirement to obtain capital may reduce the firm's cost of capital and convey economic advantage to owners of incumbent installations that receive allowances for free relative to investors in new installations, in cases where they have to buy all the allowances they need.[1]

Second, most Member States implicitly subsidize existing installations by withdrawing the allocation to existing installations that decide not to operate (e.g. Neuhoff et al., 2006). Under this policy, the operator of an installation will not only maximize profits with respect to the cost of production and market price of the products, but also has to take into account the value of the allowances that will be lost should the installation be closed. This puts new entrants, which could potentially replace existing installations, at a disadvantage.

It can be shown that if the value of the allowances that are lost equal the allocation to the new investment, this effect is diminished (Åhman et al., 2006). One approach that approximates this prescription is illustrated by the transfer rules used by, for instance, Germany and Austria: the allowances from an installation that closes can be transferred to a new installation. However, Bode et al. (2005) have argued that the German transfer rule still discriminates against new entrants and causes large profits for incumbent generators. Furthermore, the Austrian rules explicitly state that the new installation has to have the same owner as the old one; thus the rule provides little help to new investors wanting to enter the market.

Thus, it is our view that there may be some justification for allocating free allowances to new entrants, particularly considering the effects of the current rules on closures.

3. Comparison of new entrant allocation methodologies

Although in theory there are an infinite number of options to compare allocation methodologies, as well as many different terminologies, the allocation methods can be structured in a few different approaches:

- *Input- or output-based.* Input-based allocation is calculated by multiplying input or production factors such as fuel use or installed capacity with a benchmark (e.g. 1,710 EAU/MW). Output-based allocation is calculated by multiplying e.g. emissions or generated energy with a benchmark. The major advantage of choosing output-based allocation over input-based is that it rewards high-efficiency technologies.
- *Fuel-neutral or fuel-specific.* Some countries use different benchmarks for different fuels, or groups of fuels. The major advantage with fuel neutral benchmarks is that they provide incentives to use low-carbon fuels. Fuel-specific benchmarking provides incentives that are similar to allocation based on emissions only, thus does not encourage investments in low-carbon fuels.[2]
- *Technology-neutral or technology-specific.* This means using different methodologies for electricity generated in condensing plants and in combined heat and power (CHP) systems. This can be used in order to promote one specific technology or to accommodate for the different conditions in which different technologies are used. If the objective is to create incentives for least-cost emissions reductions, however, there is little justification for technology-specific benchmarks.[3]
- *Product-specific or product-neutral* ('product' in this context being electricity or heat). In the context of competition for investments between countries, heat and power have very different characteristics. The advantage of using different benchmarks for heat and electricity is that it would allow this difference to be taken into account. Harmonization is a higher priority for electricity than it is for heat.

The NAPs of the Member States in this study contain examples of all the approaches listed above, in various combinations. In addition, even when the same basic approach is used, for instance output-based, fuel-specific benchmarking, the actual number of allocated allowances differs significantly between countries. The Nordic countries all apply different benchmarks for electricity and heat.

Depending on which approach is used, different incentives are created for investments. This will affect the competitiveness of different fuels, products and technologies. Even if two different approaches can result in identical allocation, the investment incentives can still be different.

For the competitiveness of a country, the total volume of allocated allowances for a given installation may be as important as what incentive structure is created by the allocation methodology. That is, an operator who has already chosen which fuel or technology to use only cares about how many allowances he will receive upon entering the market.

For a more comprehensive analysis of phase I NAPs, see, e.g., Åhman and Holmgren (2006), Kolshus and Torvanger (2005), DEHSt (2005), Matthes et al. (2005), Zetterberg et al. (2004) and Ecofys (2004).

3.1. Quantitative examples

We have calculated the allocation that would be awarded to two hypothetical installations if they were to be started (Table 1). The first installation type is taken from an ongoing Elforsk project (Ekström et al., 2006). The second is modelled closely on the CHP currently planned by Göteborg Energi (Göteborg Energi, 2005).

Figures 1 and 2 show what allocation the installations would receive if they were built in the respective countries, in relation to expected annual emissions.

There are few signs of increased harmonization of the allocation methodologies to new entrants in phase II, and it is striking how much the allocation differs between Member States. For a natural-gas-fired condensing plant the percentage of emissions covered range from zero in Sweden in both phases, to 119 in Lithuania (phase I) and 131 in Germany (phase II). For a CHP, the allocation also differs widely across countries: in phase I ranging from 62% of emissions covered (Sweden) to 131% in Germany, and in phase II from 70% in Finland to 157% in Germany (Figure 2).

Germany has changed the allocation methodology to new entrants in phase II, resulting in significantly increasing volumes allocated on installation level. The allocation is based on so-called standard utilization factors, specifying the number of operational hours for different installation types, installed capacity and BAT (best available technology) factors. In phase I, the allocation was not based on standard utilization factors but on projected emissions. Furthermore the allocation was proposed to be subject to *ex-post* adjustments, although this proposal was rejected by the EU Commission. In phase II, the explicit *ex-post* adjustment rules have been discarded. However, the NAP states that the allocation in coming periods will be based on the actual number of hours of operation in previous periods, thus providing an updating component of the allocation methodology.

Table 1. Hypothetical standard new installation

Fuel	Technology	Power efficiency	Total efficiency	Production capacity	Operational hours
Natural gas	CC condensing	58%	58%	400 MW_e	6000 h/a
Natural gas	CHP	50%	92.5%	261 MW_e	5000 h/a
				294 MW_{heat}	

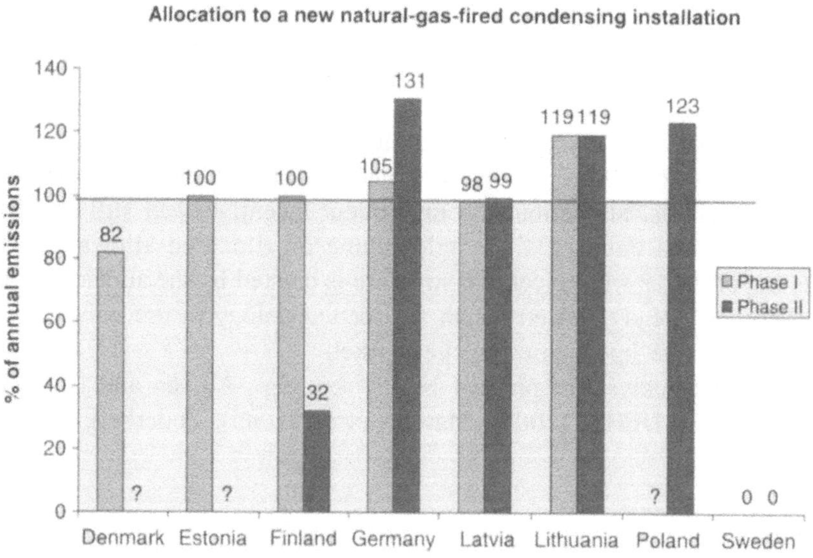

Allocation to a new natural-gas-fired condensing installation

Figure 1. The allocation to a new natural-gas combined-cycle electricity production unit (no heat) in different Member States. Results presented as percentage of expected annual emissions, i.e. the number of allowances required for compliance, covered by the allocation, with the horizontal line representing 100% of allowances needed for compliance. NAP I of Poland and NAP II of Estonia did not contain enough information to allow calculation of the allocation, while Denmark had not notified its NAP II to the European Commission at the time of writing (December 2006).

It is interesting that while both Poland and Germany claim they use benchmarks based on BAT, the benchmarks used are very different. For a natural-gas-fired power plant the Polish benchmark is 430 kg CO_2/MWh electricity whereas the corresponding German value is 365 kg CO_2/MWh electricity, a difference of almost 18%. For heat the benchmarks used are more similar, being 60 kg/GJ for a Polish natural-gas-fired CHP, corresponding to 216 kg CO_2/MWh, and 215 kg CO_2/ MWh heat for a corresponding German installation.

3.2. The role of assumptions and forecasts

Forecasts and assumptions are used frequently in the NAPs. Parameters such as assumed annual operating hours and efficiency of the installations differ significantly across Member States, which has a significant impact on the allocation.

For instance, the Danish allocation to a new natural-gas combined-cycle condensing plant (NGCC) in phase I cover approximately 82% of the estimated annual emissions. The main reason for the 20% shortfall is that the estimated number of operational hours is 20% higher in our example than the default value used for the calculation of the benchmark in the Danish NAP.

In Finland we find an opposite example. The 20% surplus of allowances allocated to the CHP can be explained by the fact that Finland in its NAP assumes 6,000 hours of operation per annum, while our standard assumption is 5,000 hours.

An interesting feature of the German NAPs is that they specifically state that the benchmarks used in the allocation will not be changed until 14 years after the installation has started its operation.

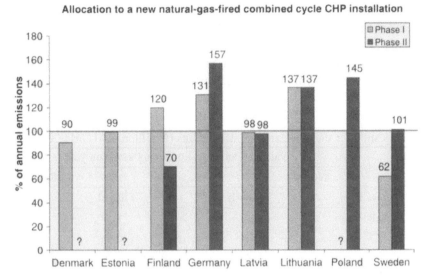

Figure 2. Allocation to a new natural-gas-based combined-cycle CHP plant assuming location in different countries. Results presented as percentage of expected annual emissions, i.e. the number of allowances required for compliance, covered by the allocation, with the horizontal line representing 100% of allowances needed for compliance. NAP I of Poland and NAP II of Estonia did not contain enough information to allow calculation of the allocation, while Denmark had not notified its NAP II to the European Commission at the time of writing (December 2006).

In the Commission decision for the first phase this was not commented on, whereas the second phase Commission decision includes language that can be interpreted as disallowing this rule.

In some Member States the regulator produces forecasts, while other Member States rely on operators to provide forecasts on which the allocation is based. This creates potentially large differences in the allocation even if the principles on which it is based are the same.

We have also found some differences between our calculated results and a previous study on allocation to energy installations (BALTREL, 2004). When analysing these differences, we found that BALTREL had applied different assumptions regarding, for instance, operating hours, efficiencies and emission factors. Some of these parameters are stated in the individual NAPs, some are to be submitted by the operator of the firm that applies for allocation. Furthermore, the BALTREL study used draft NAPs for some countries, which also may explain some of the discrepancies.

4. Does the allocation matter?

The value of the allocated allowances compared to other costs and sources of revenue of the firm is a key factor in determining whether the allocation actually has an impact on investment decisions and to what extent the observed differences between countries can distort competition.

This section illustrates the relative importance of the allocation by comparing the monetary value of the allocation to the fixed costs associated with the installations, and to the expected annual revenue from sales of electricity on the Nordic electricity market.

Table 2 shows the absolute value of the allocation to the two standard installations discussed above in different Member States. In Figures 3 and 4 these values are compared to the annualized fixed costs of the installations that are shown in Table 3, i.e. the annualized investment costs plus fixed operation and maintenance costs. Finally, in Figure 5, the value of the allocation to the condensing plant is compared to estimated annual revenues from sales of electricity from the installation.

Table 2. Value of annual allocation for the two standard installations (€million, EAU price €10)

	Value of annual allocation (€million/year)			
	NGCC		CHP	
	Phase I	Phase II	Phase I	Phase II
Denmark	6.8	n.a.	5.5	n.a.
Estonia	8.4	?	6.0	?
Finland	8.4	2.7	7.3	4.3
Germany	8.8	11.0	7.9	9.5
Latvia	8.2	8.3	6.0	5.9
Lithuania	10.0	10.0	8.3	8.3
Poland	?	10.3	?	8.8
Sweden	0.0	0.0	3.7	6.1

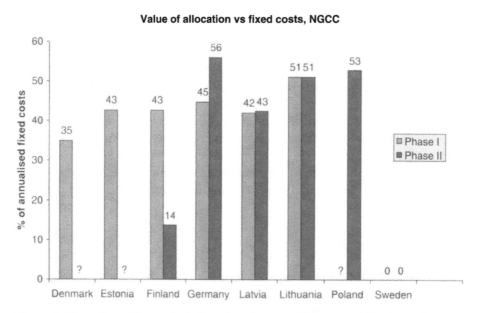

Figure 3. The value of the annual allocation shown as percentage of estimated annualized fixed costs of a natural-gas-fired condensing installation. Assumed real interest rate is 6%, depreciation time 20 years. EAU price €10. Data on investment costs and fixed operation and maintenance taken from Elforsk (2003).

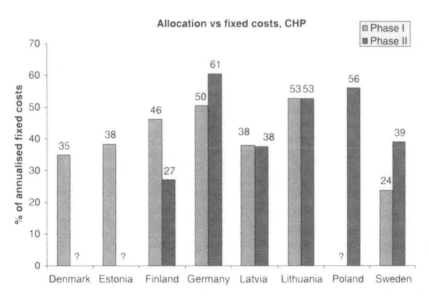

Figure 4. The value of the annual allocation shown as percentage of estimated annualized fixed costs of a natural-gas-fired combined-cycle CHP installation. Assumed real interest rate is 6%, depreciation time 20 years. EAU price €10. Data on investment costs and fixed operation and maintenance taken from Elforsk (2003).

Table 3. Estimated selected costs and revenues. The calculations on investment costs are based on data from Elforsk (2003)

Fixed annual costs NGCC	€19.5 million
Fixed annual costs gas-fired CHP	€15.7 million
Annual sales revenues NGCC	€74.4 million
Underlying assumptions	
Depreciation rate:	20 years
Real interest rate	6%
Investment costs NGCC	€560,000/MWe
Investment costs gas-fired CHP	€690,000/MWe
Fixed operation and maintenance costs	2% of investment cost
Power price	€31/MWh
Annual power generation NGCC	2.4 TWh

5. Does the allocation to new entrants affect investment decisions?

At the core of this study lies the hypothesis that the allocation does have an impact on investment decisions and competitiveness. However, this hypothesis can be challenged. The EU Commission has stated (Zapfel, 2005) that it is the price of allowances, not the allocation, which should drive new investment in CO_2-efficient technologies and changes in behaviour. According to this position, the allocation is a way to compensate for sunk costs and to facilitate the introduction of the trading scheme, not an instrument to drive technological change or strengthen the competitiveness of industry.

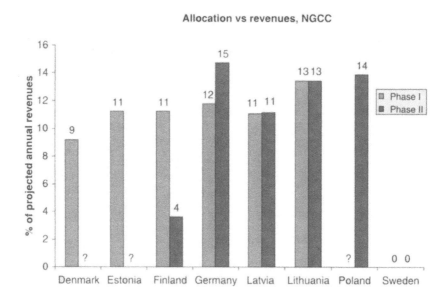

Figure 5. The value of the annual allocation shown as percentage of estimated annual sales revenue from electricity for the standard NGCC installation. Assuming 2,400 GWh annual electricity generation, allowance price €10, electricity price €31/MWh.

Behind this lies the view that since the allocation does not affect the variable costs for an installation, it has no significant impact on the competitiveness. However, this reasoning only holds as long as the allocation is not conditioned on the choices of an investor (for instance the choice to start operations or the choice of fuel or technology) and does not significantly affect the cost of capital for an operator.

The first assumption is negated by the fact that an operator can indeed affect the allocation to a new entrant: first through the decision to start operations at all, and then, depending on what allocation methodology is used, the allocation could be affected through choice of fuel, technology etc. In this respect, the allocation to a new entrant is different from allocation to existing installations based on historical measures, since the allocation can be directly affected by the operator's investment decisions.

The second assumption, that the capital costs are not a barrier to investment, is also unlikely to hold true. As discussed above, capital is a scarce resource for most firms, although the significance of this scarcity may vary between firms and settings.

Furthermore, the value of the allocated allowances in relation to other costs must be understood in order to determine its importance for investment decisions. Simply put; if the allocation represents a significant source of revenue for an installation, and the value of the allocation depends on the investment decisions, the allocation is likely to affect the decisions taken by the investor.

For a more formal presentation of incentive distortion caused by different allocation methodologies see, e.g., Sterner and Muller (2006). A general conclusion is similar to the one suggested above: when the firm can influence the allocation, the allocation does affect the firm's behaviour.

In Table 2, the annual values of the allocated allowances are presented. As shown in Figure 4, the annual value of the allocation is comparable to the estimated annualized investment cost for the installation. This implies that the allocation is an important source of revenue for the operator of an installation. It is also worth pointing out that the results are very sensitive to the EAU price. If the price increases from €10 to levels around €20 (which is close to the average price during the first two years of the trading scheme) the value of the allocation will in fact be higher than the fixed investment costs in several Member States. In addition, we see significant differences between countries in the outcome of the allocation, thus distorting competition between countries.

However, in order to get a more complete assessment of the importance of the allocation, several other factors have to be taken into account. While a full analysis is beyond the scope of this article, a few issues that are likely to be important can be pointed out:

– Uncertainty in the allocation. The operator can only be certain of receiving a 5-year allocation under current rules.
– Variable costs, such as fuel prices and salaries.
– Market factors such as energy prices and access to customers vary over time and between countries, which affects the role of the allocation in determining the investment decision. The large differences in power prices that currently exist between Germany and the Nordic countries are likely to have a significant impact on investment decisions.
– Uncertainty in other energy policies. The European energy system is affected by a wide range of policy instruments that differ between Member States, for instance subsidies for renewables, guaranteed feed-in tariffs, green certificates and restrictions on nuclear power. Many of these policies are important for ensuring which fuels or technologies are profitable, and they are all subject to more or less predictable changes.

Therefore it is difficult to precisely estimate to what extent the allocation will impact the decisions on where to invest and in what type of installations. But all this said, we conclude that the sheer magnitude and value of the allocation, in combination with the incentive structure the current methodologies provide, makes it very likely that the allocation to new entrants does affect investment decisions and competitiveness of countries, firms and technologies in northern Europe.

6. Transition from new entrants to existing installations

The treatment of new entrants is closely related to the general issue of updating allowance allocations over time. Although this does not directly affect the competitiveness between Member States, it is an important issue for the efficiency of the trading scheme as a whole. As such, it should be addressed when discussing how to harmonize the allocation rules between the Nordic countries.

The questions are how long should a new installation receive allocation according to some special allocation methodology before it is regarded as an existing installation, and how can the transition between different allocation methodologies be made without providing incentives for firms to act strategically in order to increase their future allocations. According to the EU Directive on Emissions Trading (European Union, 2003) a 'new entrant' is an installation that starts its operations after the NAP has been submitted to the EU Commission.[4] This would suggest that a new installation could only be regarded as a new entrant for one trading period.

In general, the economics literature indicates that changing or updating allowance allocations over time may have a distorting effect on company decisions. For example, Burtraw (2001) and

Fischer (2001) found that updating output-based allocation methodologies serves as an economically inefficient subsidy for production that lowers product prices for consumers. Similarly, in an analysis of a potential emissions trading programme in Alberta, Canada, Haites (2003) found that an output-based updated allocation provides an incentive for production.

These considerations have clearly guided the Commission's prohibition on updating within each phase of the EU ETS. Nevertheless, it is not clear how this should be applied to the treatment of new entrants. One option suggested by Åhman et al. (2006) would be to introduce a 10-year time delay in the allocation. Under such a scheme, a new entrant would first be allocated based on some projected measures, but then, after 10 years, the allocation would be updated. For instance, an installation starting in operation in 2006 would receive free allocation based on forecasts until 2015. From 2016 onwards the allocation would be based on actual activity 10 years previously. A 10-year time delay would significantly weaken the tendency of updating to produce perverse incentives for operators and thus reduce some of the distortions of free allowance allocation. A similar approach, but with a 4-year time delay, is used in the US NO_x SIP Call, a programme that requires summertime reductions in NO_x in the eastern half of the USA.[5]

7. What about auctioning?

According to the Emissions Trading Directive (European Union, 2004), a Member State only has to explain how new entrants can gain access to allowances; it does not need to provide special allocation to them. Furthermore, up to 10% of the total volume of allowances may be sold, for instance in an auction, in the second trading period. This means that there would be room to use full auctioning of allowances to new entrants. The Directive also allows for forcing new entrants to buy allowances on the open market. The discussion regarding free allocation or not to new entrants is analogous to the one on whether new entrants are discriminated against compared with existing installations, presented above. For a full discussion on the advantages of auctioning versus grandfathering, see, for instance, Cramton and Kerr (2002) and Hepburn et al. (2006). The major advantage of auctioning is that it provides efficient incentives for investments in efficient technologies and low-carbon fuels. It also eliminates the creation of windfall profits in the energy sector. Moreover, it avoids the problems of obtaining accurate data that are associated with benchmarking methodologies. However, if allocation is not harmonized across Member States with a common energy market, competition for investments may be distorted. Thus, if other northern European countries continue to apply free allocation, this adds weight to the arguments favouring free allocation to new electricity producers in the Nordic countries.

8. Framing the discussion: input from authorities and industry

In order to gain a better understanding of the rationale behind the current allocation methodologies and the potential changes that could be possible and politically realistic in future phases, we sought input from policy-makers in Denmark (Sigurd Lauge Pedersen), Finland (Timo Ritonummi) and Sweden (Truls Borgström). We also interviewed representatives from the energy associations from the respective countries: Danish Energy Companies (Charlotte Söndergren), Finnish Energy Industries (Jukka Leskelä) and Swedenergy (Maria Sunér Fleming).

All of the people we interviewed have extensive experience of working with the design of phase I NAPs, and several were also involved in phase II NAPs. The respondents acted in their personal capacity and were not asked to give the official position of their respective countries or industry associations. For reasons of confidentiality we have summarized the respondents' comments in the sections below, only disclosing individual views in a few cases. At the time of the interviews, no Member States had notified their phase II NAPs to the European Commission. Thus the views expressed primarily refer to phase I allocation.

8.1. Views from policy-makers

There seems to be agreement that, should the current allocation methodologies remain unaltered, it will distort competition between the Nordic countries. However, since the allocation is only determined for a short period of time in relation to the life-span of a power plant, it is difficult to judge the importance of the allocation compared with other factors determining investment decisions. Furthermore, both Sigurd Lauge Pedersen and Truls Borgström expect that the allocation will be decreased in future trading periods, and thus its importance and impact on competitiveness will also decrease.

There seem to be no fundamental or principal reasons that would prohibit the countries from adjusting their allocation principles in order to harmonize them with each other. The main barriers are probably political. What other Member States, in particular Germany, do is very important for what is feasible in the Nordic countries.

None of the respondents ruled out the option to force new entrants to pay for their allowances, although this will probably be politically difficult to pursue if other neighbouring countries continue with free allocation.

8.2. Views from industry

All respondents believed that the current allocation methodologies distort competition and that harmonizing them is of high priority. However, allocation is expected to be decreased in coming trading periods, and thus this effect is likely to decrease also. All respondents also pointed out that there are differences in other energy policies between the Nordic countries that strongly affect investment decisions, including taxation and application process. There is a need to harmonize other policies as well in order to achieve a level playing field.

There seem to be no fundamental barriers to adjusting the allocation principles in future phases. However, a critical condition for almost any changes is that the Nordic countries would in fact implement harmonized allocation methodologies. Further, since all allocation methodologies create winners and losers, it may be difficult to get general support for any one system. Auctioning would probably meet great resistance unless at least Germany, Poland and Estonia also radically decreased the allocation to new entrants.

The first priority, according to all respondents, is to get a harmonized system, preferably across the entire EU or at least on the northern European energy market. A harmonized Nordic system would be a step forward, but the approach used in particular in Germany should be considered. The exact design of the allocation is important, but is a secondary priority. It would probably be easiest to get wide support for a common benchmarking methodology that would take technology and fuel into account, thus avoiding the creation of major winners and losers, although not all respondents favoured this methodology.

9. Conclusions

Given the current allocation methodologies, and the discussion above, several options for a harmonized allocation methodology exist. But first, a few general conclusions can be drawn:

– Current allocation rules do have an impact on investment decisions, and can significantly distort competition if they remain unchanged.
– Under current allocation rules, the annual value of the allocation is comparable to the fixed investment costs for a new installation. Furthermore, it is not insignificant compared with expected revenues from sales of energy from the installation.
– There seem to be no fundamental obstacles in any Nordic country to changing the allocation system to new entrants as part of a harmonizing process.
– Although it would be an important accomplishment if Denmark, Finland and Sweden could harmonize their allocation methodologies, the Nordic countries must also consider policies in other neighbouring countries when deciding allocation methodology. This is also stressed by both policy-makers and industry representatives. Although the transmission capacities between the Nordic countries are significantly higher than they are to other countries, the Nordic energy sector is already part of the larger northern European energy market. Germany, Poland and Estonia are of particular importance, since the transmission capacities to those countries are relatively large.
– Harmonizing allocation is a higher priority for electricity generation than for heat, due to the higher sensitivity of electricity generators to competition.
– Since the energy sector can pass on the majority of the cost for emission allowances to clients, a stringent allocation is easier to justify in this sector than in others.

The primary reasons for allocating free allowances to new entrants in the energy sector are:

– *A level playing field vis-à-vis existing installations.* Under current regulations on closures, Sweden excepted, incumbents are favoured over new entrants. If rules on closures are changed so that a plant that closes does not lose its allocation, this argument fails.
– *A level playing field vis-à-vis neighbouring countries.* As long as neighbouring countries (in particular Germany, Poland and Estonia) allocate free allowances to new entrants, there may be a reason to allocate free allowances to electricity producers in order to avoid discouraging investments in the Nordic electricity sector. For heat generation, the argument is less relevant since the market is local, although, in the choice between investing in heat generation in two different countries, the allocation may be a factor if capital is a constraining factor.
– *Stimulating investments in new capacity.* Since capital is a scarce resource, allocating free allowances may have a positive impact on the rate of new investments. However, setting a 'correct' level of subsidy is difficult, and subsidizing investments through the allocation risks distorting the market in other ways.

Although we include both electricity and heat generation in the 'energy sector', the need for a harmonized allocation methodology is greatest for electricity generation. However, as heat and power are often co-generated, and to some extent can be substituted for one another, a harmonized allocation methodology for heat generation would also carry advantages.

A few observations can also be made regarding the changes in allocation between phase I and phase II. First, no harmonization of allocation methodologies between Member States can be detected.[6] Rather, there are still striking differences in how Member States allocate allowances to new entrants. This includes differences in general principles, but also in underlying assumptions such as emission factors and activity rates for energy installations.

Second, the use of fuel- and technology-specific benchmarks is still widespread. No Member State applies a uniform benchmark regardless of fuel or technology used.

Third, Finland is the only Member State that significantly reduces the allocation to new entrants. Instead, we see important increases in the allocation to new entrants in Germany and Sweden.

These findings are particularly disturbing when considering the growing economics literature showing that the efficiency of EU ETS would benefit from a much more stringent allocation to new entrants, as well as from more harmonized allocation methodologies across Member States, fuels and technologies (e.g. Åhman et al., 2006; Gagelmann, 2006; Grubb and Neuhoff, 2006; Hepburn et al., 2006; Betz et al., 2006, this issue).

We conclude that the preferred and most cost-effective solution would be that the Nordic countries do not allocate free allowances to new entrants in the energy sector. It is crucial to avoid updating, i.e. allocations must not depend on some variable that the firms can influence. Instead operators would have to buy allowances, either from the government or on the open market. Combined with adjusted rules on allocation to existing installations and to installations that close, this would give the most efficient incentives for new investment. However, this solution may not be the most appropriate, or even efficient, if Germany and Poland[7] do not follow or radically decrease their allocation to new entrants.

A full discussion on allocation rules to existing installations is beyond the scope of this article. However, a restrictive allocation to the entire energy sector can be justified considering the possibility of energy producers to pass on costs to clients. Furthermore, a level playing field between existing and new installations and between technologies would be achieved if auctioning to incumbents was applied, if the rules on closures were changed or if identical, fuel- and technology-independent, benchmarks were used for both existing and new installations.

This solution would eliminate the distortion of competition between the Nordic countries and decrease windfall profits created by the allocation to the energy sector.[8] It would also provide incentives to invest in efficient technologies and low-carbon fuels.

Free allocation to electricity producers in the Nordic countries may be justified in order to avoid distorting the competition in relation to Germany, Estonia and Poland if those countries continue with a generous allocation to new electricity producers, and if the rules on allocation to incumbent emitters and closures remain unaltered. In such a scenario, a second option would be to use harmonized fuel- and technology-independent benchmarks based on output. The allocation should be kept as restrictive as possible, in particular for heat producers. There should also be harmonized assumptions and guidelines on how to forecast production and, if compliance factors are used, of course these should be harmonized as well. This solution, while definitely in the realm of second best, would eliminate the distortion of competition between the Nordic countries created by the allocation. It would also give incentives to invest in low-carbon fuels and efficient technology. However, there would still be windfall profits created by the allocation to energy producers. Moreover, if other neighbouring northern European countries continue to use fuel- and/or technology-specific benchmarks, there will still be distortion of competition between those countries and the Nordic countries. However, the benefits of preserving correct incentives for investments could well be greater than the potentially negative effects created by some distortion in competition. A 'race to the bottom', where the Nordic countries apply allocation methodologies that create perverse incentives for fear of losing investments to neighbouring countries, would be regrettable. In the long term, this would risk shifting the structure of the energy system in the wrong direction. Furthermore, the magnitude of the distortion in competition, and the impact this will have on investments, depends not only on the allocation principle but also on the actual level of allocation.

A third option would be to use harmonized, fuel- and/or technology-dependent benchmarks, keeping the allocation as restrictive as possible. This would probably meet less resistance from industry and some policy-makers than the first or second options. It would also fulfil the objective of removing distortion of competition from the allocation. However, the incentives to invest in low-carbon fuels and efficient technologies would be reduced, and windfall profits would still be created by the allocation. In this case, the benefits of having harmonized allocation methodologies have to be weighed against the negative effects of not having incentives to invest in low-carbon energy generation.

9.1. Further research

Although the allocation as shown in this study has a large monetary value, it is only determined for 5 years into the future. Considering the long investment cycles in the energy sector, increased certainty over the allocation would carry significant benefits. If auctioning is used for the allocation to existing installations as well as to new entrants in the energy sector, this issue is dealt with. An area identified for future research is therefore to explore the options to provide higher certainty, for instance by extending the allocation periods.

This also relates to the issue of how the transition from status as a new entrant to existing installation is to be done. If free allocation to existing installations is kept, we find that a solution where a new installation is treated as a new entrant in the allocation for two successive trading periods would be preferable to the current regulations. It would weaken the perverse incentives to increase production and/or emissions created by updating the allocation at the beginning of each trading period. For further discussion of this topic, see Åhman et al. (2006). An argument against an approach with longer allocation periods would be if there is an intention to move away from free allocation in future trading periods. Such a transition may be more difficult to make if allocation to certain installations is determined many years into the future. As we find that auctioning carries significant advantages over free allocation, there is a need for research that could facilitate a transition to such a scheme. The power of policy and political path dependency should not be underestimated, which adds to the urgency of changing the allocation system.

Finally, a question that is beyond the scope of this article but is important to understand, is *why* it is important to have the same incentives for new investments across Member States and to what extent this objective should be given priority over others. In an integrated electricity market such as that in the Nordic countries, harmonizing incentives makes economic sense and is intuitively appealing. But when markets are only semi-integrated, like the northern European electricity market, or even completely separated like the market for district heating, there may be other considerations that are more important when designing the allocation, for instance security of supply, volatility in energy prices, and the structure of the energy system. Thus the interaction between the EU ETS and other policy instruments, and the potential trade-off between the objectives of the trading programme and other priorities, are areas where further research is needed.

Acknowledgements

The research was performed under the Emissions Trading in Climate Policy project (ETIC) as part of Mistra's Climate Policy Research Programme (CLIPORE). Additional funding was provided by the Swedish Energy Agency and the Nordic Council of Ministers. The researchers appreciate helpful comments from members of the climate group at the Nordic Council of Ministers. We also thank the following people, who agreed to be interviewed for this research: Peter Zapfel (DG Environment, EU Commission), Inga Valuntiene (Ekostrategija), Sigurd Lauge Pedersen (Denmark), Timo Ritonummi (Finland), Truls Borgström (Sweden), Charlotte Söndergren (Danish Energy Companies), Jukka Leskelä (Finnish Energy Industries), and Maria Sunér Fleming (Swedenergy). The authors appreciate helpful comments from Åsa Löfgren and two anonymous reviewers.

Notes

1   One reviewer suggested a countervailing effect: the volatility of sales revenue minus allowance costs and thus investment risk could be lower if electricity prices are positively correlated with allowance prices and allowances are auctioned frequently.

2   If a common benchmark is used for all fossil-based energy generation, but no allocation is given to energy based on biofuels, as is the dominating methodology in the EU ETS, this is an example of fuel-specific allocation, since it discriminates between different categories of fuels.

3   In the case of CHP, it has been argued that two reasons can justify generous allocation: first, generation of energy is more efficient in CHPs than in condensing plants and, second, heat generated in CHPs competes with small-scale heating installations that are not covered by the EU ETS. The first argument is weak as long as each technology bears the full costs of production; a higher efficiency is then rewarded in the market. The second argument is relevant, but it can be questioned whether one distortion should be fixed by creating another.

4   The technical definition is given in Article 3(h) of the Directive: 'Any installation carrying out one or more of the activities indicated in Annex I, which has obtained a greenhouse gas emissions permit or an update of its greenhouse gas emissions permit because of change in the nature or function or an extension of the installations, subsequent to the notification to the Commission of the national allocation plan.'

5   Of course, there are risks associated with longer allocation periods; committing to policies that turn out to be bad, for a long time into the future, can be worse than updating. Since the EU ETS is still in its infancy, there may be reasons to conduct more frequent reviews, although it should be a priority to keep correct incentives in place.

6   This said, one can speculate whether individual Member States may have adjusted their allocation methodology in phase II in response to how other Member States set up their allocation in phase I. Two possible examples of this are the significant increase in allocation to new CHPs in Sweden and the introduction of compliance factors in Finland.

7   We base our conclusion on the figures given in the Polish NAP submitted to the Commission in July 2004. We have not been able to obtain any official confirmation of changes to these in response to the Commission decision.

8   However, it would not address 'secondary' windfall profits created by electricity producers being able to sell *all* electricity, not just fossil-based, at higher price due to the price on carbon. This secondary effect is probably at least as important as direct windfalls from the allocation.

References

Åhman, M., Holmgren, K., 2006. Harmonising New Entrant Allocation in the Nordic Energy Sectors: Current Principles and Options for Phase II. TemaNord 2006:515, Report for the Nordic Council of Ministers, Copenhagen.

Åhman, M., Zetterberg, L., 2005. Options for allowance allocation under the EU emissions trading directive. Mitigation and Adaptation Strategies for Global Change 10, 597–645.

Åhman, M., Burtraw, D., Kruger, J., Zetterberg, L., 2006. A Ten-Year Rule to guide the allocation of EU emission allowances. Energy Policy 35(3), 1718–1730.

BALTREL, 2004. Emission Trading Task Force of BALTREL: Final Report. Presented at BALTREL Committee meeting, Riga, 4 November 2004.

Betz, R., Rogge, K., Schleich, J., 2006. EU emissions trading: an early analysis of national allocation plans for 2008–2012. Climate Policy 6(4), 361–394.

Bode, S., Hubl, L., Schaffner, J., Twelemann, S., 2005. Discrimination Against Newcomers: Impacts of the German Emission Trading Regime on the Electricity Sector, Hamburgisches Welt-Wirtschafts-Archiv Discussion Paper 316.

Burtraw, D., 2001. The Effect of Allowance Allocation on the Cost of Carbon Emission Trading. Resources for the Future Discussion Paper 01-30. RFF, Washington, DC.

Cramton, P., Kerr, S., 2002. Tradable carbon permit auctions: how and why to auction not grandfather. Energy Policy 30, 333–345.

DEHSt, 2005. Implementation of Emissions Trading in the EU: National Allocation Plans of All EU States. UBA, Berlin.

Ecofys, 2004. Analysis of the National Allocation Plans for the EU Emissions Trading Scheme. Ecofys Report, London.

Elforsk, 2003. El från nya anläggningar, Elforsk, Stockholm.

Ekström, C., Bröms, G., Eidensten, L., Hammarberg, A., Herbert, P., Kapper, R., Krohn, P., Larsson, S., Rydberg, S., Nyström. O., Olsson, F., 2006. Kostnader och potential för att minska CO2-utsläppen i Sverige. Elforsk-report 05:47, Stockholm.

European Union, 2003. Directive 2003/87/EC of the European Parliament and the Council of 13 October 2003 establishing a Scheme for Greenhouse Gas Emission Allowance Trading within the Community and amending the Council Directive 96/61/EC.

European Union, 2004. COM (08/III/2005). Commission Decision concerning the National Allocation Plan for the Allocation of Greenhouse Gas Emission Allowances notified by Poland in accordance with Directive 2003/87/EC of the European Parliament and of the Council.

Fischer, C., 2001. Rebating Environmental Policy Revenues: Output-Based Allocations and Tradable Performance Standards, Resources for the Future Discussion Paper 01-22. RFF, Washington, DC.

Gagelmann, F., 2006. Innovation effects of tradable emission allowance schemes: the treatment of new entrants and shutdowns. UFZ (Centre for Environmental Research), Department of Economics Discussion Papers (4/2006).

Göteborg Energi, 2005. Definition of New Power Plant under Construction, November 2005. [Available at http://www.goteborgenergi.se/Om_Goteborg_Energi/Var_verksamhet/Rya_Kraftvarmeverk_DXNI-5363_.aspx].

Grubb, M., Neuhoff, K., 2006. Allocation and competitiveness in the EU Emissions Trading Scheme: policy overview. Climate Policy 6(1), 7–30.

Haites, E., 2003. Output-based allocation as a form of protection for internationally competitive industries, Climate Policy 3(Supplement 2), S29–S41.

Haites, E., Hornung, R., 1999. Analysis of Options for Gratis Distribution of Allowances, National Roundtable on the Environment and the Economy, Canada.

Harrison, D., Radov, D., 2002. Evaluation of Alternative Initial Allocation Mechanisms in a European Union Greenhouse Gas Emissions Allowance Trading Scheme, National Economic Research Associates, prepared for DG Environment, European Commission.

Hepburn, C., Grubb, M., Neuhoff, K., Matthes, F., Tse, M., 2006. Auctioning of EU ETS phase II allowances: how and why? Climate Policy 6(1), 137–160.

Kolshus, H.H., Torvanger, A., 2005. Analysis of EU Member States' National Allocation Plans, Working Paper No. 2, CICERO, Oslo.

Matthes, F., Graichen, V., Repenning, J., Doble, C., Macadam, J., Taylor, S., Zanoni, D., Chodor, M., 2005. The Environmental Effectiveness and Economic Efficiency of the European Union Emissions Trading Scheme: Structural Aspects of Allocation. WWF Report.

Neuhoff, K., Keats Martinez, K., Sato, M., 2006. Allocation, incentives and distortions: the impact of EU ETS emissions allowance allocations to the electricity sector. Climate Policy 6(1), 73–91.

Schleich, J., Betz, R., 2005. Incentives for energy efficiency and innovation in the European emission trading system. In: European Council for an Energy-Efficient Economy (Paris): Proceedings of the 2005 ECEEE Summer Study. Energy Savings: What Works & Who Delivers? ECEEE, Mandelieu, Côte d'Azur, France.

Sterner, T., Muller, A., 2006. Output and abatement effects of allocation readjustment in permit trade. RFF Discussion Paper 06-49. Resources for the Future, Washington, DC.

Zapfel, P., 2005. Personal communication 24 October. DG Environment, EU Commission.

The environmental and economic effects of European emissions trading

Claudia Kemfert[1,2]*, Michael Kohlhaas[1], Truong Truong[3], Artem Protsenko[1]

[1] *German Institute for Economic Research, 14191 Berlin, Germany*
[2] *Humboldt University of Berlin, Unter den Linden 6, 10099 Berlin, Germany*
[3] *School of Economics, University of New South Wales, NSW 2052, Australia*

Abstract

In this article, we analyse the effects of emissions trading in Europe, with special reference to Germany. We look at the value of the flexibility gained by trading compared to fixed quotas. The analysis is undertaken with a modified version of the GTAP-E model using the latest GTAP version 6 database. It is based on the national allocation plans (NAP) as submitted to and approved by the EU. We find that, in a regional emissions trading scheme, Germany, Great Britain and the Czech Republic are the main sellers of emissions permits, while Belgium, Denmark, Finland and Sweden are the main buyers. The welfare gains from regional emissions trading – for the trading sectors only – are largest for Belgium, Denmark and Great Britain; smaller for Finland and Sweden, and smallest for Germany and other regions. When we take into account the economy-wide and terms-of-trade effects of emissions trading, however, (negative) terms-of-trade effects can offset the (positive) allocative efficiency gains for the cases of the Netherlands and Italy, while all other regions end up with positive net welfare gains. All regions, however, experienced increases in real GDP as a result of regional emissions trading.

Keywords: European emissions trading; Computational general equilibrium; Economic assessment

1. Introduction

The European Union considers climate change as 'one of the greatest environmental, social and economic threats facing the planet'. It therefore took a leading role in the negotiations for international action against climate change, in particular the Kyoto Protocol. In order to set an example, it accepted relatively ambitious targets. Whereas all Annex B countries were to reduce the emissions of greenhouse gases by about 5%, the EU has committed to an 8% reduction.

Compliance with this target, however, is not easy for the EU. Figure 1 depicts the development of the emissions of CO_2 and of all greenhouse gases (GHGs). It shows that although emissions in

---

* Corresponding author. Tel.: +49-30-897-89-663; fax: +49-30-897-89-113
E-mail address: ckemfert@diw.de

the EU were reduced quite effectively in the first half of the 1990s, this was due to a large extent to the massive breakdown of the economy and the modernization of industries in the former East Germany. Since then, emissions have been fluctuating and, since the end of the 1990s, they have actually been increasing (EEA, 2005).

Therefore, in 2000 the EU Commission launched the European Climate Change Programme (ECCP), a continuous multi-stakeholder consultative process which serves to identify cost-effective ways for the EU to meet its Kyoto commitments, to set priorities for action, and to implement concrete measures.[1] One of the main elements of this programme was the establishment of a European CO_2 emissions trading scheme (EU ETS) (Babiker et al., 2001, 2002). The EU considers this as 'a cornerstone in the fight against climate change', which will help its Member States to achieve compliance with their commitments under the Kyoto Protocol and the EU burden-sharing at lower costs. The basic idea of emissions trading is to limit the amount of emissions by creating rights to emissions and to make these rights – which are called allowances – tradable. The scarcity of emission allowances gives them a market value and those emitters whose avoidance costs are lower than the market value of allowances will reduce their emissions and buy fewer certificates or sell excess emissions rights, and vice versa for other emitters.

There is a fundamental difference between the EU ETS and the emissions trading scheme as envisaged under the Kyoto Protocol. In the latter case, emissions trading is to occur between the Parties to the protocol at the level of the States. Under the EU ETS, however, trading is to occur between individual emitters, which comprise 11,428 installations in 25 Member States. There have been other studies which look at the effects of emissions trading in Europe. Böhringer et al. (2004), for example, used a set of 'reduced form' equations which represent marginal abatement costs derived from a general equilibrium model to conduct simulation experiments to analyse the efficiency and equity aspects of different allocation rules for the EU ETS (European Commission, 2001, 2004). In these studies, the approach adopted is often 'partial equilibrium' in nature, which implies that important market interactions (including terms-of-trade effects) are not taken into account.

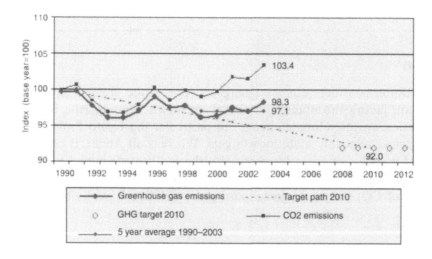

Figure 1. Total EU greenhouse gas emissions in relation to the Kyoto target.
Source: EEA (2005).

In this article we use a general equilibrium multi-sectoral and multi-regional trade model to analyse the effects of the EU ETS and, in particular, examine the cost reduction that may be obtained by the establishment of this trading scheme. Because of the nature of the general equilibrium modelling approach adopted, we can take account of the important interactions between changes in fuel prices, fuel and factor substitution, terms-of-trade effects, and therefore we can evaluate the efficiency and equity aspects of emissions trading in a more realistic fashion than by using partial equilibrium analysis. In fact one of the most important findings of our results is that terms-of-trade effects cannot be ignored, as they can sometimes mask the domestic efficiency aspects.

We conduct three simulation experiments to analyse the effects of the EU ETS. In all experiments, we maintain the same emissions reduction target but each experiment has a different set of rules regarding trading which account for different degrees of trading flexibility. In Experiment 1, fixed quotas are assumed, which do not permit any trading flexibility at all. In Experiment 2, emissions trading is allowed between the sectors within a national economy but not across the national borders. The results of this experiment are to be compared with those of Experiment 3, where emissions trading is allowed also across national borders of the EU Member States. The difference between the results of Experiments 2 and 3 will show the combined efficiency and terms-of-trade gains (or losses) from such emissions trading schemes. In both experiments, we have assumed that the emissions reduction targets have already been fixed at the national Member State level. This means there is to be no further 'optimal adjustment' of these national targets to achieve the same total level of emissions at the EU level.[2]

2. The European emissions trading scheme

The EU ETS started on 1 January 2005. The first trading period – which has been nicknamed the 'warming-up phase' or 'learning phase' – covers the years 2005–2007. The second phase corresponds to the Kyoto period 2008–2012.

The framework for EU ETS has been defined by a Directive in October 2003,[3] which outlines the basic features of the scheme, but leaves substantial scope for the Member States to decide on important aspects of the implementation. The most important features set by the EU are the following:[4]

- The European ETS is a cap-and-trade system; i.e. the absolute quantity of emission rights (rather than relative or specific emissions) is fixed at the beginning.
- Only one of the six greenhouse gases of the Kyoto Protocol (CO_2) is subject to the ETS, at least during the first period from 2005 to 2007. The main reason for this is that CO_2 is the greenhouse gas which is easiest to monitor, since the emissions are directly related to the use of fossil fuels for which most countries have already established a monitoring system in order to levy energy taxes.
- The EU ETS is implemented as a *downstream* system; i.e. the users (rather than the producers and importers of fossil fuels) will be obliged to hold emission allowances.[5]

This has some fundamental consequences. All users of fossil fuels which are covered by the ETS have to be monitored and can participate actively in the trading system. In order to limit the administrative costs of the ETS, the system is restricted to large installations. Therefore, only installations belonging to one of four broad sectors, which are listed in the Directive and which exceed a sector-specific threshold, are subjected to emissions trading. The four sectors are:

- Energy activities (such as electric power, direct emissions from oil refineries)
- Production and processing of ferrous metals (iron and steel)
- Mineral industry (such as cement, glass and ceramic production)
- Pulp and paper.

The thresholds refer to the production capacity of the installation, e.g. in the case of combustion installations these are installations with a rated thermal input exceeding 20 MW. The emissions trading scheme will cover around 45% of the EU's total CO_2 emissions, or about 30% of its overall greenhouse gas emissions. This partial coverage of the ETS is likely to produce inefficiencies which can only be avoided if the total quantities of allowances are set at a level which equalizes the marginal avoidance costs between the emissions trading sector and other emitters. This, however, is unlikely to be the case because the marginal avoidance costs of these emitters are not known.

- Allowances are issued by each Member State, but trading can take place between any EU participants.
- The so-called 'linking Directive' will allow participants in emissions trading to count credits from Clean Development Mechanism and Joint Implementation emission reduction projects around the world toward their obligations under the European Union's emissions trading scheme, even if the Kyoto Protocol did not enter into force.

Within this framework, the Member States have three important tasks. First, they have to decide which quantity of emissions should be allocated to the installations participating in the ETS. This decision must take into consideration the burden-sharing target of the country and must list the policies and measures which are to be applied in the sectors which are not part of the ETS. However, in almost all countries, business representatives have made strong lobbying efforts to ensure that emissions trading will not impair their competitive position. This has led to very generous allocations in some cases. Second, they have to draw up a list of all installations which are subject to emissions trading. Third, they have to decide how to allocate the total quantity to individual installations. The Directive sets some general rules according to which the allocation has to be made, but there is substantial scope for national priorities. These decisions have to be set down in a national allocation plan (NAP).

3. Quantitative impact assessment

3.1. Model, data, and description of experiments

In this study we use a version of the GTAP-E model (Burniaux and Truong, 2002) which is based on the latest version 6.2 of the standard GTAP model (Hertel, 1997) (see Figure 2). The model uses version 6 of the GTAP database, which consists of 57 commodities/sectors and 87 regions including the 25 European Member states (Dimaranan and McDougall, 2006). The regional and sectoral aggregation used for this study is shown in Table 1. It includes most of the EU Member States except for those States with small allocations.[6]

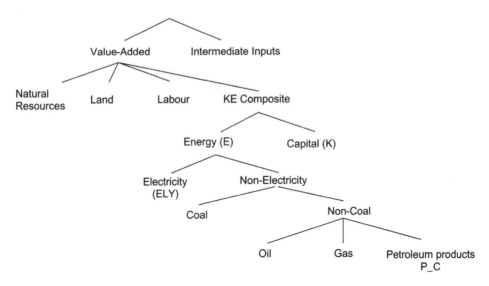

Figure 2. Standard GTAP-E production structure.

Table 1. Categorization of regions/countries and sectors

Regions/ Countries	Description	Sectors	Description
aut	Austria	Coal	Coal mining
bel	Belgium	Oil	Crude oil
dnk	Denmark	Gas	Natural gas extraction
fin	Finland	Electricity	Electricity
fra	France	Oil_Pcts	Refined oil products
deu	Germany	Metals	Metals products
grc	Greece	Min_Prod	Mineral products
gbr	Great Britain	Paper	Paper
ita	Italy	Motor_Equip	Motor machine & equipment
nld	Netherlands	Constr	Construction
prt	Portugal	Textile	Textile
esp	Spain	Oth_Ind	Other industries
swe	Sweden	ROE	Rest of the economy
cze	Czech Republic		
hun	Hungary		
pol	Poland		
REU	Rest of European Union		
CHIND	China and India		
JPN	Japan		
USA	United States of America		
RoW	Rest of the World		

The percentage differences between the CO_2 emissions in the reference case and the allocation of allowances in the respective NAPs for the various sectors in the period 2005–2007 are shown in Table 2.

These data have been derived from the information available in the NAPs.[7] Most countries made projections of emissions in a 'business-as-usual' (BAU) scenario. In these cases, percentage changes have been derived from the projected emissions and the allowances allocated to the sectors by the NAPs for this period.

For Germany, a different procedure was applied, as there are no data available either on historical or on projected emissions of the ET sector. Therefore, reference emissions were calculated from the quantity of allocated allowances, taking into account the allocation rules of the German NAP.[8] As a basic rule, the allocation to installations commissioned before 2003 is based on historical emissions in the base period (usually 2000–2002). The quantity of the allowances is determined by multiplying the historical emissions data by compliance factors which are necessary to balance the Macroplan with the Microplan. In some cases more generous rules could be applied, e.g. for 'early action',[9] CHP plants or process-related emissions.[10] Moreover, hardship provisions could be applied to compensate for economic burdens. As a consequence, a compliance factor between 0.926 and 1.00 was applied to base-period emissions. New entrants (including extensions of existing installations) obtain free allowances based on the production capacity and a product-specific benchmark.[11] For them, a compliance factor of 1.00 was applied. From the number of allowances allocated by the diverse rules, the reference emissions were calculated by applying the reverse compliance factors.

The Directive does not refer to economic sectors, but rather to activities. Only installations belonging to one of four broad activities and which exceed a sector-specific threshold are subject to emissions trading.

Table 2. Percentage deviation of emissions from projected level for period 2005–2007 according to the NAP(*)

Sector/Region	Electricity	Oil_Pcts	Metals	Min_Prod	Paper	Motor_Equip	Constr	Textile	Oth_Ind	ROE
aut	−8.9	−7.9	−3.5	−4.3	−3.6	−4.9	−4.6	−5.9		
bel	−27.4	−5.3	−5.3	−5.3	−5.3	−5.3	−5.3	−5.3	−5.3	
dnk	−26.2	−7.1	−7.1	−7.1	−7.1	−7.1	−7.1	−7.1	−7.1	
fin	−12.5									
fra	−0.4	−2.8	−10.3	−8.1						
deu	−3.1	−2.6	−0.5	−0.4	−1.0	−2.2	−2.2	−2.2	−2.2	
grc	−6.5	−16.8		−6.6						
gbr	−8.7	−0.9	−18.4	−5.7	−3.3	−3.3	−2.9	−2.5		
ita	−5.5		−4.2	−1.7	−3.4					
nld	−7.8	−7.8	−7.8	−7.8	−7.8	−7.8	−7.8	−7.8	−7.8	
prt	−6.2			−1.2						
esp	−6.5	−3.6	−2.9	−5.4	−4.5					
swe	−13.9	−13.9	−13.9	−13.9	−13.9	−13.9	−13.9	−13.9	−13.9	
cze	−4.5	−4.3	−4.6	−4.5	−4.1					
hun	−3.1	−5.1	−5.1	−5.1	−5.1					
pol	−9.3	−3.8	−10.3	−2	−7.5					

(*) (Allocated emissions − Projected emissions)/(Projected emissions) * 100

Three of the 'activities' (production and processing of ferrous metals, mineral industry, pulp and paper) correspond (more or less) to economic sectors. The fourth category, energy activities, however, may be undertaken by any sector. Due to the threshold of a rated thermal input exceeding 20 MW, installations of this type are concentrated in electricity generation and manufacturing. Some large installations (e.g. hospitals with CHP plants above 20 MW, which are subject to ET too) belong to other sectors. Often, NAPs do not contain sectoral information on projected and allocated emissions. If no information was available, we assumed uniform percentage shocks to all ET sectors.

From Table 2, we can see that if we adhere strictly to the NAP, then some shocks to the emissions would be positive (shaded areas). A positive emission shock would imply that no abatement effort is involved, and furthermore, a *negative* abatement cost may result, which does not make sense in practice. Therefore, to avoid this situation, we have chosen to swap a positive emissions shock with a zero shock for the marginal abatement cost (i.e. zero carbon tax) and let the emissions levels be determined endogenously within the model. The resulting emissions will then be positive but often less than the actual NAP allocations (see results in Table 3).

Table 3. Percentage change in emissions for period 2005–2007 in various experiments

Sector/ Region	Coal	Oil	Gas	Elec- tricity	Oil_ Pcts	Met- als	Min_ Prod	Pap- er	Motor Equip	Con- str	Tex- tile	Oth_ Ind	ROE	To- tal
Experiment 1 (No emissions trade)														
aut	−5.3	−0.7	−0.4	−8.9	−7.9	−3.5	−4.3	−3.6	−4.9	−4.6	−5.9	0.7	−1.5	
bel	−1.8	−0.8	−1.6	−27.4	−5.3	−5.3	−5.3	−5.3	−5.3	−5.3	−5.3	−5.3	−0.9	
dnk	−2.1	−0.2	−6.9	−26.2	−7.1	−7.1	−7.1	−7.1	−7.1	−7.1	−7.1	−7.1	−0.2	
fin	−7.6	−0.2	−1.2	−12.5	4.1	3.3	1.0	2.1	2.9	0.9	1.7	1.8	0.8	
fra	−3.0	−0.3	−0.2	−0.4	−2.8	−10.3	−8.1	0.3	0.2	−1.0	−0.2	0.2	−0.9	
deu	−3.2	−0.5	−1.0	−3.1	−2.6	−0.5	−0.4	−1.0	−2.2	−2.2	−2.2	−2.2	−1.3	
grc	−5.8	−2.5	−16.1	−6.5	−16.8	−4.9	−2.9	−6.6	−4.5	−4.8	−6.6	−7.0	−5.9	
gbr	−3.6	−0.3	−1.5	−8.7	−0.9	−18.4	−5.7	−3.3	−3.3	−2.9	−2.5	0.0	0.1	
ita	−2.4	−0.2	−0.3	−5.5	0.4	−4.2	−1.7	−3.4	1.0	0.9	1.0	1.1	0.5	
nld	−2.0	−0.3	−0.2	−7.8	−7.8	−7.8	−7.8	−7.8	−7.8	−7.8	−7.8	−7.8	0.0	
prt	−2.3	−0.5	−1.7	−6.2	0.8	0.6	−1.2	0.2	0.4	0.1	0.1	0.3	0.1	
esp	−3.6	−0.4	−0.4	−6.5	−3.6	−2.9	−5.4	−4.5	−0.4	−1.4	0.2	−1.7	−1.1	
swe	−5.6	−1.0	−13.9	−13.9	−13.9	−13.9	−13.9	−13.9	−13.9	−13.9	−13.9	−13.9	−2.4	
cze	−3.0	−0.5	0.2	−4.5	−4.3	−4.6	−4.5	−4.1	1.2	−0.8	2.3	1.8	−0.8	
hun	−3.0	−0.4	−0.3	−3.1	−5.1	−5.1	−5.1	−5.1	0.2	−0.4	0.7	0.6	−0.7	
pol	−5.1	−0.1	−0.1	−9.3	−3.8	−10.3	−2.0	−7.5	6.4	2.1	7.0	3.9	1.1	
Experiment 2 (Domestic emissions trade)														
aut	−5.3	−0.7	−0.4	−8.9	−7.9	−3.5	−4.3	−3.6	−4.9	−4.6	−5.9	0.7	−1.5	−4.3
bel	−1.8	−0.8	−1.6	−27.4	−5.3	−5.3	−5.3	−5.3	−5.3	−5.3	−5.3	−5.3	−0.9	−8.5
dnk	−2.1	−0.2	−6.9	−26.2	−7.1	−7.1	−7.1	−7.1	−7.1	−7.1	−7.1	−7.1	−0.2	−15.1
fin	−7.6	−0.2	−1.2	−12.5	4.1	3.3	1.0	2.1	2.9	0.9	1.7	1.8	0.8	−6.2
fra	−3.0	−0.3	−0.2	−0.4	−2.8	−10.3	−8.1	0.3	0.2	−1.0	−0.2	0.2	−0.9	−1.5
deu	−3.2	−0.5	−1.0	−3.1	−2.6	−0.5	−0.4	−1.0	−2.2	−2.2	−2.2	−2.2	−1.3	−1.8
grc	−5.8	−2.5	−16.1	−6.5	−16.8	−4.9	−2.9	−6.6	−4.5	−4.8	−6.6	−7.0	−5.9	−3.4

Table 3. Percentage change in emissions for period 2005–2007 in various experiments *(Cont'd)*

Sector/ Region	Coal	Oil	Gas	Elec-tricity	Oil_ Pcts	Met-als	Min_ Prod	Pap-er	Motor Equip	Con-str	Tex-tile	Oth_ Ind	ROE	To-tal
gbr	−3.6	−0.3	−1.5	−8.7	−0.9	−18.4	−5.7	−3.3	−3.3	−2.9	−2.5	0.0	0.1	−5.0
ita	−2.4	−0.2	−0.3	−5.5	0.4	−4.2	−1.7	−3.4	1.0	0.9	1.0	1.1	0.5	−2.5
nld	−2.0	−0.3	−0.2	−7.8	−7.8	−7.8	−7.8	−7.8	−7.8	−7.8	−7.8	−7.8	0.0	−3.7
prt	−2.3	−0.5	−1.7	−6.2	0.8	0.6	−1.2	0.2	0.4	0.1	0.1	0.3	0.1	−2.5
esp	−3.6	−0.4	−0.4	−6.5	−3.6	−2.9	−5.4	−4.5	−0.4	−1.4	0.2	−1.7	−1.1	−3.2
swe	−5.6	−1.0	−13.9	−13.9	−13.9	−13.9	−13.9	−13.9	−13.9	−13.9	−13.9	−13.9	−2.4	−6.3
cze	−3.0	−0.5	0.2	−4.5	−4.3	−4.6	−4.5	−4.1	1.2	−0.8	2.3	1.8	−0.8	−3.5
hun	−3.0	−0.4	−0.3	−3.1	−5.1	−5.1	−5.1	−5.1	0.2	−0.4	0.7	0.6	0.7	−2.4
pol	−5.1	−0.1	−0.1	−9.3	−3.8	−10.3	−2.0	7.5	6.4	2.1	7.0	3.9	1.1	−6.4
Experiment 3 (Regional emissions trade)														
aut	−3.9	−0.1	−0.3	−4.0	−0.6	−3.9	−1.7	−5.0	−3.2	−1.9	−3.7	0.8	0.3	−2.0
bel	−2.1	0.0	−1.1	−5.9	−0.3	−6.6	−2.1	−3.5	−1.8	−1.7	−3.3	−1.3	0.1	−2.4
dnk	−1.9	0.0	−3.1	−7.0	−0.3	−41.9	−10.0	−74.6	−53.4	−1.4	−72.5	−65.4	0.6	−6.2
fin	−2.9	0.0	−0.5	−2.8	0.2	1.8	0.6	1.0	0.8	0.3	0.7	0.6	0.2	−1.2
fra	−2.2	0.0	−0.2	−7.0	−0.5	−4.9	−1.4	0.5	0.4	0.0	0.2	0.6	0.0	−1.6
deu	−4.4	0.0	−0.7	−4.4	−0.3	−3.9	−2.5	−3.3	−2.0	−1.3	−2.5	−0.9	0.1	−2.7
grc	−4.4	−0.2	−0.9	−4.4	−0.4	1.3	1.3	−0.9	1.3	0.0	0.4	0.3	0.1	−1.9
gbr	−3.7	0.0	−1.4	−8.2	−0.2	−36.9	−30.4	−73.6	−70.8	−10.6	−72.9	0.5	0.5	−8.7
ita	−2.2	0.0	−0.2	−4.0	−0.3	−4.2	−1.5	−4.6	0.7	0.6	0.7	0.8	0.3	−1.9
nld	−1.7	0.0	−0.2	−4.2	−0.5	−9.2	−1.6	−14.9	−53.9	−30.9	−34.1	−1.1	0.2	−2.2
prt	−2.3	0.0	−1.7	−6.3	−0.3	0.6	−1.9	0.2	0.4	0.1	0.1	0.4	0.1	−2.6
esp	−3.2	0.0	−0.2	−5.7	−0.5	−4.2	−1.4	−2.4	0.3	0.3	0.4	0.1	0.0	−2.4
swe	−2.6	−0.1	−3.9	−5.4	−0.2	−2.1	−1.4	−1.5	−1.9	−1.0	−1.4	−2.4	0.1	−1.6
cze	−4.0	0.1	0.4	−10.6	−0.3	−7.4	−2.7	−4.9	3.0	0.6	3.7	2.4	1.0	−7.4
hun	−4.0	0.0	−0.4	−6.6	−1.0	−5.2	−2.4	−4.9	1.3	0.8	1.3	0.5	0.6	−3.9
pol	−4.3	0.2	−0.1	−8.7	−0.1	−6.6	−4.0	−5.1	5.8	2.5	6.2	3.8	2.0	−6.0

For non-NAP sectors (i.e. sectors which are not part of the NAP), we assume that there will be no abatement cost (zero carbon tax) imposed on these sectors. This means that their emissions levels will be determined endogenously within the model, according to the production and relative price relationships between these sectors and the NAP sectors. In general, we may expect a positive increase in emissions from these non-NAP sectors, which represents a 'leakage' of emissions from NAP to non-NAP sectors.[12]

We carried out three experiments. In Experiment 1 ('No trading'), we shock the emissions of each designated trading sector of each region by the projected percentage change to satisfy the NAP requirement, and let the model estimate the required carbon price (marginal abatement cost). In Experiment 2 ('Domestic emissions trading' only), we allow all designated sectors of each region with a NAP allocation to trade in emissions with each other. This will result in a uniform MAC across all trading sectors for each region, but the MAC will be different for different regions.

In Experiment 3 ('Regional emissions trading'), we allow not only domestic trading, but also trading between regions (EU Member States). This will result in a uniform MAC across all NAP sectors and regions. The changes in MACs between the three experiments are used to measure the potential gains (reduction in MAC) that can result from either domestic trading or from domestic plus regional trading. The results of the experiments are shown in Table 4. All costs are reported in 1995US$.

Table 4. Marginal abatement cost (tCO_2) in various experiments

Sector/Region	Coal	Oil	Gas	Electricity	Oil_Pcts	Metals	Min_Prod	Paper	Motor Equip	Constr	Textile	Oth_Ind	ROE
Experiment 1 (No emissions trade)													
aut	0.0	0.0	0.0	3.8	42.2	1.6	3.0	1.0	2.0	3.2	2.0	0.0	0.0
bel	0.0	0.0	0.0	11.5	32.3	1.6	4.4	3.2	5.7	6.4	3.5	7.7	0.0
dnk	0.0	0.0	0.0	7.5	50.5	0.2	1.1	0.1	0.0	9.4	0.0	0.1	0.0
fin	0.0	0.0	0.0	8.0	0.0	0.0	0.0	0.0	0.0	0.0	0.0	0.0	0.0
fra	0.0	0.0	0.0	0.5	17.3	4.1	11.6	0.0	0.0	0.0	0.0	0.0	0.0
deu	0.0	0.0	0.0	1.6	22.5	0.7	0.5	0.7	1.5	2.4	1.4	1.8	0.0
grc	0.0	0.0	0.0	2.8	137.0	0.0	0.0	0.7	0.0	0.0	0.0	0.0	0.0
gbr	0.0	0.0	0.0	2.2	13.3	0.4	0.3	0.0	0.0	0.2	0.0	0.0	0.0
ita	0.0	0.0	0.0	2.8	0.0	2.1	2.6	1.7	0.0	0.0	0.0	0.0	0.0
nld	0.0	0.0	0.0	3.8	30.7	1.8	8.7	1.1	0.2	0.0	0.4	13.9	0.0
prt	0.0	0.0	0.0	2.0	0.0	0.0	1.6	0.0	0.0	0.0	0.0	0.0	0.0
esp	0.0	0.0	0.0	2.3	19.2	1.3	6.8	3.4	0.0	0.0	0.0	0.0	0.0
swe	0.0	0.0	0.0	5.1	163.1	10.7	16.2	15.0	13.4	26.9	18.7	8.8	0.0
cze	0.0	0.0	0.0	1.1	53.8	1.3	2.5	1.4	0.0	0.0	0.0	0.0	0.0
hun	0.0	0.0	0.0	1.0	28.6	1.9	3.9	1.9	0.0	0.0	0.0	0.0	0.0
pol	0.0	0.0	0.0	2.3	45.8	2.9	1.3	2.6	0.0	0.0	0.0	0.0	0.0
Experiment 2 (Domestic emissions trade)													
aut	0.0	0.0	0.0	3.7	3.7	3.7	3.7	3.7	3.7	3.7	3.7	0.0	0.0
bel	0.0	0.0	0.0	8.0	8.0	8.0	8.0	8.0	8.0	8.0	8.0	8.0	0.0
dnk	0.0	0.0	0.0	6.1	6.1	6.1	6.1	6.1	6.1	6.1	6.1	6.1	0.0
fin	0.0	0.0	0.0	8.0	0.0	0.0	0.0	0.0	0.0	0.0	0.0	0.0	0.0
fra	0.0	0.0	0.0	2.0	2.0	2.0	2.0	0.0	0.0	0.0	0.0	0.0	0.0
deu	0.0	0.0	0.0	1.5	1.5	1.5	1.5	1.5	1.5	1.5	1.5	1.5	0.0
grc	0.0	0.0	0.0	3.5	3.5	0.0	0.0	3.5	0.0	0.0	0.0	0.0	0.0
gbr	0.0	0.0	0.0	0.8	0.8	0.8	0.8	0.8	0.8	0.8	0.8	0.0	0.0
ita	0.0	0.0	0.0	2.6	0.0	2.6	2.6	2.6	0.0	0.0	0.0	0.0	0.0
nld	0.0	0.0	0.0	3.5	3.5	3.5	3.5	3.5	3.5	3.5	3.5	3.5	0.0

Table 4. Marginal abatement cost (tCO_2$) in various experiments *(Cont'd)*

Sector/ Region	Coal	Oil	Gas	Elec- tricity	Oil_ Pcts	Metals	Min_ Prod	Paper	Motor Equip	Constr	Textile	Oth_ Ind	ROE
prt	0.0	0.0	0.0	2.0	0.0	0.0	2.0	0.0	0.0	0.0	0.0	0.0	0.0
esp	0.0	0.0	0.0	2.8	2.8	2.8	2.8	2.8	0.0	0.0	0.0	0.0	0.0
swe	0.0	0.0	0.0	8.4	8.4	8.4	8.4	8.4	8.4	8.4	8.4	8.4	0.0
cze	0.0	0.0	0.0	1.2	1.2	1.2	1.2	1.2	0.0	0.0	0.0	0.0	0.0
hun	0.0	0.0	0.0	1.3	1.3	1.3	1.3	1.3	0.0	0.0	0.0	0.0	0.0
pol	0.0	0.0	0.0	2.2	2.2	2.2	2.2	2.2	0.0	0.0	0.0	0.0	0.0
Experiment 3 (Regional emissions trade)													
aut	0.0	0.0	0.0	2.0	2.0	2.0	2.0	2.0	2.0	2.0	2.0	0.0	0.0
bel	0.0	0.0	0.0	2.0	2.0	2.0	2.0	2.0	2.0	2.0	2.0	2.0	0.0
dnk	0.0	0.0	0.0	2.0	2.0	2.0	2.0	2.0	2.0	2.0	2.0	2.0	0.0
fin	0.0	0.0	0.0	2.0	0.0	0.0	0.0	0.0	0.0	0.0	0.0	0.0	0.0
fra	0.0	0.0	0.0	2.0	2.0	2.0	2.0	0.0	0.0	0.0	0.0	0.0	0.0
deu	0.0	0.0	0.0	2.0	2.0	2.0	2.0	2.0	2.0	2.0	2.0	2.0	0.0
grc	0.0	0.0	0.0	2.0	2.0	0.0	0.0	2.0	0.0	0.0	0.0	0.0	0.0
gbr	0.0	0.0	0.0	2.0	2.0	2.0	2.0	2.0	2.0	2.0	2.0	0.0	0.0
ita	0.0	0.0	0.0	2.0	0.0	2.0	2.0	2.0	0.0	0.0	0.0	0.0	0.0
nld	0.0	0.0	0.0	2.0	2.0	2.0	2.0	2.0	2.0	2.0	2.0	2.0	0.0
prt	0.0	0.0	0.0	2.0	0.0	0.0	2.0	0.0	0.0	0.0	0.0	0.0	0.0
esp	0.0	0.0	0.0	2.0	2.0	2.0	2.0	2.0	0.0	0.0	0.0	0.0	0.0
swe	0.0	0.0	0.0	2.0	2.0	2.0	2.0	2.0	2.0	2.0	2.0	2.0	0.0
cze	0.0	0.0	0.0	2.0	2.0	2.0	2.0	2.0	0.0	0.0	0.0	0.0	0.0
hun	0.0	0.0	0.0	2.0	2.0	2.0	2.0	2.0	0.0	0.0	0.0	0.0	0.0
pol	0.0	0.0	0.0	2.0	2.0	2.0	2.0	2.0	0.0	0.0	0.0	0.0	0.0

4. Results

Table 3 shows the percentage changes in emissions for all sectors and regions in Experiment 1 (No emissions trading). For the sectors subjected to the NAP, these are the same as in Table 2 (i.e. negative) except for those sectors with *positive* emissions changes according to the NAP constraints, which have been replaced with a zero MAC constraint. For these sectors, as well as all other non-NAP sectors which are subject to a zero MAC constraint, the estimated changes in emissions can be positive, which implies a 'leakage' from NAP to these sectors. Table 4 shows the estimated MACs for the NAP sectors in this case of no emissions trading (Expt 1). These estimated MACs can range from a very low figure of less than a dollar per tonne of CO_2 ($/tCO$_2$) for some sectors, to a high figure of 163 ($/tCO$_2$) for the oil refining (Oil_Pcts) sector in Sweden (swe). The high figures of the MACs, mostly in the oil refining sector, reflect the fact that there is limited capacity for fuel substitution or fuel efficiency improvement in this sector (as compared to other sectors such as electricity generation).

Tables 3 and 4 also show the results for Experiment 2. In this experiment, emissions trading is allowed but only between the sectors, and no trading occurs between the regions. The MACs in this case are now uniform for a given region but vary across different regions. They can range from a low figure of less than $1/tCO$_2$ for Great Britain (gbr) to a high figure of $8.4/tCO$_2$ for Sweden (swe).

From Table 3, we can observe that some sectors will show positive changes in emissions levels when moving from Experiment 1 to Experiment 2. This indicates a 'buying sector'; i.e. one which buys the permits for the extra emissions from those sectors with negative changes in emissions. The 'buying sectors' are those with high MACs, which will acquire more permits to increase their emissions rather than incurring a higher MAC to reduce their emissions. The reverse is true for the sectors with low MACs. Both, however, will gain from emissions trading. These gains are measured (approximately) by the 'efficiency triangle' bordered by the changes in emissions quantities and prices, i.e. by 0.5 × (Change in emissions) × (Change in MAC). The change in emissions and change in MAC are normally opposite in direction except for those cases where the output effect may dominate the price or substitution effect. When we estimate the efficiency gains for regions when moving from the 'No trading' to the 'Domestic sectoral trading' experiments, we find that regions that gain the most from domestic emissions trading are those which have large variations in MACs across the trading sectors (and also large target reductions in emissions). Those regions are: Greece (grc) followed by the Netherlands (nld), Sweden (swe), France (frc) and Great Britain (gbr). Germany (deu) and Spain (esp) only gain moderately from domestic emissions trading.[13]

Results for Experiment 3 are also shown in Tables 3–4. In Experiment 3, emissions trading is allowed to take place not only between the sectors but also between regions. The MAC in this case ($2/tCO$_2$) is uniform not only across NAP sectors but also across trading regions. The small figure of MAC reflects the non-ambitious nature of the NAPs in the existing EU ETS.[14] From Table 3, it can be seen that the regions with positive changes in emissions levels between Experiment 2 and Experiment 3 are: Austria, Belgium, Denmark, Finland, Greece, Italy, The Netherlands, Spain, Sweden and Poland. These represent '(permit) buying regions', while regions with negative changes (Germany, Great Britain, the Czech Republic, Hungary) are 'selling regions'. The buying regions are those with relatively high MACs. All regions will gain in efficiency from emissions trading, however. The gains are generally smaller when we move from Experiment 2 to Experiment 3, as compared to the gains when we move from Experiment 1 to Experiment 2. This implies that the differences in MACs across different EU ETS regions are generally smaller than the differences in MACs across the trading sectors within these regions. The gains are also seen to be larger for Belgium, Denmark, Great Britain, Finland and Sweden, which reflects the fact that variations in MACs between these regions are greater when compared to other regions.

Finally, Table 5 shows the overall macroecoomic effects of emissions trading. Firstly, compared to the case of no trading, emissions trading (across sectors as well as across regions) will bring about an improvement in GDP level for all EU regions (first column of Table 5). The effects of emissions trading will bring about some positive trade balance for some regions (Great Britain, Germany and the Czech Republic – see second column of Table 5), and a negative trade balance for others (Belgium, Denmark, the Netherlands, Sweden). This means that even though emissions trading will bring about substantial efficiency gains for most regions (columns 3 and 4 of Table 5) the combined trade and efficiency effects can be negative for some regions, such as Italy (ita) and the Netherlands (nld) (see the last column in Table 5). This implies that even though the combined welfare effects of emissions trading for all NAP regions as a whole is positive, the distribution of these welfare gains across the regions may result in some regions having a net welfare loss (the Netherlands and Italy) rather than a welfare gain from emissions trading.

Table 5. Macroeconomic effects of domestic and regional emissions trading(*)

Region	Real GDP change (%)	Trade balance due to emissions trading ($millions)	Welfare decomposition: equivalent variation (ev) due to various components ($millions)			
			Allocative effects due to CO_2 tax	Other Allocative effects	Terms-of-trade effects	Total(**)
aut	0.10	−2.4	10.5	181.7	−20.4	171.9
bel	0.11	−13.4	43.2	209.5	−127.7	125.2
dnk	0.12	−11.7	33.8	163.8	−10.0	187.1
fin	0.04	−5.7	14.2	35.2	−7.7	37.9
fra	0.05	0.0	31.9	660.2	−85.3	606.0
deu	0.06	11.6	39.7	1155.7	118.0	1312.4
grc	0.33	−2.4	30.6	357.2	−99.5	286.1
gbr	0.02	34.6	−7.7	249.4	14.4	259.1
ita	0.00	−4.1	3.5	−40.8	−13.1	−49.8
nld	0.05	−5.9	21.8	183.5	−377.2	−171.8
prt	0.00	0.1	0.6	1.1	9.2	10.2
esp	0.06	−3.7	9.1	334.6	−68.7	275.9
swe	0.13	−4.4	28.3	264.0	−122.2	174.1
cze	0.05	8.5	−4.3	31.3	−6.9	19.4
hun	0.10	1.5	3.0	49.7	−5.6	47.0
pol	0.02	−2.7	6.9	30.3	11.9	50.1

(*)   The values shown in this table are *changes* from Experiment 1 (No emissions trading) to Experiment 3 (Regional emissions trading).

(**) Including a small effect due to changes in the price of capital goods.

5. Conclusions

Our study has shown that emissions trading is an important policy instrument to achieve a particular climate policy objective such as the fulfilment of the Kyoto obligations by the EU at minimum costs. The use of this 'flexible' policy instrument is seen to result in significant efficiency gains, measured either in terms of the reduction in marginal abatement costs or in terms of the efficiency gains for both (permit) buying and selling sectors. For buying sectors (those with high MACs without trading), the efficiency gains represent reductions in overall compliance costs. For selling sectors (those with low MACs without trading), increases in income from emission trading overcompensate additional abatement costs. As a result, real GDP is seen to increase for all regions. However, the efficiency gains in some cases may not be sufficient to offset the losses in revenue due to emissions trading (emissions permit purchasing); hence some regions may still experience a net welfare loss. For these regions, a net welfare loss implies a negative change in net national income even if there is a positive change in gross domestic product. This uneven distribution of the total welfare gains (income from emissions trading) across regions may warrant some attention being given to the initial distribution of the burden of emissions reductions across regions.

Acknowledgements

We wish to thank Peter Zapfel and Axel Michaelowa for many helpful comments on an earlier draft of this article, and two anonymous reviewers for many suggestions and useful comments.

Notes

1 Communication from the Commission to the Council and the European Parliament on EU policies and measures to reduce greenhouse gas emissions: Towards a European Climate Change Programme (ECCP), Com(2000)88 final.
2 In terms of the Böhringer et al. (2004) experiments, we do not consider the scenario of 'NAP_Opt', where national allocation plans (NAPs) are coordinated between EU Member States to exploit the full potential of efficiency gains from 'where-flexibility'. This is because we want to focus attention on the existing nature of the NAPs rather than on the issue of optimal allocation between Member States, which is beyond the scope of this article and can be left for a future study.
3 Directive 2003/87/EC of the European Parliament and of the Council of 13 October 2003 (EC, 2003) establishing a scheme for greenhouse gas emission allowance trading within the Community and amending Council Directive 96/61/EC, Official Journal of the European Union, L 275/32, 25.10.2003.
4 For a more detailed description and good discussions of the ETS see Kruger and Pizer (2004).
5 This means that the oil refining (Oil_Pcts) sector has to hold allowances, but only for their own emissions and not the emissions which are 'incorporated' in their product.
6 These are aggregated into a single 'Rest of European Union' (REU) region (see Table 1).
7 For an overview of the NAPs, see DEHSt (2005b).
8 Federal Ministry for the Environment, Nature Conservation and Nuclear Safety (2004): National Allocation Plan for the Federal Republic of Germany 2005–2007. Berlin, 31 March 2004. For an overview of the German allocation see DEHSt (2005a).
9 This rule applies to installations which have been modernized or newly built between 1994 and 2002 and which demonstrated a predefined reduction in emissions.
10 Process-related emissions are defined as the atmospheric release of CO_2 resulting from a chemical reaction other than combustion.
11 Operators of an existing installation can opt to be allocated allowances on the basis of their production capacity and the benchmark for new installations as well (option rule).
12 The alternative is to impose some emission restrictions on these non-NAP sectors, but this will require some price mechanisms (such as carbon tax). Given that most NAPs are unclear with respect to these mechanisms for the non-trading sectors, it was decided that for the purpose of our illustrative experiments, the non-trading sectors are subjected to no restrictions. This will allow a main focus on the trading sectors.
13 The results on efficiency gains are not shown in the article, but are available from Tables A and B, accessible via the Internet.
14 However, in Germany we currently observe much higher prices which do not seem to reflect market prices. An oligopolistic market situation, high fuel prices and market uncertainties seem to drive the prices above the competitive market price.

References

Babiker, M., Viguier, L., Reilly, J., Ellerman, D., Criqui, P., 2001. The Welfare Costs of Hybrid Carbon Policies in the European Union. MIT Report 74.
Babiker, M., Reilly J., Viguier L., 2002. Is International Emissions Trading Always Beneficial? MIT Report 93.
Böhringer, C., Hoffmann, T., Lange, A., Löschel, A., Moslener, U., 2004. Assessing Emission Allocation in Europe: An Interactive Simulation Approach. Discussion Paper No. 04-40.
Burniaux, J.M., Truong, P.T., 2002. GTAP-E: An Energy-Environmental Version of the GTAP Model. GTAP Technical Paper No. 16 (revised), January.
DEHSt [German Emissions Trading Authority], 2005a. Emissions Trading in Germany: Allocation of Allowances for the first Commitment Period 2005–2007. 2nd edition: 28.02.2005 [available at http://www.dehst.de/cln_007/nn_76354/SharedDocs/Downloads/EN/e_Zuteilung/Allocation_of_Allowances,templateId=raw,property=publicationFile.pdf/Allocation_of_Allowances].

DEHSt [German Emissions Trading Authority], 2005b. Implementation of Emissions Trading in the EU: National Allocation Plans of all EU States, in cooperation with the Fraunhofer Institute for Systems and Innovation Research, Karlsruhe and the Öko-Institut, Berlin [available at http://www.dehst.de/cln_007/nn_593634/SharedDocs/Downloads/EN/ETS/EU__NAP__Vergleich,templateId=raw,property=publicationFile.pdf/EU_NAP_Vergleich].

Dimaranan, B.V., McDougall, R.A. (Eds), 2006. Global Trade, Assistance, and Production: The GTAP 6 Database. Center for Global Trade Analysis, Purdue University [available at https://www.gtap.agecon.purdue.edu/databases/v6/v6_doco.asp].

EC [European Commission], 2001. Proposal for a Directive of the European Parliament and the Council establishing a scheme for greenhouse gas emission allowance trading within the Community and amending Council Directive 96/61/EC, COM (2001) 581 final. Commission of the European Communities, Brussels.

EC [European Commission], 2003. Directive 2003/87/EC of the European Parliament and of the Council of 13 October 2003 establishing a scheme for greenhouse gas emission allowance trading within the Community and amending Council Directive 96/61/EC. Official Journal of the European Union, L 275/32, 25.10.2003.

EC [European Commission], 2004. Emissions trading: National allocation plans. Final national allocation plans and available drafts of national allocation plans. [Available at http://europa.eu.int/comm/environment/climat/emission_plans.htm].

EEA [European Environment Agency], 2005. Annual European Community greenhouse gas inventory 1990–2003 and inventory report 2005. Revised final version, 27.05.2005 [available at http://reports.eea.eu.int/technical_report_2005_4/en].

Federal Ministry for the Environment, Nature Conservation and Nuclear Safety, 2004. National Allocation Plan for the Federal Republic of Germany 2005–2007. Berlin, 31.03.2004, Translation: 07.05.2004 [available at http://www.bmu.de/files/pdfs/allgemein/application/pdf/nap_kabi_en.pdf].

Hertel, T.W. (Ed.), 1997. Global Trade Analysis: Modeling and Applications. Cambridge, Cambridge University Press.

Kruger, J., Pizer, W.A., 2004. The EU emissions trading directive: opportunities and potential pitfalls. Resources for the Future. Discussion Paper 04–24.

Table A. Efficiency gains ($ millions) when moving from 'No trade'(Experiment 1) to 'Domestic emissions trade' (Experiment 2) (*)

Sector/ Region	Electricity	Oil_ Pcts	Metals	Min_ Prod	Paper	Motor Equip	Constr	Textile	Oth_Ind	Total
aut	0.0	3.0	0.2	0.0	0.1	0.0	0.0	0.0	0.0	3.7
bel	3.3	2.2	5.4	0.4	0.1	0.0	0.0	0.0	0.0	11.5
dnk	1.1	1.6	0.5	0.8	0.5	0.6	0.0	0.2	1.8	7.5
fin	0.0	0.0	0.0	0.0	0.0	0.0	0.0	0.0	0.0	0.0
fra	2.2	3.1	1.0	6.6	0.0	0.0	0.0	0.0	0.0	12.9
deu	0.0	5.7	0.3	0.3	0.0	0.0	0.0	0.0	0.0	6.3
grc	0.2	29.4	0.0	0.0	0.0	0.0	0.0	0.0	0.0	29.8
gbr	8.2	1.2	0.3	0.6	1.0	1.4	0.0	0.5	0.0	13.1
ita	0.0	0.0	0.1	0.0	0.1	0.0	0.0	0.0	0.0	0.2
nld	0.0	12.4	0.5	1.5	0.2	1.3	0.3	0.3	0.1	16.5
prt	0.0	0.0	0.0	0.0	0.0	0.0	0.0	0.0	0.0	0.0
esp	0.2	3.1	0.2	1.5	0.0	0.0	0.0	0.0	0.0	5.0
swe	1.2	13.3	0.2	0.6	0.5	0.1	0.5	0.1	0.0	16.4
cze	0.0	0.9	0.0	0.1	0.0	0.0	0.0	0.0	0.0	1.0
hun	0.0	1.0	0.0	0.1	0.0	0.0	0.0	0.0	0.0	1.2
pol	0.0	1.8	0.2	0.2	0.0	0.0	0.0	0.0	0.0	2.2

(*) Efficiency gain is calculated as –0.5 × (Change in emissions) × (Change in MAC), where the changes will be opposite in directions (except where the output effect dominates the substitution effect).

Table B. Efficiency gains ($ millions) when moving from 'Domestic emissions trade' (Experiment 2) to 'Regional emissions trade' (Experiment 3) (*)

Sector/ Region	Electricity	Oil_ Pcts	Metals	Min_ Prod	Paper	Motor Equip	Constr	Textile	Oth_Ind	Total
aut	0.7	0.0	0.1	0.1	0.0	0.0	0.0	0.0	0.0	1.0
bel	12.6	0.2	4.7	1.6	0.1	0.2	0.2	0.1	0.1	19.8
dnk	10.7	0.0	0.1	0.5	0.0	0.0	0.0	0.0	0.2	11.7
fin	8.4	0.0	0.0	0.0	0.0	0.0	0.0	0.0	0.0	8.4
fra	0.0	0.0	0.0	0.0	0.0	0.0	0.0	0.0	0.0	0.0
deu	1.3	0.0	0.1	0.1	0.0	0.0	0.0	0.0	0.0	1.5
grc	0.9	0.0	0.0	0.0	0.0	0.0	0.0	0.0	0.0	0.9
gbr	6.9	0.0	1.0	2.5	0.2	0.2	0.1	0.1	0.0	10.9
ita	0.5	0.0	0.1	0.0	0.0	0.0	0.0	0.0	0.0	0.6
nld	1.5	0.1	0.3	0.2	0.1	0.1	0.0	0.0	0.0	2.2
prt	0.0	0.0	0.0	0.0	0.0	0.0	0.0	0.0	0.0	0.0
esp	0.6	0.0	0.0	0.0	0.0	0.0	0.0	0.0	0.0	0.7
swe	5.3	0.1	0.7	0.3	0.3	0.1	0.1	0.0	0.1	6.9
cze	1.5	0.0	0.2	0.0	0.0	0.0	0.0	0.0	0.0	1.8
hun	0.2	0.0	0.0	0.0	0.0	0.0	0.0	0.0	0.0	0.3
pol	0.1	0.0	0.0	0.0	0.0	0.0	0.0	0.0	0.0	0.1

(*) Efficiency gain is calculated as –0.5 × (Change in emissions) × (Change in MAC), where the changes will be opposite in directions (except where the output effect dominates the substitution effect).

Harmonization versus decentralization in the EU ETS: an economic analysis

Pablo del Río González*

Department of Spanish and International Economics, Universidad de Castilla-La Mancha, C/ Cobertizo de S. Pedro Mártir s/n, Toledo 45071, Spain

Abstract

Although certain guidelines have been put forward by the European Commission, Member States (MS) have had a considerable degree of freedom to elaborate their national allocation plans (NAPs) and decide on key elements for the first commitment period of the EU emissions trading scheme (EU ETS)(2005–2007). While some favour this decentralized approach, arguing that it provides flexibility and allows the consideration of 'national circumstances', it may also bring many problems, in particular a possible distortion of sectoral competition. This article reviews and analyses the arguments for and against delegating the decision on key allocation elements to the MS, it discusses different degrees and alternatives for harmonization of those key elements, and analyses their pros and cons according to several criteria. The article concludes that harmonization is generally preferable to a decentralized approach, although this preference depends on the specific elements and on the assessment criteria considered.

Keywords: EU ETS; Allowance allocation; Harmonization; Cost-efficiency

1. Introduction: aims, scope and methodology

The EU emissions trading scheme (EU ETS) set out in the emissions trading Directive 87/2003/EC (ET Directive) shows a unique combination of harmonization and decentralization; i.e. decisions on key design elements taken at either Community or Member State (MS) level. While the choice of some important elements has been left for MS to decide, other issues were decided at EU level and through EU 'guidelines'. Allowances were not allocated top-down, i.e. from the European Commission, but MS themselves had to elaborate national allocation plans (NAPs) and decide on the number of allowances that they would allocate and on the treatment of other key provisions relevant to the use of those allowances.

The decision on other elements was left at the discretion of MS. This has led to a continuous discussion since the inception of the scheme on the need for EU harmonization of several of those

* Corresponding author. Tel.: +34-925-268800
E-mail address: pablo.rio@uclm.es

elements. While many have favoured a 'decentralized' approach, arguing that it provides flexibility and allows the consideration of 'national circumstances', others claim that this brings many problems with it, including a distortion of sectoral competition. This article analyses the economic implications of delegating the decision on key allocation elements to the MS in their NAPs, it discusses several different alternatives for harmonization of NAPs and analyses their pros and cons. Other studies have dealt with the allocation topic in the EU ETS, but mainly to compare different allocation methods (see, among others, Harrison and Radov, 2002; Matthes et al., 2005; Carraro et al., 2006). The issue of harmonization versus decentralization has often been mentioned but not usually analysed in depth. This article tries to cover this gap in the literature.

Accordingly, the article is structured as follows. The next section provides an interpretation of the term 'harmonization'. Section 3 shows how harmonization was dealt with in the ET Directive. The criteria to assess the harmonization options are put forward in Section 4, whereas the analysis of the different alternatives in the light of relevant criteria is carried out in Sections 5 and 6. The article closes with some concluding remarks.

2. Interpreting harmonization

The term 'harmonization' in the EU context can have different meanings, but it is generally used to denominate a common approach applied top-down from EU institutions to MS. In the EU ETS context, it can be interpreted as NAPs following a homogeneous approach concerning key provisions (allocation, banking, etc.). Different degrees and interpretations of this term are possible, however. Furthermore, we can distinguish the general approach to harmonization (including cap setting) from harmonization of several key elements in order to highlight the pros and cons of different options.

2.1. Different choices on the general structure of allocation in the EU ETS

The setting of the total cap (i.e. the total number of allowances to be allocated) should be distinguished from the method used to allocate this cap and other key choices to address particular situations (i.e. the treatment of new entrants or consideration of early actions). The term 'general' harmonization designates the administrative level at which decisions on the setting of the total number of allowances and the other key elements are taken. These other issues are considered as 'specific provisions' and will be tackled later. General harmonization can show different degrees of involvement from the European Commission and the MS. In principle, there are four alternatives, covering a wide range of possibilities:

- *Absolute harmonization*. The decision on key EU ETS design choices is taken at the EU level and MS have a very low degree of discretion. By considering a path to Kyoto, the Community sets the aggregate quantity of allowances allocated to the trading and non-trading sectors on an EU-wide basis and determines the allowances distributed to each MS for specific sectors.
- *Relative harmonization*. NAPs are elaborated by countries, but based on obligatory and detailed guidelines set up by the Commission, with very limited leeway for MS.
- *Soft harmonization*. NAPs are carried out by countries. The allocation method is decided at Community level but MS are free to decide on other NAP provisions.
- *No harmonization*. MS have total freedom to decide on key design provisions.[1] In fact, this would lead to different domestic trading schemes linked to each other through intra-Community

cooperation. The Community's role would be to ensure that domestic systems conform to Community law.[2]

2.2. Choice of elements and provisions

Following the ET Directive and the Commission guidelines, MS were required to take a decision on certain elements in their NAPs. It was inevitable that the degree of harmonization would differ between the different elements:

- *Allocation method.* MS may choose the allocation method, but at least 95% of the allowances have to be distributed free. Most countries used grandfathering based on historical emissions, although a few also used benchmarks for specific sectors.[3]
- *New entrants reserve (NER).* The ET Directive states that installations entering into operation in the commitment period should have access to allowances. Some experts argue that newcomers should buy those allowances in the market. Others have argued that a number of allowances (a 'reserve') should be set aside initially and be distributed to new entrants either through auction or freely (i.e. with benchmarks or on a first-come-first-served basis). This was the option chosen by all MS.
- *Closures.* Cancelling the allowances given to the operator of the installation when the emission permit is also cancelled is one option to deal with the allowances from installations which close within a commitment period. Other options include allowing the operators to retain them (i.e. Sweden) or devising a 'transfer rule' whereby the allocation to old plants is transferred to new plants with some conditions (i.e. Germany).
- *Opt-out.* MS could ask the Commission to exclude certain installations from the EU ETS if they limit their emissions to the same extent than if they were covered by the EU ETS.
- *Early action.* This refers to measures taken in the past aimed at emissions reductions. MS may wish to reward early action either by using benchmarks or grandfathering allowances based on emissions with a distant base-year, or even by creating a reserve of allowances which are allocated to those installations proving that early action measures were taken.
- *Banking.* Allowances issued for one year could be used to comply with targets in a later year, either within the same commitment period (i.e. intraperiod banking) or between different commitment periods (i.e. interperiod banking). Banking is allowed from the first EU ETS period to the second and is compulsory from the second to the third.
- *Process emissions.* Process emissions are difficult to reduce and some MS give them a special treatment. For example, in Spain, installations have been given as many allowances as they are likely to need to cover those emissions.
- *Mandatory/voluntary inclusion of sectors and activities.* Although a voluntary scheme was initially considered as an option in the Green Paper on GHG emissions trading (CEC, 2001), a mandatory scheme was finally implemented.
- *Degree of auctioning.* MS could auction up to 5% of their total allocation. However, only three countries have used this possibility (Hungary, Denmark and Ireland).

Table 1 indicates how the different elements rate against the four levels of harmonization in the EU ETS.

Table 1. Degrees of harmonization of different elements in the EU ETS

	Absolute harmonization	Relative harmonization	Soft harmonization	No harmonization
Allocation method		X	X	
NER	X (requirement that new entrants have access to allowances)			X*
Closures				X
Opt-out		X	X	X
Early action				X
Banking	X (intraperiod)			X (interperiod)
Process emissions				X
Inclusion of activities	X (except opt-in)			
Degree of auctioning	X (max. 5%)			

* Discretionality for Member States (in the manner in which they ensure that new entrants have access to allowances).

3. What was harmonized in the first EU ETS allocation period?

Several choices were made by the ET Directive regarding harmonization/decentralization of key elements. Harmonization was initiated in several official documents. The discussion started in the aforementioned Green Paper (CEC, 2000). The ET Directive stated how some issues should and should not be tackled and also set general criteria for allocation, whereas later documents were more precise regarding harmonization. As Table 2 shows, some issues were left for MS to decide, the most important of which was the total amount of allowances to be issued and allocated (i.e. the setting of the cap), although the Community retained a verification role to ensure that allocations were consistent with a path to Kyoto. Since every MS had different emission targets and differing degrees of compliance with those targets, it was believed that MS should be allowed to decide how to reach their commitments.

Harmonization was also implemented through other Commission documents, such as the so-called 'non-paper' (CEC, 2003) and the 'Commission guidelines' (CEC, 2004b). The non-paper includes a set of recommendations on how to elaborate the NAP, stating that 'the Common Position leaves Member States some freedom to allocate the quantities of allowances appropriate to their national circumstances', reflecting the burden-sharing agreement (BSA) targets agreed by MS.[4] Other issues are also left at Member States' discretion (i.e. the use of benchmarking or treatment of new entrants). However, the non-paper reiterates that, in fixing the total number of allowances, MS should consider the potential to reduce emissions, other EC legislation and national energy policies, and that they may consider accommodating early action (see Table 3). Nevertheless, the non-paper explicitly states that it is not a draft for a guidance document, instead focusing on process issues.

An additional milestone was the 'Commission guidelines' document, whose purpose was to assist MS in drawing up their NAPs by indicating the scope of interpretation of the Annex III criteria of the ET Directive that the Commission deemed acceptable. It also constituted the Commission's main tool when assessing the notified NAPs. Depending on whether the MS were required to apply specific criteria or had certain leeway in doing so, the Commission distinguished between 'mandatory' Annex III criteria and 'optional' criteria. Certain criteria had both a mandatory and an optional nature (Table 4).

Table 2. Harmonized and non-harmonized provisions in the ET Directive

Issues	Article in the Directive
Harmonized	
Type of ET system, sectors and gases included	Art. 2, 24, 30 and Annexes I and II
Requirement to carry out and submit a NAP determining the total quantity of allowances to be allocated and the allocation method, based on objective and transparent criteria, including those of Annex III and considering the observations from the general public	Art. 9 (1), 11 (1), Annex III (see Table 4)
At least 95% free allocation for the first commitment period and (at least 90% for the second)	Art. 10
When deciding on the allocation, MS should consider the need to give new entrants access to allowances	Art. (3)
Penalties for non-compliance	Art. 16
Intraperiod banking allowed	Art. 13(1)
Common monitoring, verification and reporting obligations	CEC (2004a)
Linked/harmonized national registries with independent transaction log	Art. 19
At Member States' discretion	
Emissions reduction targets/allocation of allowances at different levels	Art. 9 and Annex III
Interperiod banking	Art. 13(2)
Opt-in	Art. 24(1)
Opt-out	Art. 27
Pooling	Art. 28
Inclusion of additional gases and activities	Art. 24
Use of credits from the Kyoto flexible mechanisms	Art. 30
Verification of emissions is delegated to MS, which should consider the criteria included in Annex V	Art. 15, Annex V

Nevertheless, even when issues were formally harmonized, a considerable degree of interpretation often resulted. This was the case with the list of installations in Annex I, particularly with combustion installations. As stressed by Betz et al. (2004, p. 4) most MS based the interpretation of the activities to be included in the ETS (Annex I of the ET Directive) on their national implementation of the EU IPPC Directive. However, since MS differed in their implementation of the IPPC Directive and, thus, of Annex I of the ET Directive, unequal treatment of otherwise equal installations resulted, potentially leading to competition distortions. Furthermore, differences in the accumulation rule existed, such as the criteria governing which of the installation capacities below the 20 MW threshold had to be accumulated and included in the EU ETS. This considerable degree of interpretation was the result of pressures from MS to have final control over the key issues, the complexities of the criteria included in Annex III, and the short time-frame to deal with them in depth.

Nevertheless, a certain degree of convergence in the treatment of some non-harmonized NAP elements can be observed in the NAPs as a result of the decisions of MS themselves.[5]

Table 3. Items that the NAP should include

- The share of the MS' emissions cap under the Kyoto Protocol intended to be allocated in the form of allowances
- Principles, assumptions and data applied to determine that share
- Consideration of early action
- Whether the installations in the 'trading population' benefit from environmental tax exemptions and whether they are covered by any environmental investment aid scheme
- Whether the installations that are to benefit from 'early action' received state aid for the investment concerned
- Consideration of clean technologies and energy policies
- How the number of allowances intended to be allocated to each installation have been determined
- List of installations and their respective quantitative allocation
- Data per installation (including annual emissions)
- How new entrants will be able to begin participating in the GHG emissions trading scheme in the MS
- How public comments are taken into account

Source: CEC (2003).

4. Criteria for assessment

The literature on the assessment of climate policy instruments provides several criteria (see, among others, Stavins, 1989; OECD, 1997; Pelchen, 1999). These criteria can also be used to evaluate the accuracy of harmonization versus decentralization.

4.1. Environmental effectiveness

Instruments should be assessed according to their contribution to emission reduction targets. Therefore, the extent to which harmonization or non-harmonization of key provisions in an ETS may contribute to environmental effectiveness is a relevant criterion.

4.2. Cost-efficiency and market functioning of the scheme

Reaching the aforementioned targets at lower social costs is also important. Ideally, an emissions trading scheme ensures cost-efficiency, because it is a flexible mechanism following the equimarginality principle. To achieve this, however, the market has to function well, with high liquidity in terms of traded volume, frequent transactions and numerous active traders. An EU-wide ETS ensures additional abatement cost savings compared with domestic systems. A segmented market may not lead to the fulfilment of the equimarginality principle at the EU level if national allocations distort the incentives to reduce emissions in the low-cost abatement sectors.[6]

4.3. Dynamic efficiency

The extent to which climate policy instruments encourage the development and diffusion of less CO_2-emitting technologies is another relevant criterion, because new carbon-friendly investments

Table 4. Categorization of the Annex III allocation criteria on the basis of mandatory (M) or optional (O) implementation

Annex III criteria	Mandatory or optional	Content
(1) Kyoto commitments	(M)/(O)	The total quantity of allowances to be allocated shall be consistent with the Member State's obligation to limit its emissions, considering the proportion of these allowances represented in comparison with emissions from non-covered sources. The quantity shall be consistent with a path towards achieving compliance with the Kyoto Protocol (M). Distribution of effort between covered and non-covered sectors is optional (O).
(2) Assessments of emissions development	(M)	The total quantity of allowances shall be consistent with assessments of actual and projected emissions.
(3) Potential to reduce emissions	(M)/(O)	The quantity of allowances to be allocated shall be consistent with the technological potential of activities covered by this scheme to reduce emissions (M). MS may base their distribution of allowances on average emissions of GHG by product and achievable progress in each activity (O).
(4) Consistency with other legislation	(M)/(O)	The NAP shall be consistent with other Community legislation (M). Unavoidable emissions increases resulting from new legislation should be considered (O).
(5) Non-discrimination between companies or sectors	(M)	The NAP shall not discriminate between companies or sectors as to unduly favour certain installations or sectors.
(6) New entrants	(O)	The NAP shall inform on the treatment of new entrants.
(7) Early action	(O)	The NAP shall inform on the treatment of early action.
(8) Clean technology	(O)	The NAP shall inform on the treatment of clean technology.
(9) Involvement of the public	(M)	The NAP shall inform on how public comments are considered.
(10) List of installations	(M)	The NAP shall contain the list of covered installations with the quantities of allowances allocated to each.
(11) Competition from outside the Union	(O)	The NAP may inform on how the existence of competition from countries or entities outside the EU will be considered.

Source: Elaboration from CEC (2004b).

will allow the climate change challenge to be met at the lowest cost in the future. Different degrees of harmonization may affect the incentives to implement new technologies, since this depends on key variables affected by the allocation (i.e. price of EUAs, allocation method, new entrants reserve and banking rules).

4.4. Administrative and firm transaction costs

The administrative procedure to allocate allowances is costly, given the deeply political nature of the allocation process involving the transfer of valuable assets. Total administrative costs are the sum of the Commission and MS costs. Emissions trading may involve additional costs for firms (costs of seeking purchasers and sellers of allowances, negotiation, approval of transactions, and monitoring, execution and insurance costs) (see Stavins, 1995).

4.5. Political feasibility

Different designs of an ETS may be more or less acceptable to political constituencies and to polluting sources covered by the scheme. Mitigating the conflict with the stakeholders is necessary in order to ensure that the system will finally be implemented and will function smoothly. Transparent and simple rules and consideration of the opinions of stakeholders may be key to ensuring their support.

4.6. Minimizing the competitive distortions between sectors in different countries as a result of specific provisions

A level playing field is necessary for the accurate functioning of the internal market and this justifies Community involvement.[7] Competitive distortions may be either internal (i.e. sectors and firms within the EU) or external (i.e. firms in the EU versus those located in non-EU countries).

4.7. Consideration of national peculiarities versus Community interests

The singularities of countries might be taken into account when carrying out the allocation in an international ETS.[8] This may provide some flexibility but may conflict with European Community interests and with other criteria.

4.8. Equity (cost distribution)

How costs are distributed between actors (countries, sectors, firms and consumers) is another relevant criterion. An excessive burden on a particular actor should be identified and mitigated.

Obviously, there might be trade-offs between different criteria. These should be identified and, if possible, mitigated through the choice of appropriate design options.

5. Assessing general harmonization

This section assesses the pros and cons of the 'general' harmonization alternatives according to the aforementioned criteria, while the following section analyses the harmonization of specific allocation choices.

A major feature of the Directive is that national targets (caps) are left for MS to decide, considering a 'Kyoto path'. Although Annex III of the Directive states that the total quantity of allowances to be allocated shall not be more 'than is likely to be needed', it leaves a lot of leeway for MS to decide. This subsidiarity element has been criticized by some actors, notably environmental NGOs. For others, allowing MS to decide on targets was probably the right decision at the time, considering the difficulty in reaching an agreement on MS targets at the EU level and the delays in negotiations that this could cause.[9]

5.1.Cost-efficiency and market functioning

The theory of emissions trading usually stresses that it does not matter how allowances are allocated to attain cost-efficiency of the scheme, since the equimarginality principle is attained regardless of the method used. Therefore, in principle, the cost-efficiency of the scheme is not affected by the decision on allocation (harmonization or decentralization). In practice, however, the allocation decision may distort the incentives to reduce emissions where it is more cost-efficient to do so. If this is so because, for example, a large amount of allowances have been distributed to the high-cost sectors, then the cost-efficiency of the scheme might be affected. Since transaction costs and market power could also affect the cost-efficiency of the scheme, then allocation may affect cost-efficiency through its impact on these two aspects. For example, if allocation based on grandfathering was entirely left for MS to decide, some companies might be able to use a favourable allowance allocation to gain market shares in the power market (Svendsen, 2003). On the other hand, allocation always entails unavoidable transaction costs. The point is to know whether harmonization or decentralization leads to a higher increase in those transaction costs (we return to this discussion in Section 5.4).

In general, it can be expected that absolute harmonization increases the cost-efficiency of the scheme with respect to the other alternatives because there is a risk that the NAPs will not be submitted on time. This would lead to uncertainties and an imperfect market functioning and also affect cost-efficiency. Absolute harmonization would mitigate this risk. For political reasons (lobbying pressures for national governments), a decentralized allocation would probably lead to more allowances to high-cost sectors than a harmonized alternative. In contrast, absolute harmonization would probably result in allocation more closely resembling the equimarginality principle. Finally, the fact that the decision to allocate allowances is decentralized means that the total number of allowances in the scheme can not be known *ex ante*. This lack of information on scarcity makes it difficult to obtain a market price signal, creating market uncertainty and also affecting the dynamic efficiency of the scheme.

5.2. Environmental effectiveness

The allowances allocated to polluting sources are a key factor determining the emissions reduced in an ETS. The decentralization–harmonization options could thus affect the environmental effectiveness of the scheme through their different impact on the allocation of allowances. In this context, the no-harmonization case would probably not ensure as many emissions reductions as the other three cases because MS would be more directly exposed to pressure from the firms and more likely to argue that their 'special circumstances' should result in more allowances being allocated to a specific sector. Therefore, they would tend to be more generous in their allocations.[10] In contrast, although subject to MS pressures, top-down decisions on allocation from the European Commission would tend to lead to a less generous allocation. Thus, in general, a higher level of harmonization is likely to increase the environmental integrity of the scheme. We assume that country targets agreed at Community level would be more ambitious than targets unilaterally set by MS themselves because lobbying pressures for governments would be more intense in the latter than the former case, since they can 'sell' it to their political constituencies by arguing that the (greater) reductions were the unavoidable result of compromises in the negotiations with other MS and with the EU.

5.3. Dynamic efficiency

Since allowances at EU level would tend to be scarcer with harmonization, the allowance price would be higher. This would provide a greater incentive for the development and diffusion of less-emission-intensive technologies, which could allow the achievement of long-term emissions targets at lower costs. On the other hand, if the NER is not harmonized at the EU level, MS could be particularly generous through this 'back-door', and then more allowances would reduce the incentives to adopt cleaner technologies (see next section).

5.4. Administrative transaction costs

Given the different sources of transaction costs, the discussion of the administrative transaction costs of different choices is subject to uncertainty. These costs include those incurred by the MS directly (i.e. in their negotiations with their firms or with the European Commission) and the costs incurred by the European Commission itself. In the no-harmonization case, intensive negotiations between the MS and their firms would significantly increase Member States' transaction costs. As we move from absolute harmonization to decentralization, the negotiation costs between the MS and the Commission would probably decrease and those between MS and their firms increase because:

(a) In the absolute harmonization case, countries have to negotiate with the Commission and with the firms. The Commission decides on the allocation of allowances, which leads to conflicts with MS and, thus, to costs.
(b) Under relative harmonization, the Commission would still incur significant administrative costs because it has to elaborate the guidelines for allocation, which involves negotiations with MS and dedicating resources for these tasks. The MS would incur high administrative costs, although the tight EU guidelines would minimize their conflict with firms compared with cases (c) and (d) because the government can claim that it has little capacity to manoeuvre.
(c) In the soft harmonization case, in contrast, the Commission bears lower administrative costs because, although it has to elaborate the aforementioned guidelines and approve allocation decisions, the MS decide on key elements of the NAP.
(d) Under no-harmonization, the costs are negligible for the Commission but they are high for MS, since their governments have to negotiate with their firms.

Therefore, the results of the different harmonization options according to this criterion are highly inconclusive.

5.5. Firms' transaction costs

Companies invest resources in order to influence allocation decisions. Therefore, the greater the capacity of firms to influence institutions, the greater this investment and, thus, the higher the firms' transaction costs. We assume that firms have a greater capacity to influence national than Community institutions. This makes lobbying activities more likely in the decentralization case and less likely as we move to absolute harmonization. Therefore, absolute harmonization would probably lead to the lowest transaction costs and no-harmonization to the highest.

5.6. Political feasibility

The widespread call for some harmonization makes the no-harmonization decision a difficult one to take. But, on the other hand, the claim for consideration of national circumstances and the interests of countries in keeping sovereignty also makes absolute harmonization an unrealistic option. Therefore, the alternatives 'in the middle' are likely to receive the greatest political support. Harmonization may increase the acceptability of the scheme if rigorous rules for transparency (including proper public consultation requirements) are put forward.

5.7. Distortion of competition

Internal
The no-harmonization case entails the highest risk for competition distortion because different allocation methods might be chosen, but also because different amounts of allowances (in relation to the different sectors' 'needs') could be grandfathered between sectors in different countries. Absolute harmonization with allocation based on sectoral European benchmarks could lead to lower competitive distortions, but this allocation method might be problematic (see next section).

External
Distortion of competition between EU and non-EU firms is defined as the competitive advantage for the latter due to their lack of CO_2 emissions restrictions. Under the assumption that the Commission would be less generous than the MS, external competition distortions would be less severe in the no-harmonization case. The no-harmonization case allows MS to be more generous with their firms. Installations receiving a generous allocation are more likely to mitigate competitive disadvantages.

5.8. Consideration of national circumstances

The greater the ability of MS to influence the allocation decisions, the greater the possibility that MS consider their 'national peculiarities'; this being a legitimate part of national interests or a result of intense company lobbying. One benefit of delegating the elaboration of NAPs to MS is that it has managed to bring the main components of the allocation debate to the MS level, avoiding lengthy allocation discussions at the EU level and setting time limits for the debate within the MS (Lefevere, 2005, p. 282). Of course, this 'consideration of national circumstances' provides flexibility but makes the system more liable to capture by special interest groups and adds complexity and transaction costs.

5.9. Equity

Many argue that allocation is fundamentally an equity issue. It is not easy to identify *a priori* the equity impacts of different harmonization alternatives. For example, the distribution of costs between producers and consumers depends on cost pass-through into prices. Cost pass-through at a sectoral EU level is probably more likely under harmonization than under decentralization because, in this case, the same sector is more likely to be treated differently in different MS (i.e. receive a different allowance allocation), which makes translating the extra EU ETS costs into prices risky for the competitiveness of those firms receiving a lower allocation. However, this also depends very much on the features of the sector (i.e. openness to international competition and elasticities). Harmonization could be designed to mitigate distributional impacts between different countries.

To sum up, the case for (absolute) harmonization can be justified according to three criteria: distortion of competition, dynamic efficiency and environmental effectiveness; whereas the argument against absolute harmonization mainly rests on the low degree of flexibility it gives MS to consider their national circumstances. Table 5 summarizes the above discussion.

6. Assessing the harmonization of specific provisions and choices

6.1. New entrants reserve (NER)

Within the harmonization–decentralization debate, three cases are worth considering concerning the treatment of new entrants: (1) *total harmonization* (allocation to new entrants based on each sector's growth rates and sectoral benchmarks, both provided by the Commission), (2) *relative harmonization* (allocation to new entrants based on EU sectoral benchmarks but sector growth rates calculated by MS), and (3) *each MS deciding* on the criteria for allocating allowances to new entrants. In this latter case, newcomers in some MS are likely to receive more allowances (compared to their needs) than those in other MS. This option, finally chosen by the ET Directive, could have negative effects on several criteria. In principle, cost-efficiency would not be affected because it does not depend on how allowances are distributed but on the attainment of the equimarginality rule. However, a negative impact on this criteria would result if newcomers are treated differently in different MS and reductions by firms with lower abatement costs are discouraged (more

Table 5. Summary of the assessment of different harmonization alternatives

Criteria	Harmonization choice			
	Absolute	Relative	Soft	No-harmonization
1. Cost-efficiency	++	++	++	++
2. Environmental effectiveness	++	+	=	--
3. Dynamic efficiency	++	+	=	-
4. Administrative transaction costs	-/-- (- nat; -- Com)	- (- nat; - Com)	- (-- nat; = Com)	= (-- nat; ++ Com)
5. Firm transaction costs	+	=	-	--
6. Political feasibility	-	+	+	--
7a. Distortion of competition (internal)	++	=	=	--
7b. Distortion of competition (external)	-	=	=	++
8. Consideration of national circumstances	-	=	=	++
9. Equity	++	=	=	--

Note: ++ (very good score), + (good), = (intermediate), - (poor), - - (very poor).

allowances are given to high-cost abatement emitters). Therefore, harmonization is likely to score better under this criterion. Environmental effectiveness might not be affected. In the short term, if more allowances are reserved for future entrants, there will be fewer allowances for existing installations. More scarcity will be created in the short term. Higher allowance prices would result, but overall emissions would be similar when considering the whole period (i.e. it is a zero-sum game between emissions in the short and medium terms). Therefore, harmonization makes no difference to decentralization in this regard.

Concerning dynamic efficiency, under decentralization some MS would tend to give relatively more allowances to new entrants, which discourages the introduction of new technologies compared with the harmonization cases. The non-harmonization of the NER could have negative competitive distortions. If a country requires newcomers to buy the allowances it needs and another MS reserves an amount of allowances to be distributed free, this would affect companies' investment decisions. Countries with a free NER would be more attractive to investors. This may lead to a 'race to the bottom' as MS compete to attract investments (Grubb and Neuhoff, 2006). Therefore, this element should be harmonized according to this criterion, for instance through EU-wide sectoral benchmarks, by making new entrants buy the allowances in the market.

Decentralization is obviously preferable concerning the consideration of national circumstances. Countries could allocate allowances to new entrants according to their own projections of emissions growth in sectors and installations. This is a prisoner's dilemma because once a country decides to give new entrants allowances for free, others are likely to follow. Therefore, the case between harmonization and decentralization boils down to a trade-off between the latter two criteria. Insofar as the competition distortions are more pervasive than the impacts resulting from the non-consideration of national circumstances, harmonized rules for the NER would be preferable. Nevertheless, devising appropriate methods to harmonize the NER is a difficult task. One option is to use benchmarks, as done by some MS to allocate allowances to newcomers in the first commitment period. However, European benchmarks entail technical difficulties (see Section 6.6). Another option is to make newcomers buy the allowances in the market.[11] This could be an appropriate long-term solution because new entrants would then internalize the CO_2 cost as another input cost, which would be the same in all MS, avoiding the aforementioned competitive distortions. All in all, some *de-facto* harmonization occurred in the treatment of new entrants across MS in the first commitment period, with all of them providing free allowances.

6.2. Closures

In a similar way to the previous case, the different treatment of closures across countries may allow the consideration of MS peculiarities, but may also create competitive distortions and tilt the investment incentives between incumbents and new firms to the benefit of the former.[12] For most MS, the closure of an installation is defined as the ending of permanent operation resulting in the return of the allowances. However, some MS allow the transfer of those allowances to a new installation (Germany, Slovenia and Italy), avoiding the disincentive to close down an existing (inefficient) installation and build a new one.

If allowances from closures are given to the operator of the old installation which closes down and he uses those allowances for a new installation, then this new installation would have a competitive advantage over a new entrant in the same sector (but in a different country) which would have to buy the allowances in the market, favouring incumbents. Note that this could also affect the dynamic efficiency criteria and the long-term cost-efficiency of the scheme if it is assumed that new entrants would introduce newer and more efficient technologies than incumbents. A competitive distortion problem can also occur if the allowances from closures are auctioned by one MS whereas they accrue to the NER to be distributed freely in another MS. Therefore, harmonization of this issue is advisable according to the competitive distortion and the dynamic efficiency criteria.

6.3. Treatment of small installations

The treatment of small installations was harmonized through the setting of a common minimum threshold. This was a right choice for reasons of competitive distortion. Otherwise, small installations in one MS could have a competitive disadvantage over small installations in the same sector in another MS. However, the thresholds were set at such a low level that some very small installations were included in the scheme. This increases transaction costs with little additional environmental benefit.

6.4. Early action and process emissions

The harmonization/decentralization of other provisions would only affect the distribution of allowances between installations, i.e. it is merely a distributional issue which does not affect other assessment criteria. For example, if some countries allocate more allowances to reward early action or to cover process emissions than other countries, the environmental integrity of the scheme would not be affected, since it is a zero-sum game between installations.

6.5. Banking

The banking of allowances between years within a commitment period (intraperiod banking) is explicitly allowed by the Directive. However, banking between commitment periods (interperiod banking) is left at Member States' discretion and only France and Poland have allowed it.[13] Interperiod banking has its pros and its cons. The drawbacks call for a harmonized approach for this element. On the one hand, banking facilitates 'when' flexibility for firms to reach their targets and increases the economic efficiency of the scheme. It also tends to create greater scarcity in the first period (from which allowances are banked) and to increase liquidity in the second period (when banked allowances are used). If this scarcity translates into price signals, prices would tend to be higher in the first commitment period (and lower in the second) than if banking were not allowed. However, prices would effectively be affected only if the allowances banked represented a significant share of total allowances in either of the two periods and this could only happen if relatively large countries allowed banking and large firms within these countries used it. In addition to these price effects, constraining banking could undermine longer-term mitigation plans. This is because firms may have little incentive to implement mitigation strategies that create additional emissions reductions and which lead to the 'free-up' of allowances that cannot be used in the future. Finally, the lack of interperiod banking could reduce a key incentive for EU firms to support the continuation of the ETS into subsequent periods (namely, the holding of a valuable portfolio of banked allowances) (Kruger and Pizer, 2004).

However, according to environmental effectiveness criteria, interperiod banking could bring some problems for MS if not harmonized. Those countries allowing unrestricted banking between periods could have problems in complying with their BSA targets in the following commitment period if other countries did not follow suit, because excess allowances from MS with banking restrictions could flow into MS without banking provisions.[14] In fact, this is a real problem because it only takes one MS to allow banking in order for surplus allowances to flow to that state to be banked forward.[15] These problems led to *de-facto* harmonization, since most MS decided to prohibit banking between the first and the second EU ETS commitment periods. Therefore, the problems that banking may bring and its benefits in terms of 'intertemporal' efficiency call for a harmonized approach.

6.6. Allocation method

As with other elements, harmonizing the allocation method has its pros and cons according to different assessment criteria. Furthermore, it may be a difficult task.

Some commentators argue that if the allocation method is not harmonized, competitive distortions between installations may occur because if a MS auctioned its allowances while others grandfathered them, firms in the first country would be competitively disadvantaged. Even if all countries were required to allocate the allowances for free, there could still be competitive distortions due to the application of different methods. Harmonization based on auction would certainly mitigate competitive distortions between firms in different MS. It would also provide an allowance price signal and allow countries (and firms) to profit from the 'double dividend', increasing overall economic efficiency. It would also avoid the problem of obtaining data on which to base the allocation, which is the case with other allocation methods and which has been a hurdle when elaborating the NAPs, as shown by Carraro et al. (2006). Paradoxically, auction could be favoured by firms in countries far from their Kyoto targets, because in this case grandfathering would lead to fewer allowances for those firms compared with their competitors in other countries. This has been an argument used by Danish electricity generators, for example. However, auction could negatively affect the competitiveness of EU firms with respect to firms in countries without carbon restrictions (as shown by Grubb et al., 2007) and this allocation method could be politically unfeasible if implemented in the short term.[16] An alternative would be to harmonize free allocation using benchmarks (rather than basing the allocation on past emissions), but developing EU-wide benchmarks is a cumbersome exercise in most sectors, given the heterogeneity of their processes and products. In addition, it is unlikely to be a feasible option given the heterogeneous character of firms within most sectors and their different specific emissions (tCO_2/tonne of product). A more feasible alternative would then be to gradually increase the percentage of allowances auctioned in each commitment period, leading to a 100% auction in the long term. Therefore, overall economic efficiency and competitive distortion criteria provide an argument for the harmonization of the allocation method.[17]

However, totally harmonizing the allocation method is difficult and may even be undesirable. First, this could only take place from the third commitment period of the EU ETS. Second, harmonization of the method would not avoid the problem of competitive distortions between firms in different MS, because the different stringency of Kyoto targets would still lead to different sector allocations.[18] Third, it should be taken into account that sectors are very different in structure and that countries have different national policy settings. On the other hand, diversity of products, processes and national circumstances is the norm in the EU sectors. Harmonization in this context should be able to adapt to those differences, which would certainly be an impossible task.

Furthermore, Grubb and Neuhoff (2006) suggest that the (internal) competitive distortions may not be large and that the competitiveness impact of different allocations should be put into this context. For example, at a carbon price of €15/tCO$_2$, a 5% differential allocation in the iron and steel and refining sectors would only represent a 0.25% change in the sector value added, while this percentage rises to barely 1% in the case of cement and electricity. These are trivial figures compared to existing price differentials between products in MS.

6.7. Compliance and enforcement regime (minimum penalties for non-compliance)

The compliance and enforcement regime (and, particularly, penalties for non-compliance) has been harmonized at the EU level. This is a correct decision according to the environmental effectiveness, competitive distortion and equity criteria. If sanctions for non-compliance were not imposed by some MS, then the environmental effectiveness of the scheme would be at risk.[19] If different enforcement regimes and penalty levels were implemented in different MS, competitive distortions could result, since there would be an incentive for firms and installations to locate in countries where penalty levels are lower and enforcement regimes weaker. In addition, allowances would be systematically sold abroad by companies in the country with the lowest level of sanctions, endangering the MS compliance with its own target (FIELD, 2000; Gagelmann and Hansjürgens, 2002). Verification of emissions has been delegated to the MS, with some harmonization of minimum verification rules to avoid distortion of the internal market. This was also a correct decision, since this is the level at which this activity could be undertaken with the lowest administrative costs (using the existing administrative infrastructure), while preserving the environmental integrity of the scheme.[20]

6.8. Definition of installations

Different interpretations of the term 'installation' in different MS may cause competitive distortions in the EU ETS and would violate the equity criteria if, for example, one installation was covered by the ETS while the same type of installation in a different country was not. The latter would not have to control its emissions, while the former would incur additional costs. In fact, this could have been a problem in the first EU ETS commitment period. Combustion installations have heterogeneous definitions across countries to a certain extent, with some countries using a narrow definition and others using a broader one.[21] Therefore, the definition of the installations covered by the scheme (and, particularly, combustion installations) should be fully harmonized in the next periods.

6.9. Inclusion of sectors and activities

The participation of sectors and activities in the EU ETS was harmonized through the implementation of a mandatory system. This was a proper decision for reasons of environmental effectiveness, static and dynamic efficiency. Although a voluntary system would have been politically more feasible for the MS, it would have failed to include a sufficiently large number of emitters, would have restricted market efficiency and liquidity, and the functioning of the scheme would have been negatively affected (Christiansen and Wettestad, 2003). Only companies interested in selling would probably have taken part, whereas potential buyers would not have done so. The limited coverage would have affected the liquidity of the market and led to a low allowance price which, in turn, would have negatively affected the incentives for technological change (dynamic efficiency). It would have also reduced the environmental effectiveness of the scheme because emissions reductions would be greater with a mandatory system than with a voluntary one.

7. Concluding remarks

The EU ETS combines harmonized and non-harmonized elements as a result of negotiations between MS and the Community. This division of competencies between the Community and the MS could be a reflection of their respective areas of comparative advantage. This article has analysed the pros and cons of different harmonization alternatives in this system according to different criteria put forward in the emissions trading literature.

Harmonization was followed concerning some relevant provisions (such as allocation method, sectors included, etc.) and the general structure of the scheme. Nevertheless, harmonization of other key provisions (national caps, NERs, closures) was difficult to achieve and a 'decentralized' approach was adopted. This was a result of political negotiations requiring agreement and the fact that MS preferred to keep control over key areas. Nevertheless, a certain degree of *de-facto* harmonization of some non-harmonized issues could be observed (i.e. treatment of interperiod banking, more generous allocation for the industrial sectors compared to the electricity generation sector, free allowances for new entrants, and the use of recent emissions to allocate allowances to existing installations).

This qualitative article shows that, even if flexibility and consideration of national circumstances provide an argument for decentralization, harmonization is preferable according to some criteria and concerning some key elements (NER and banking). Decentralization adds complexity to the scheme and thus increases transaction costs, although it also increases the political viability of implementing such a system in the first place. The smooth functioning of the market, dynamic efficiency gains and, most importantly, the absence of distortions to (internal) competition are certainly the major factors that justify harmonization.

Finally, it was also shown that the implementation of harmonization often results in a trade-off between different criteria and elements. In fact, harmonizing some key elements might prove to be a difficult (if not worthless) task, given that MS want to keep control of certain decisions. Future empirical work should use the experience gained with the elaboration of the NAPs and the actual functioning of the ETS to derive conclusions and lessons on the most appropriate degree of harmonization.

Acknowledgments

I am grateful to Felix Hernández (CSIC, Spain) and two anonymous referees for their comments. Of course, the usual disclaimer applies.

Notes

1 In fact, the EU ETS was proposed by the Commission as a remedy to the possibility of dealing with several incompatible national trading schemes, which was perceived as a threat to the internal market.
2 This basically corresponds to scenario 1 in FIELD (2000).
3 It is not the purpose of this article to discuss the pros and cons of different allocation methods but to analyse the advantages and disadvantages of harmonizing different design elements of an ETS. For an analysis of different allocation methodologies in the context of the EU ETS, see the references cited in Section 2.

4 For example, MS may prefer to favour emissions reductions in some sectors more than in others.

5 Sometimes, this *de-facto* harmonization has taken place because MS looked at what others were doing and copied the choices made in other NAPs. In other cases *de-facto* harmonization was due to the unavailability of data and to the Commission review. Placing the burden of emissions reductions on the electricity sector was also a common choice (given its low-cost abatement alternatives and its relatively low degree of international competition). Other non-harmonized issues did not experience a *de-facto* harmonization, however.

6 Market segmentation could be the result of either domestic schemes or of an EU-wide market with national allocation of allowances.

7 In fact, the equalization of competition across sectors in all MS has been one of the most important justifications for European environmental legislation (FIELD, 2000).

8 For example, through distribution of allowances, MS can deal with inequities resulting from higher energy prices and other economic impacts of GHG regulation.

9 'It is difficult to see how the ET Directive could have been adopted within such a short period of time if targets would have been included' (Lefevere, 2005, p. 275).

10 It is doubtful whether many MS would demand considerable contributions from the larger emitters without a coordinated initiative at the EU level (Gagelmann and Hansjürgens, 2002).

11 An interesting issue is what MS plan to do with unused allowances from their NERs. Harmonization of this issue is desirable.

12 The treatment of closures may lead to perverse effects. For instance, if operators do not keep their allowances after the installation closes, they may have an incentive to keep inefficient installations running. However, this issue exceeds the remit of the harmonization–decentralization discussion.

13 More precisely, banking is allowed from the first EU ETS period to the second, while it is compulsory from the second to the third.

14 For example, if country X allows banking between periods and country Y does not, and if a firm from country Y sells allowances to a firm in country X which banks these allowances into the following commitment period, this could cause a compliance problem for country Y in this period.

15 We thank an anonymous referee for this observation.

16 Kruger and Pizer (2004) report that it was politically very difficult to convince industry groups to support auctions in the different US emissions trading schemes.

17 If auction is chosen as the harmonized allocation method, however, the issue of external competitive distortions would remain.

18 We thank an anonymous referee for this observation.

19 Installations operating in a MS without adequate enforcement could emit CO_2 without handing over allowances. They could then sell their allowances to installations in other MS, thus increasing the emissions in another MS.

20 The Green Paper favours this approach on the argument that 'the checking and enforcement of compliance by companies with Community environmental legislation is mostly carried out by the MS' (CEC, 2000, p. 25).

21 Three different definitions resulted: one included all combustion plants producing electricity, heat or steam, even if their main purpose was not energy production; another encompassed only those installations producing electricity, heat or steam with the purpose of energy production; a third only included power generation combustion plants.

References

Betz, R., Eichhammer, W., Schleig, J., 2004. Designing national allocation plans for EU emissions trading: a first analysis of the outcome. Energy and Environment 15(3), 375–425.

Carraro, C., Ellerman, D., Buchner, B. (eds.), 2006. Lessons Learnt from the National Allocation of Allowances in the EU ETS. Cambridge University Press, Cambridge, UK.

CEC [Commission of the European Communities], 2000. Green Paper on Greenhouse Emissions Trading within the EU. CEC, Brussels.

CEC, 2003. The EU Emissions Trading Scheme: How to develop a National Allocation Plan. Non-paper. CEC, Brussels.

CEC, 2004a. Commission Decision Establishing Guidelines for the Monitoring and Reporting of Greenhouse Gas Emissions pursuant to Directive 2003/87/EC of the European Parliament and of the Council. CEC, Brussels.

CEC, 2004b. Communication from the Commission on Guidance to Assist Member States in the Implementation of the Criteria Listed in Annex III to Directive 2003/87/EC Establishing a Scheme for Greenhouse Gas Emission Allowance Trading within the Community and Amending Council Directive 96/61/EC, and on the circumstances under which force majeure is demonstrated. CEC, Brussels.

Christiansen, A., Wettestad, J., 2003. The EU as a frontrunner on greenhouse gas emissions trading: how did it happen and will the EU succeed? Climate Policy 3, 3–18.

FIELD, 2000. Designing Options for Implementing an Emissions Trading Scheme for Greenhouse Gases in the EC. Foundation for International Environmental Law and Development (FIELD). Final Report to the European Commission. 22 February 2000.

Gagelmann, F., Hansjürgens, B., 2002. Climate protection through tradable permits: the EU proposal for a CO_2 emissions trading system in Europe. European Environment 12, 185–202.

Grubb, M., Neuhoff, K., 2006. Allocation and competitiveness in the EU emissions trading system: policy overview. Climate Policy 6(1), 1–26.

Grubb, M., Sato, M., Cust, J., Chan, K.L., Korppoo, A., Ceppi, P., 2007. Differentiation and dynamics of competitiveness impacts from the EU ETS. Climate Policy, forthcoming.

Harrison, D., Radov, D., 2002. Evaluation of Alternative Initial Allocation Mechanisms in a European Emission Allowance Trading Scheme. National Economic Research Associates, Report for the European Commission, March.

Kruger, J., Pizer, W.A., 2004. The EU Emissions Trading Directive: Opportunities and Potential Pitfalls. Discussion Paper 04-24, Resources for the Future, Washington, DC.

Lefevere, J., 2005. The EU greenhouse gas emission allowance trading scheme. In: M. Bothe, E. Rehbinder (Eds), Climate Change Policy. Routledge, London.

Matthes, F., Graichen, V., Repenning, J., 2005. The Environmental Effectiveness and Economic Efficiency of the European Union Emissions Trading Scheme: Structural Aspects of Allocation. Öko-Institut. Report to WWF, Berlin, November 2005.

OECD, 1997. Evaluating Economic Instruments for Environmental Policy. OECD, Paris.

Pelchen, A., 1999. A framework for the evaluation of political and economical instruments for global warming mitigation. In: J. Hacker, A. Pelchen (Eds), Goals and Economic Instruments for the Achievement of Global Warming Mitigation in Europe. Kluwer, Dordrecht, The Netherlands.

Stavins, R.N., 1989. Harnessing market forces to protect the environment. Environment 31(1), 28–35.

Stavins, R.N., 1995. Transaction costs and tradable permits. Journal of Environmental Economics and Management 29, 133–148.

Svendsen, G.T., Vesterdal, M., 2003. How to design greenhouse gas trading in the EU? Energy Policy 31(14), 1531–1539.

www.climatepolicy.com

Simple rules for targeting CO_2 allowance allocations to compensate firms

Karen Palmer, Dallas Burtraw, Danny Kahn*

Resources for the Future, 1616 P Street NW, Washington, DC 20036, USA

Abstract

Policies to cap emissions of carbon dioxide (CO_2), such as the recently announced agreement among the northeastern states of the USA, are expected to have important effects on the electricity industry and on the market value of firms that own electricity generation assets. A study of the economics literature reveals potentially large efficiency advantages for initial distribution of tradable emissions allowances through an auction and direction of allowance value to public purposes. However, an auction raises the costs for the regulated firms. This article identifies rules for free distribution of a portion of the allowances that satisfy a compensation goal for firms while maximizing the value of allowances that can be directed to public purposes. The article employs a detailed simulation model to calculate numerical results for the market value of generation assets under the CO_2 cap-and-trade programme in the northeastern USA.

Keywords: Emissions trading; Allowance allocations; Electricity; Auction; Grandfathering; Asset value

1. Introduction

One reason for global warming being a tremendously complex problem is that policies to mitigate its effects necessarily involve the actions of millions of actors. In some cases, these policies would impose high costs on severely affected parties. A frequently cited principle of public policy is that government should 'do no direct harm' (Schultze, 1977); that is, public policy needs to respond to the direct harm that may be concentrated on severely affected parties. Compensation can take a variety of forms. One form is the time delay between the announcement of a public policy and its implementation, which provides for the realization of economic value from previous investments while giving investors the opportunity to realign their decisions going forward. Years that have transpired between the announcement of policy goals and the implementation of policy provide such an opportunity. Within a cap-and-trade programme, another fundamental form of compensation is in the initial distribution of emissions allowances, because the free distribution of emissions allowances conveys substantial economic value to recipients.

* Corresponding author. Tel.: +1-202-328-5134
E-mail address: kahn@rff.org

In this article, we first examine the claim for compensation from electricity producers that are affected directly by the regional proposal in the northeastern USA known as the Regional Greenhouse Gas Initiative (RGGI). The RGGI represents the first mandatory policy requiring the reduction of emissions of greenhouse gases in the USA. Secondly, we investigate ways to deliver compensation to electricity producers through free allocation of emissions allowances, while simultaneously attempting to minimize the amount of compensation that would be received undeservedly. To the extent that the compensation target can be achieved at minimum cost, this leaves more revenue (in the form of valuable emissions allowances) that can be directed toward other complementary public policy goals such as improving efficiency or compensating other parties.

The burden of the cost of emissions reductions, as well as the cost of paying for the use of emissions allowances, forms the basis for stakeholder claims for compensation. In addition, the regional approach could put electricity producers within the region at a competitive disadvantage with respect to competing generators operating outside the region. In order to gain acceptance of such a regional policy, policy makers will need to find a way to compensate firms for some or all of their increased costs.

Emissions allowances represent an enormous economic value that arises due to the value placed on emissions within a cap-and-trade system, and the initial distribution of emissions allowances to electricity generators represents a significant potential source of compensation. However, others, including residential, commercial and industrial electricity consumers, and fuel suppliers, also face the prospect of losses under a greenhouse gas cap-and-trade policy. Free allocation of emissions allowances to generators diverts revenues that otherwise could be directed to compensating other parties or be dedicated to general tax relief, which offers tremendous efficiency gains and forms broad-based compensation for the diffuse effects of the policy on households. It also diverts revenues from other purposes, such as research initiatives or efficiency programmes linked to climate policy. Policy makers need to be cognizant of likely impacts on all affected parties, and they may want to limit and narrowly target free distribution of emissions allowances in order to be better able to address the broader set of efficiency and compensation goals.

One approach to the initial distribution of emission allowances that could address a mix of efficiency and compensation goals would be to combine free allocation to electricity generators with an auction. Indeed, we find that under an allowance auction several firms, including (but not limited to) those that rely heavily on nuclear and other non-emitting generating technologies, will actually realize profits in excess of those received in the absence of a CO_2 cap-and-trade policy. The value of the emissions allowances in the regional programme that we model is at least four times the cost to producers of mitigating CO_2 emissions. Thus, ideally only a portion of the allowances need to be given away for free to compensate adversely affected generators, which would leave the remainder to be auctioned.

As a point of departure, we calculate the change in market value of existing generation assets were the policy to take effect immediately without warning. We identify a benchmark of 100% compensation for the worst-off firm. This benchmark enables the reader to scale our results to achieve any compensation target for the industry.

We find that the policy has an important effect on facilities outside the RGGI region, which typically gain value due to the change in the regional wholesale power price. Taking changes outside the RGGI region into account, the industry is fully compensated for the costs of the policy under an auction through the change in electricity prices and increased revenues paid by consumers.

From this industry-wide perspective, we find that regulators could direct 100% of the emissions allowances to an auction and dedicate the revenues to compensating consumers or to other purposes, with no free allocation to producers, and the industry would suffer no loss in market value.

However, changes at the industry level mask the effects on individual firms, some of which gain value and some of which lose value, and the effect on individual firms plays an important role in the policy dialogue. Therefore we seek to find ways to tailor compensation to firms' known losses without providing undue compensation to firms that benefit under the policy. The contribution of this article is to solve a highly parameterized simulation model of the US electricity sector to identify changes in the market value of existing electricity generation assets. We organize the change in market value of those assets according to ownership by firms as of January 2005, and thereby calculate the effect of various policies on investors. Using this information, we explore various approaches to compensating investors, including free initial distribution of emission allowances.

A crucial question is whether the regulator can successfully use a revelation strategy to identify the winners and deny them compensation and thereby limit and target the free allocation of emissions allowances to firms that lose value. One mechanism through which the regulator might be able to entice firms to reveal their true costs is through a process analogous to the stranded cost recovery proceedings that were part of deregulation of the electricity industry in many parts of the country. If this were possible, we suggest that it would be sufficient for the regulator to freely allocate 34% of the allowances and thereby maintain fully the market value of all firms generating electricity in the RGGI region, while still allowing many firms actually to gain substantial value. Such complete compensation would itself be controversial; and often public policy aims to achieve an average level of compensation rather than targeting the worst-off party. Nonetheless, under this approach the remaining 66% of the emissions allowances could be auctioned or otherwise directed toward other compensation goals or public purposes.

In the alternative scenario, the regulator might not be able to identify the gains and losses of individual firms. To address this possibility, we investigate decision rules that are simple to understand and execute, and that make use of information that is generally available to state regulators. The decision rules that we envision would condition the initial distribution of emissions allowances to incumbent generators on variations of historic measures that, for the most part, have been used in previous cap-and-trade programmes. These measures involve a formula for allocation based on historic generation at the facility level, with variations including different formulas for different fuels and for different gas-fired generating technologies and mechanisms to account for the portion of a firm's generation that is non-emitting. We formulate a mathematical problem with the objective of finding an approach to allocation that provides the maximum amount of revenue available for public purposes subject to the constraint that the worst-off firm suffers no decline in market value. Using readily available information about the fuel type and size of firms, it appears that the regulator would need to freely distribute about 77% of the allowances in order to maintain at least a break-even value for the worst-off firm, while also enabling, in this case, a substantial increase in value for many firms and for the industry as a whole. The regulator could auction the remaining 23% of the emissions allowances. It is noteworthy that this value is proximate to the requirement in the Memorandum of Understanding (MoU) in the RGGI region that stipulates that states should reserve for public purposes (equivalent to an auction) at least 25% of the emissions allowances.[1] These calculations do not take into account changes that might result from the implementation of policy in other regions or at the national level, and they are based on a specific metric for calculating the portion of free allocation – i.e. production in 1999. Also, we evaluate allocation rules for the RGGI region as a whole, although decisions are ultimately left to states within the RGGI.

Typically the delay between the time when a policy is announced and when it is implemented delays the cost of compliance and gives firms an opportunity to depreciate existing capital and to adjust their investment strategies. We find that the share of allowance value that would need to be given away for free in order to achieve a compensation goal does not change with delay; however, the absolute magnitude of the economic impact of the policy is reduced. Therefore, were the goal to limit harm to producers in absolute magnitude, the delay in the policy would reduce the justification for a free allocation.

This research sets the stage for a meaningful discussion about the appropriate goal for compensation. While some would argue that to 'do no harm' to investors is a reasonable accommodation to achieve political will around climate policy, others would argue that investors should assume responsibility for risks stemming from changes in policy or market conditions, especially since other firms would have made investments in anticipation of climate policy. One might argue, for instance, that firms deserve less than full compensation for disadvantageous investments made since the date when global warming emerged onto the policy agenda. We illustrate how the allocation rules we calculate can be scaled to achieve whatever level of compensation is the goal of regulators.

2. The design of a cap-and-trade policy

The RGGI represents an effort by nine northeastern and mid-Atlantic states to develop a regional, mandatory, market-based cap-and-trade programme to reduce greenhouse gas emissions. The effort was initiated formally in April 2003 when Governor George Pataki of New York sent letters to governors of the northeastern and mid-Atlantic states. Each of the nine participating states (Connecticut, Delaware, Maine, Massachusetts, New Hampshire, New Jersey, New York, Rhode Island, and Vermont) assigned staff to a working group to develop a Memorandum of Understanding and a model rule by the end of 2005. On 20 December 2005, seven of the original nine states (excluding Massachusetts and Rhode Island) announced an agreement on a Memorandum of Understanding to implement the RGGI programme. A draft model rule was released for comment in March 2006. In April, legislation was signed by the governor of Maryland to bring the state into the programme. Initially, the programme will address carbon dioxide (CO_2) emissions from the electric power sector. If successful, the programme could serve as a model for a national cap-and-trade programme for GHG emissions.

Several approaches to the initial distribution of emissions allowances have been considered in other regulatory contexts and in analyses of the RGGI programme (Burtraw et al., 2005, 2006; Sterner and Muller, 2006). One is to distribute allowances on the basis of **historic** measures of electricity generation; this approach is often called grandfathering because it distributes allowances without charge to incumbents in the industry. Another approach is to regularly **update** the calculation underlying the allowance distribution based on current- or recent-year data. Like distribution based on historic data, an updating approach distributes allowances free of charge and could also distribute them according to various measures, such as the share of electricity generation or heat input (a measure related to fuel use and CO_2 emissions) at a facility. The primary alternative to these free distribution approaches is the sale of allowances through an **auction**, directly or indirectly (e.g. allowances may be sold by the government or distributed for free to third parties such as energy consumers or their trustees, which then sell allowances through an auction).

Burtraw et al. (2002) and Bovenberg and Goulder (2001) have found that, in the case of nationwide CO_2 regulation, the free allocation of emissions allowances can dramatically overcompensate the electricity industry on aggregate, although different parts of the industry are affected very differently. Analysis of the CO_2 emissions trading system in Europe, which began in 2005, has reached a similar conclusion (Sijm et al., 2005; UK House of Commons, 2005). In RGGI, earlier work (Burtraw et al., 2005, 2006) suggests that giving away 100% of the allowances for free to emitting generators based on historic output (or other measures) will more than compensate generators for the costs of the programme. Using a simple model with fixed capacity and fixed demand in the RGGI programme, the Center for Energy, Economic and Environmental Policy (2005) finds that all three approaches to allocation – historic, updating and auction – would lead to increased profitability for the electricity sector as a whole in RGGI relative to no policy, with the historic approach resulting in the greatest increase in profits.

Using the same detailed simulation model as one that we use in this article, with endogenous investment and price-responsive demand, Burtraw et al. (2006) analyse a regional CO_2 cap-and-trade policy that generates roughly twice the emissions reductions as the proposed RGGI policy. Also, unlike the RGGI policy, the policy that is modelled will be announced in 2008 and implemented immediately, albeit with a phased-in reduction in emissions over time. They find that the industry as a whole sees a substantial increase in value when emissions allowances are distributed for free under a historic approach. Furthermore, under any approach, the value of the industry will be greater when the analysis includes the effect of the policy on the value of generation assets located outside the RGGI region.

The changes in the value of generation assets are illustrated in Figure 1, which depicts the effects of an auction approach to allocation on the 23 largest generating firms that sell electricity within the RGGI region. A number of firms profit and some experience important losses in the value of generation assets owned inside the RGGI region. Nearly all firms show an increase in the value of the generation assets they own outside the region, and some of these increases are sizeable.

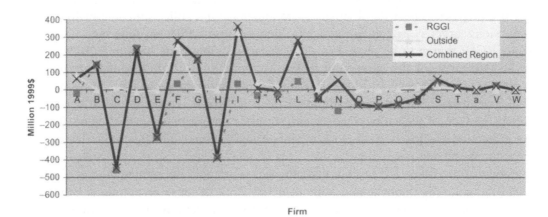

Figure 1. Change in market value for the 23 largest firms in the RGGI region under an auction. The modelled scenario does not match any specific proposal that is part of RGGI and is roughly twice as stringent as that adopted in the model rule.

Taking the unified assets of the firms inside and outside the RGGI region into account, almost half of the 23 largest firms increase in value even when they purchase emissions allowances in an auction. Therefore, limiting free allocation so as to compensate only losing firms provides the opportunity to compensate other affected parties, including consumers.

Another compelling reason to limit free allocation of emissions allowances is efficiency. Many economists and other analysts suggest that auctioning provides a source of revenue that may have economy-wide efficiency benefits if it is used to reduce taxes, with potentially dramatic efficiency advantages compared to free distribution (Bovenberg and de Mooij, 1994; Parry, 1995; Bovenberg and Goulder, 1996; Goulder et al., 1999; Parry et al., 1999; Smith et al., 2002). Moreover, an auction has a dramatic efficiency advantage in regions of the country where electricity prices differ substantially from marginal costs due to cost-of-service regulation, because the auction approach tends to reduce the difference between price and marginal cost in this case (Beamon et al., 2001; Burtraw et al., 2001, 2002; Parry, 2005).

In addition to its implications for how allowance allocation affects efficiency, how electricity prices are set also is a key issue that determines how well firms will fare under an emissions trading programme (Burtraw et al., 2001). In the RGGI region, electricity markets are deregulated, and retail prices are based on marginal costs rather than regulated average cost of service. In this case, there is little difference to electricity price between auction and historic approaches to distributing allowances because investment and compliance behaviour are expected to be nearly identical. The difference is that in one case, the revenues (allowance value) go to government; in the other, they go to industry. An updating approach leads to lower electricity prices than an auction or historic approach, and therefore it is expected to have greater social costs because it does not provide the same incentive (through higher prices for consumers) to improve the efficiency of energy use.

3. Overview of the model

Our analysis is based on a detailed national electricity market simulation model developed at Resources for the Future.[2] The scenarios employ specific assumptions about the potential design of a regional CO_2 policy in the original nine-state RGGI region, including Massachusetts and Rhode Island, and not including Maryland. These assumptions are not intended to mirror precisely the specific proposals under development or to anticipate the policy outcome of RGGI. Our annual CO_2 emissions target is calculated as a 20% decline from 2008 baseline emissions levels in the nine-state RGGI region to be phased in on a linear basis between 2008 and 2025, which is about twice the stringency of the agreement in the Memorandum of Understanding among the seven states announced in December 2005.[3] The simulation model predicts how our representation of a regional greenhouse gas cap-and-trade system in the RGGI region would affect generation and investment by type of technology and electricity price and demand in the region. The results also predict effects on electricity trade with neighbouring regions and effects on electricity producers and consumers outside the region.[4]

As a point of departure, we assume that allowances are sold through auction at a market-clearing price and the policy is implemented without delay. Both of these assumptions help to identify an upper bound on the financial impact on the industry. Our central question is how to compensate shareholders in firms in a manner that is sufficient to maintain a specified market value through free allocation of a portion of the allowances, while still preserving as much value as possible in the auction.

The effect of the policy on the value of generation assets varies significantly across types of generators and is a reflection of the change in revenues and costs. The model accounts for the change in revenues that depends on the change in electricity price, which is determined by the change in the cost at the marginal generation facility. It also depends on the change in quantity produced at a particular facility, which in turn depends on both the change in the relative costs of generation among different facilities and also on the changes in demand that occur in response to the change in electricity price.[5] The costs of coal and natural gas also change in response to the change in the use of these fuels. Also important to asset value is the value of the allocation of emissions allowances, including both the new allocation of CO$_2$ emissions allowances and the change in the value of the allocation for other programmes such as the SO$_2$ and NO$_x$ emissions allowance trading programmes. The change in market value for each facility is the present discounted value of the changes in net revenue over the period 2008–2030 measured in 1999 dollars (1999$). The generating assets planned and built through 2005 are assigned to firms using information on plant ownership as of 1 January 2004.

To find the net present discounted value of the allowance pool, we calculate the present discounted value of the predicted CO$_2$ permit price in each future year and multiply by the number of allowances allocated in that year to obtain the present discounted value of the allowances in each year. Summing over the time period of 2008–2030 yields the net present value of the entire allowance pool to be allocated over the forecast horizon. Dividing this by the total number of allowances under the RGGI cap over the entire time period yields a weighted average of the present discounted value of one allowance in the RGGI programme.

4. Compensation when regulators have complete information

We model individual facilities in order to calculate the effects of the policy. However, typically investors do not own individual facilities. Rather, investors own portfolios of facilities organized either at the industry level through mutual funds and institutional investments or by holdings of stocks and bonds of a specific firm. In Section 4.1, we consider the case when regulators seek to compensate on an industry-wide basis. In Section 4.2, we consider the expected financial impacts of the trading system on individual firms. In Section 5, we consider the case when regulators seek to compensate individual firms but have only imperfect information about the performance of firms. In Section 6, we consider the delay between announcement and implementation of the policy.

4.1. Compensation at the industry level

Inside the RGGI region the change in electricity price in 2025, when the policy we model is fully implemented, is expected to be about $3.80/MWh (1999$) or 3.7% above the baseline, as reported in Table 1.[6] Outside the RGGI region we focus on the eastern USA, an area that includes much of the Ohio Valley and mid-Atlantic region.[7] In this area outside the RGGI region, average electricity price rises are expected to be around $0.72/MWh or 1.0%. As indicated in the table, this policy yields a reduction of 47 million tons of CO$_2$ in 2025 and an allowance price of about $18 per ton. Even after taking into account the small reduction in electricity demand that would result, as captured in the simulation model, the increase in electricity price provides a sizeable new source of revenue to electricity generators. The industry realizes new costs from mitigating carbon emissions and, in the case of an auction, from the purchase of emissions allowances. Accounting for changes inside and outside the region, we find that, even with an auction at the industry level, the increase in revenue is greater than

Table 1. Overview for allocation cases, 2025[a]

RGGI region (nine states)	Baseline	Historic	Auction
Average electricity price (1999$/MWh)	$103.4	$107.1[b]	$107.2
Total generation (billion kWh)	393	348	348
Coal	73	48	48
Gas	130	115	116
Nuclear	107	108	108
Renewable	34	40	40
Total new capacity[c] (GW)	28	31	31
Gas	23	24	24
Renewable	5	6	6
CO_2 price (1999$/t)	n/a	$18.1	$18.3
Emissions			
CO_2 (million t)	147	100	99
NO_x (thousand t)	118	70	70
SO_2 (thousand t)	193	101	107
Mercury (t)	1.2	0.8	0.8

[a] The modelled scenario does not match any specific proposal that is part of RGGI and is roughly twice as stringent as that adopted in the model rule.
[b] The difference between historic and auction approaches in the table stems strictly from slight differences in stranded cost recovery from industry deregulation.
[c] Numbers may not sum because of rounding.

the increase in costs. That is, if the industry is viewed as whole, we find no claim for compensation through free allocation of emissions allowances. This result is recorded in the upper left cell of Table 2. If the increase in the value of assets at some facilities were to be used to offset the decrease in value at other facilities and the effects inside and outside the RGGI region were taken into account, then the industry as a whole would require no allocation in order to preserve its market value. If one views the principals who are directly affected by the emissions trading system as shareholders in mutual funds that may be invested in electricity stocks generally, then one might claim that there is no need for compensation because investors actually benefit on aggregate from the emissions trading programme. That benefit comes at the expense of electricity consumers, as is evident from Table 1, who are worse off under the programme because of the increase in electricity price.[8]

Table 2. Percentage of free allocation required to achieve 100% compensation target when regulator can identify firms that are winners and provide exact compensation to losers

	Compensation of industry	Targeted compensation of firms that lose value
Unified assets in the eastern USA[a]	< 0%	34%
Assets in RGGI region only	29%	53%

[a] The eastern USA includes Indiana, Kentucky, Michigan, Ohio, West Virginia, Pennsylvania, the District of Columbia, Maryland, and the nine RGGI states.

The lower left cell of Table 2 indicates that if one limits attention only to the assets located inside the RGGI region, then the harm to the industry totals $1.13 billion, and the number of allowances needed to compensate the industry for the change in the value of assets inside the region would constitute 29% of the total value of emissions allowances. However, in this case the industry would realize gains outside the RGGI region. We estimate those gains – the net increase in the market value of the industry in the eastern USA but outside the RGGI – to be $1.27 billion (1999$). Considering the unified assets of the industry across regions, there is no claim for compensation.

4.2. Compensation of firms

If a regulator can identify the performance of individual firms under the trading programme, one can imagine that the regulator might seek to compensate firms through an individualized allocation of emissions allowances. Such compensation is not required by law but could play an important role in achieving political acceptability of the policy. One way in which the regulator may obtain such detailed information is by solving a simulation model. Another way in which the regulator may obtain information is by establishing a rebuttable presumption against compensation and inviting firms to appeal through the demonstration of harm, again presumably through the use of simulation modelling. These approaches would resemble the stranded cost recovery proceedings that accompanied the restructuring of the electricity sector in many states in the late 1990s, when regulators relied on simulation models to estimate the potential change in the value of generating assets due to restructuring.[9]

The second column of Table 2 reports the results when the regulator's goal is to compensate every adversely affected firm and when regulators can identify the winners under the trading system – for example, firms that operate a large portfolio of non-emitting generation – and can exclude these firms from compensation. The upper right cell accounts for the unified assets of firms throughout the eastern USA. We find that 34% of the value of emissions allowances is required to fully compensate all losing firms in this case. The remaining two-thirds of the allowances could be assigned to public purposes. Again, in this case, the overall market value of the industry would increase relative to the baseline because many firms that are winners would retain their gain in value and the allocation ensures that no firms would lose value. We estimate the net increase in the market value of the industry in the eastern USA including the compensation of 34% of emissions allowance value to be $1.48 billion.

The lower right cell considers only changes in the value of the firms' generating assets inside the RGGI region, disregarding the increase in asset values outside the region. In this case, 53% of the value of emissions allowances would be needed to fully compensate these firms. Again, in this case, the overall performance of the industry would also be better than break-even because there would be many winners. However, in this case the limited focus on the regional perspective creates more winners because many firms, including some firms that are losers within RGGI, would be winners outside of RGGI and the gain in value outside of RGGI would not be counted on to offset the loss inside RGGI. This approach would lead the industry in the eastern USA to gain $2.2 billion in market value, which includes the value of 53% of emissions allowances.

5. Compensation when regulators have incomplete information

In practice, the regulator may not have information about the financial performance of firms and may not be able or willing to gain this information through the regulatory process. Therefore, we investigate the design of compensation in a context of incomplete information. In this case we assume that the regulator does have information based on readily observable characteristics of firm portfolios of generating capacity and historic generation, and that this information can be used to differentiate among firms. For instance, the most obvious distinction is the type of fuel used by various facilities.

5.1. The mathematical problem

We assume that the regulator is motivated to minimize the amount of free allocation in order to achieve a compensation target. To do so, the regulator uses simple rules based on observable characteristics of the facilities owned by the firm. The mathematical problem is to find allocation rules that maximize the amount of allowances that would be left over for auction while achieving 100% compensation through free allocation for firms suffering losses under the auction. Formally, the problem is to identify allocation rates r_j, defined as allowances per MWh of 1999 generation by fuel type j (where j refers to coal, gas, oil) that minimize the value of the allowances that are allocated for free:

$$\min_{r_C, r_G, r_O} P * \left[\sum_{f=1}^{F} r_C C_f + r_G G_f + r_O O_f \right] \text{ such that } \forall f \in F : P * \left[r_C C_f + r_G G_f + r_O O_f \right] \geq \theta (V_f^{BL} - V_f^{A})$$

where $P*$ is the discounted weighted average allowance price ($/t CO_2) and F is the set of firms {f} operating in RGGI. Cf, Gf and Of denote 1999 generation (MWh) with coal, gas or oil, respectively. V_f^A is the net present value of firm f under an auction, and V_f^{BL} is its net present value in the baseline – that is, in the absence of the policy. All values are reported in 1999$.

The parameter θ can presumably vary between zero and one ($0 < \theta < 1$) and represents the portion of market value in the absence of the programme to be maintained through compensation. For instance, if $\theta = 1$, then the solution will provide 100% compensation to the most disadvantaged firm, implying that other firms and the industry as a whole would gain value.

There are about 100 firms operating in the RGGI region that are included in the analysis. Under this approach to defining compensation rules, usually there is one firm that just breaks even for each fuel category and thereby determines the allocation rule. These break-even firms typically are small firms with an idiosyncratic, unbalanced portfolio of assets. To achieve full compensation, these firms require a very high rate of allowances per MWh of generation in 1999, which leads to massive overcompensation of the other firms that also receive allowances at the same rate. Thus, these three firms (one for each fuel type) are deemed outliers and are removed from the analysis, and the allocation rules by fuel type are recalculated for the remaining firms.

The rules we identify are differentiated by fuel type so that, for example, gas- and coal-fired generators receive a different amount of allowances per MWh of historic generation. There is regulatory precedent for differentiating allowance allocation by fuel type; for example, in the Environmental Protection Agency's Clean Air Interstate Rule, where NO_x allowances are allocated to coal-fired generators at a rate equal to the total number of NO_x allowances divided by the fuel-adjusted total average annual heat input (BTU) between 1999 and 2002. However, gas-fired generators receive allowances at a rate that is 40% of the coal-fired rate (per BTU of total historic heat input) and oil-fired generators receive allowances at 60% of the coal-fired rate.

In addition to differentiating by fuel type, we explore other variations on the allocation rule, including differentiating by type of natural gas technology (turbine, steam and combined cycle) and including an adjustment to the allocation rule based on the non-emitting share of the firm's generation. Other variations include the exclusion of small- or medium-sized firms from direct compensation, instead applying a generic historic allocation approach for these firms.

5.2 Accounting for fuel and technology characteristics

The goal of the mathematical programming problem is to allocate allowances in a way that will achieve the compensation goal while minimizing the number of allowances (or equivalently the shares of net present value of allowance value) that have to be given away for free. We assume that, were the regulator to implement these simple rules, it is likely that the regulator would apply these simple rules only taking into account resources in the region, and this calculation is reported in Table 3. As shown in the first row of data, if the regulator only differentiates the allocation to individual facilities based on fuel, nearly 100% of the allowances must be given away for free in order to compensate the most adversely affected firms, even when accounting for gains outside the region. To achieve this target requires coal generation to be compensated at a rate of 27.7 allowances per MWh of generation in 1999, oil generation at 9.2 allowances per MWh, and natural gas generation at 11.2 allowances per MWh. To put these numbers in perspective, firms would be compensated at a rate of 17.9 allowances per MWh of 1999 generation under the historic allocation where all fossil generation was treated the same.

The driving factor in this result is the presence of small firms that have an unbalanced portfolio of generation assets. Even after we eliminate one firm as an outlier for each of the three fuel types, we still find additional small firms that require a very large allocation in order to avoid a decrease in their market value. Under this policy, all firms are made whole (i.e. their value under the policy is greater than or equal to their baseline value), so most gain value and the overall value of the industry in the eastern USA increases by $2.5 billion.

Table 3. Percentage of free allocation required to achieve 100% compensation when the regulator has incomplete information and uses simple rules

Historic allocation also to medium firms	Differentiate among gas technologies	Adjust for non-emitting generation	Percentage of allocation required to achieve 100% compensation target
Fuel-specific rules to fully compensate all firms[a]			
			98%
	Yes		89%
		Yes	84%
	Yes	Yes	77%
Fuel-specific rules to fully compensate all medium and large firms; historic allocation to small firms			
			90%
Yes			82%
Yes	Yes	Yes	77%

[a] Fuel-specific rules include elimination of one outlier for each fuel type.

The second row in Table 3 assumes that the regulator has additional information and can also differentiate among natural gas technologies, treating combustion turbines, steam and combined cycle as classes of facilities deserving different allocation rules. This differentiation has a useful effect on the allocation necessary for compensation, reducing the amount to 89%.

Another alternative is to account more completely for the portion of historic generation that comes from non-emitting sources. Heretofore, we have assumed that non-emitting sources do not qualify for an allocation. However, we expect that firms that own non-emitting generation realize an increase in value from those assets and hence are unlikely to need as much compensation as firms that have a less balanced portfolio. By adjusting the allocation based on the portion of the portfolio that is non-emitting, we find that we reduce the overcompensation that accrues to many firms. The third row of Table 3 combines the allocation to firms by fuel type with an adjustment in proportion with their share of generation in the region that is non-emitting. This adjustment is fairly potent and reduces the percentage of the allowances to be given away for free to 84%.

The fourth row combines all three adjustments for fuel type, gas technology and the share of generation that is non-emitting. We find that 77% of the allowances need to be given away for free in order to maintain the value of the disadvantaged firms. All the other firms in the region are winners, and the industry gains $1.71 billion in value.

Were the regulator to account for the change in the value of assets outside the RGGI region only, the results would be similar. Although electricity price goes up outside the RGGI region and firms benefit from increased power sales into RGGI, we also find that changes in payments for capacity reserve as well as changes in the price of natural gas can lead to negative effects on specific facilities outside RGGI. Several of these facilities are elements of the portfolios of the small firms that set the allocation rules for individual fuel types.

5.3. Accounting for firm size

As noted, the firms that are driving the performance of the allocation rules are typically small- and medium-sized firms. The compensation rule singles out firms that have unbalanced portfolios, and consequently, any formula based on their historic generation leads to overcompensation for the large firms that typically have a more balanced portfolio.

The bottom half of Table 3 reports performance when small firms are excluded from the identification of fuel-specific allocation rules. Instead, we assume that these firms are directly compensated with generic historic allocation. Small firms are identified as those with less than 500,000 MWh of generation inside the RGGI region in 1999. With a historic approach to allocation, these small firms realize a gain in market value.

The fifth row indicates that excluding small firms and using fuel-specific rules still requires 90% of the allowances to be allocated for free. The sixth row extends the generic historic allocation method to all medium-sized firms – those with more than 500,000 but less than 1 million MWh of generation in RGGI in 1999. There remain 23 large firms identified as those with generation of more than 1 million MWh in RGGI in 1999. In this case, using only a fuel-specific allocation rule requires that 82% of the allowances be given away for free.

The last row of Table 3 combines all of these features: small firms are excluded, allocation rules adjustment for fuel type, gas technology, and for the portion of non-emitting generation. The resulting share of allowances needed for compensation is 77%. We find that 90% of the firms are winners under this policy. On aggregate, we find that within the RGGI region, the industry gains $2.37 billion in market value.

Finally, in a sensitivity analysis, we consider what would happen if the regulator could identify firms that are winners under the auction and exclude them from further compensation. We consider the case in which the regulator uses a generic historic approach to allocation for small- and medium-size firms and applies the other rules for the large firms. Accounting for changes in the eastern USA outside the RGGI region, the regulator would need to give away 58% of the emissions allowances. In so doing, the regulator would still be creating new winners while compensating the most disadvantaged firms.

6. The level of compensation

We have maintained a 100% compensation goal for the most disadvantaged firms as a yardstick for comparing the different approaches to the distribution of allowances. Let us denote the share of the value of allowances that must be given away for free to achieve this goal as S. In reality, the regulator may decide on a goal that differs from 100% compensation. The estimates we provide can be adjusted in a linear way for any goal. For a compensation target less than 100% (that is for $\theta > 1$), the value of allowances necessary to achieve that goal is $\theta \cdot S$.

Several factors influence the compensation goal (θ). Hochman (1974) argues that individual behaviour presumes the permanence of pre-existing rules, and dealing equitably with those who suffer windfall losses may be crucial to preserving a belief in the fairness of social rules and institutions. On the other hand, investors in a competitive market are expected to anticipate uncertainties and factor them into their calculations. Some policy changes have a positive effect and some have a negative effect on investments, and some observers argue that society is better off in the absence of compensation.[10] For the most part, investors retain the payoff when gains exceed expectations, although sometimes regulators or legislators intervene to prevent the taking of profits, as in recent decisions in Maryland and elsewhere to allow consumers to phase-in adjustments in electricity rates when rate caps that survive from industry restructuring will be lifted. Fairness and efficiency may be served by a symmetrical process in which the regulator relieves the firm of some, but not all, responsibility for changes in policy that impose large losses in value. Inevitably, the final outcome will be shaped as much by political necessity as by compensation principles, but information about those principles can help inform the policy dialogue.[11]

In the RGGI example, the emergence of climate policy may have been anticipated years ago – perhaps with the signing of the Kyoto Protocol or at some other point in time at which changes in policy could have been anticipated. The time between when a policy is announced and when it is implemented gives firms that are to be regulated time to adjust their investment plans so as to avoid new investments that would be particularly disadvantaged under the forthcoming policy and to make investments that will perform better under the policy. To the extent that the loss in economic value stems from investments made between the announcement and implementation of the policy, this advance warning diminishes the claim for harm. In the RGGI region, most investments since the early 1990s were in natural gas generation technologies, some of which gain value and some of which lose value due to the policy.

A second aspect to delay is that it may allow for the realization of economic value from investments that predate the policy. As a consequence, the lost economic value will be less than if the policy is implemented in the same year it is announced, because for the intervening years the owner will continue to incur revenues and costs equivalent to those in the baseline. Therefore, the absolute magnitude of harm will be less if implementation occurs some time after the adoption of the policy. Delay does not directly affect the share of allowance value necessary to achieve a compensation goal. However, were the goal to limit harm to producers in an absolute sense, the delay in the policy would reduce the need for free allocation.

To illustrate these points, we consider a simple example with the value of existing assets in the baseline equal to v^{BL}, and equal to a reduced value under the auction policy equal to v^A. If the policy is adopted and implemented in the same year (t), the loss in value (L) is:

$$L = \sum_{t=0}^{\infty} \partial^t \left(v^{BL} - v^A \right) = \left(\frac{1}{1-\partial} \right) \left(v^{BL} - v^A \right)$$

Assume the discount factor is $\partial = 0.92$, corresponding to a discount rate of 0.08. Then the instantaneous loss in the value of existing assets from the implementation of the policy is $(12.5)(v^{BL} - v^A)$. If implementation is delayed by 5 years after the adoption of the policy, then the loss in value due to the policy is:

$$L = \sum_{t=5}^{\infty} \partial^t \left(v^{BL} - v^A \right) = (8.24) \left(v^{BL} - v^A \right)$$

The delay in implementation reduces the financial magnitude of harm by more than one-third. However, delay also reduces the present value of allowances measured at the time when the policy is adopted. Consequently, the portion of allowance value (S) required for full compensation is unchanged. Nonetheless, if viewed as a fraction of the market value of the assets in the baseline, the portion of allowances that would be necessary is affected by the delay. Hence, delay can be a useful mechanism to achieve compensation, and such delay has been an implicit part of the dialogue on climate policy in the USA.

One further consideration is relevant in considering the level of compensation. Firms can be expected to have differentiated themselves through their investment strategies in recent years. Some firms may have adopted risky investments in low-emitting technologies in anticipation of climate policy. The expectation of compensation here, as in any context, reduces the incentive to take steps to mitigate risks of such policy and erodes the reward for those who took such risks. This perspective also should be part of the policy debate.

7. Conclusions

A regional programme to cap greenhouse gas emissions from electricity generators, such as the recently adopted RGGI programme in the northeastern USA, can be expected to have important effects on the market value of firms that own electricity generation assets. This article explores rules for the initial distribution of emissions allowances that preserve all or some portion of the value of the firms, while maximizing the amount of allowances that can be allocated to other public purposes.

We find that, on aggregate, the industry gains value at the expense of consumers because the change in revenues is greater than the change in costs, even under an auction. An important portion of the gain in value happens at assets located outside the RGGI region. Nonetheless, individually some firms lose value. If the regulator has full information about the profitability of firms or is able to execute a revelation strategy to encourage firms to reveal information, and if the regulator sets a compensation target of maintaining 100% of the market value of all firms, then about two-thirds of the value of emissions allowances can be made available for public purposes and even the most adversely affected firms can be fully compensated. Many firms would be winners under this policy and the industry on aggregate gains $1.48 billion in value. If the regulator has to execute a decision rule with less information, then about one-quarter of the value of emissions allowances can be available for public purposes, while fully compensating the most adversely affected firm. Many firms enjoy an increase in value relative to the baseline and the industry on aggregate gains $2.37 billion in value.

An important source of compensation is the time that intervenes between the announcement of the policy and its implementation. The RGGI process began in 2003 and culminated in a Memorandum of Understanding in 2005. The programme is planned to begin in 2009. The delay in implementation provides time for investors to realize the value of previous commitments. As an example, we find that with a discount rate of 8%, a 5-year delay between adoption and implementation of the programme implies that the financial harm to companies is reduced by one-third. However, the present value of emissions allowances also is reduced, so the portion of allowance value that is required to achieve a compensation goal is unchanged. These calculations are organized to establish a benchmark that indicates the claim for compensation that would be based on maintaining 100% of the market value of the worst-off firm. Ultimately, the goal of compensation is a question for policy makers, and our results offer a tool for addressing this question. If the regulator decides that maintenance of the value of the worst-off firm in the industry at less than 100% is adequate, then the calculated allocation rules can be scaled in a straightforward manner.

Acknowledgements

The authors appreciate comments from Brian McLean and Wallace Oates and two anonymous referees on an earlier version of the article. David Evans provided excellent technical support. This research was funded by grants from the Energy Foundation, the Packard Foundation and the New York Community Trust. Model capability for this project was developed under the EPA National Center for Environmental Research (NCER) STAR Program, EPA Grant R828628.

Notes

1 As a part of the RGGI Memorandum of Understanding, the participating states agreed to set aside a minimum of 25% of their state allocation to fund a number of potential public purposes, including mitigating impacts on electricity ratepayers (RGGI, 2005). New York State has announced its intention to auction 100% of its emission allowances.

2 Model documentation is available in Paul and Burtraw (2002). Fuel prices for coal and oil adjust dynamically and are calibrated to EIA (2004).

3 We do not include endogenous banking of CO$_2$ emissions allowances, but instead assume that annual emissions caps decline linearly over the simulation horizon. The agreement is available on the RGGI web site at http://www.rggi.org/ (accessed April 26, 2006).

4 Transmission capability is limited based on information from the North American Electric Reliability Council, and transmission rents are split between buyers and sellers of power. Reserve requirements are met with capacity payments to all generating and reserve units in each time-block sufficient to elicit sufficient capacity into the market.

5 Constant elasticity demand functions are differentiated by customer class, time-block and region of the country. The lack of data requires that functions are often similar. The national weighted average own-price elasticity of demand is approximately –0.25.

6   It must be borne in mind that the policy we model is more stringent than the policy currently intended for the region.
7   Outside the nine-state RGGI region, we focus on the eastern USA, which we define to include the states of Indiana, Michigan, Ohio, Kentucky, West Virginia, Pennsylvania, Maryland and the District of Columbia. These are the states that trade electricity with states in the RGGI region and are also the states where generating firms that operate in RGGI tend to own assets outside of the RGGI.
8   The time horizon for these net present value calculations is from 2008 to 2030.
9   In the proceedings, regulators and utilities used three methods to estimate the potential change in value of generating assets due to restructuring (M. Kahal, personal communication, 5 May 2006). One was the measure of the change in the discounted value of revenues due to anticipated changes in prices as a result of restructuring. A second and conceptually similar method calculates the year-by-year revenues and costs of the generating assets in a deregulated market over the assumed remaining lives of the assets. The net present value (discounted cash flow) of this stream of profits was assumed to be the market valuation. The difference between the market valuation and the net book value of the assets (i.e. the value under regulation) measured the gain or loss from deregulation. In the later stages of restructuring, the comparable transaction approach became widely used. This much simpler method involves compiling a database on generation plant sales (usually associated with utility divestitures) and then, through the use of expert judgement, identification of comparable generation assets that had been sold and sales prices announced. In many cases, this method produced much higher post-restructuring asset valuations than those produced by simulation models, perhaps because asset buyers were willing to pay premium prices to enter newly deregulated markets quickly.
10 For example, Polinsky (1972) suggests that a single policy should be viewed as part of a larger social agenda in which government pursues many policies to improve the welfare of society generally.
11 A 'public choice' view is that appropriate compensation is discovered in a political market place, with bartering commencing in the form of political negotiations (Buchanan, 1973). Compensation serves a practical purpose by this rationale, affecting a political buy-out of groups opposing changes in social policy (Tullock, 1978).

References

Beamon, J.A., Leckey, T., Martin, L., 2001. Power Plant Emission Reductions Using a Generation Performance Standard [Draft]. US Department of Energy, Energy Information Administration, Washington, DC.

Bovenberg, A.L., Goulder, L.H., 1996. Optimal Environmental Taxation in the Presence of Other Taxes: General Equilibrium Analyses. American Economic Review 86, 985–1000.

Bovenberg, A.L., Goulder, L.H., 2001. Neutralizing the adverse industry impacts of CO_2 abatement policies: What does it cost?, in C.Carraro and G.Metcalf (Eds), Behavioural and Distributional Effects of Environmental Policies, University of Chicago Press, Chicago, IL, USA.

Bovenberg, A.L., de Mooij, R. 1994. Environmental levies and distortionary taxation. American Economic Review 94, 1085–1089.

Buchanan, J.M., 1973. The Coase theorem and the theory of the state. Natural Resources Journal 13(4), 579–594.

Burtraw, D., Palmer, K., Bharvirkar, R., Paul, A., 2001. The Effect of Allowance Allocation on the Cost of Carbon Emissions Trading. Discussion Paper 01-30. Washington, DC: Resources for the Future.

Burtraw, D., Palmer, K., Bharvirkar, R., Paul, A., 2002. The effect on asset values of the allocation of carbon dioxide emission allowances. Electricity Journal 15(5), 51–62.

Burtraw, D, Palmer, K., Kahn, D., 2005. Allocation of CO_2 emissions allowances in the regional greenhouse gas cap-and-trade program. Discussion Paper 05-25. Resources for the Future, Washington, DC.

Burtraw, D., Kahn, D., Palmer, K., 2006. CO_2 allowance allocation in the regional greenhouse gas initiative and the effect on electricity investors. Electricity Journal 19(2), 79–90.

Center for Energy, Economic and Environmental Policy, 2005. Evaluation of CO_2 Emission Allocations as Part of the Regional Greenhouse Gas Initiative: Final Report. Edward J. Bloustein School of Planning and Public Policy at Rutgers University, Newark, NJ, USA.

EIA [US Energy Information Administration], 2004. Annual Energy Outlook 2004. DOE/EIA-0383 (2004), Washington, DC (January).

Goulder, L.H., Parry, I.W.H., Williams, R.C., D. Burtraw, D., 1999. The cost-effectiveness of alternative instruments for environmental protection in a second-best setting. Journal of Public Economics 72(3), 329–360.

Hochman, H.M., 1974. Rule change and transitional equity. In: H. Hochman, G.E. Peterson (Eds), Redistribution through Public Choice. Columbia University Press, for the Urban Institute, New York, pp. 321–341.

Parry, I.W.H., 1995. Pollution taxes and revenue recycling. Journal of Environmental Economics and Management 29, 564–577.

Parry, I.W.H., 2005. Fiscal interactions and the costs of controlling pollution from electricity. Rand Journal of Economics 36(4), 850–870.

Parry, I.W.H., Williams, R.C., Goulder, L.H., 1999. When can carbon abatement policies increase welfare? The fundamental role of distorted factor markets. Journal of Environmental Economics and Management 37(1), 52–84.

Paul, A., Burtraw, D., 2002. The RFF Haiku Electricity Market Model. RFF Report. Resources for the Future, Washington, DC.

Polinsky, A.M., 1972. Probabalistic compensation criteria. The Quarterly Journal of Economics 86(3), 407–425.

RGGI [Regional Greenhouse Gas Initiative], 2005. Memorandum of Understanding (December 20) [available at www.rggi.org/docs/mou_12_20_05.pdf (accessed January 9, 2006)].

Schultze, C.L., 1977. The Public Use of Private Interest. Brookings Institution Press, Washington, DC.

Sijm, J.P.M, Bakker, S.J.A., Chen, Y., Harmsen, H.W., Lise, W., 2005. CO₂ price dynamics: the implications of EU emissions trading for the price of electricity. Energy Research Center of the Netherlands, ECN-C-05-081.

Smith, A.E., Ross, M.T., Montgomery, W.D., 2002. Implications of Trading Implementation Design for Equity-Efficiency Trade-offs in Carbon Permit Allocations. Charles River Associates, Washington, DC.

Sterner, T., Muller, A., 2006. Output and Abatement Effects of Allocation Readjustment in Permit Trade. Resources for the Future, Washington, DC.

Tullock, G., 1978. Achieving Deregulation: A Public Choice Perspective. Regulation Nov/Dec: 50–54.

UK House of Commons, Environmental Audit Committee, 2005. The International Challenge of Climate Change: UK Leadership in the G8 & EU. Fourth Report of Session 2004–2005, HC 105. The Stationery Office, London.

False confidences: forecasting errors and emission caps in CO$_2$ trading systems

Michael Grubb*, Federico Ferrario

Faculty of Economics, Cambridge University, Sidgwick Avenue, Cambridge CB3 9DD, UK

Abstract

This Commentary sets out four lines of evidence to argue both that emission forecasts are intrinsically *uncertain*, and that there is clear evidence of *projection inflation* in the forecasts of sector emissions used to underpin the setting of sector caps in emission trading systems. From a limited evidence base, we conclude that uncertainty is at least ±2%/year, overlaying an upward bias (projection inflation) on the order of 1%/year, cumulative. The Commentary concludes that this has important implications both for allocation approaches, and for some other design elements in the EU ETS. Forecasting uncertainty is not an inconvenience which is best ignored, but a fundamental fact that must be accommodated in the future design of the EU ETS and other CO$_2$ emission trading schemes.

Keywords: Emissions trading; Forecasting; Emission projections; EU ETS

Introduction

> Energy forecasting was invented to make economic forecasting look good.
>
> *Anon.*

So wrote one cynic, looking at the history of energy forecasts from the 1970s in the aftermath of the oil shocks. Yet understanding the 'science of forecasting' has assumed a wholly new significance in the context of allocating allowances for emissions trading. If allocation risks being the 'Achilles' Heel' of emissions trading, then projections of sector emissions form the protective hand responsible for a false sense of confidence.[1]

The EU ETS has hinged upon imposing cutbacks of just a few per cent, usually relative to projections of 'business as usual' emissions. The politicians who make the ultimate decisions around allocation tend to trust the numbers provided by their technical experts, who put long hours into economic modelling of projections and, increasingly, discussion with representatives of the sectors affected by allocation decisions. When the cutbacks are small relative to projections,

---

* Corresponding author. Tel.: +44-1223-335290; fax: +44-1223-335299

E-mail address: michael.grubb@econ.cam.ac.uk

the entire carbon market then hinges upon the accuracy of these projections. It is, consequently, remarkable how little critical analysis there has been of the reliability of such forecasts, despite questions being increasingly raised.

This Commentary sets out four lines of evidence to shed light on forecasting errors, and concludes by discussing implications for the future development of CO_2 cap-and-trade systems.

Scenario projections

Scenario projections are used because of acknowledged uncertainty about the future. They shed light on the range of uncertainty that forecasters themselves acknowledge to be plausible, and imply a wide range of possible emission levels. For the long-term global scenarios, the IPCC Third Assessment (IPCC, 2001) charted 'non-mitigation' scenarios ranging from under 10 to over 30 GtC/year emissions by mid-century – corresponding to average growth rates in the range 0.5–3%/year. The Fourth Assessment (IPCC, 2007) scarcely narrows the range. Moreover, by definition, the more disaggregated the focus – by sector, region and/or time-span – the wider the range of uncertainty within the global envelope.

At a national level, on time periods relevant to the EU ETS phase-II allocations, a recent study by the UK Department of Trade and Industry (DTI, 2006a) warned that UK national emission forecasts may vary by ±6% just because of modelling and statistical uncertainties. In this Special Issue, Neuhoff et al. (2006) show how, by adopting the four different fossil fuel price scenarios in the DTI study and accounting for a range (±0.75%) of expected economic growth, projections for EU ETS sectors for phase II (2008–2012) may vary as much as ±9% of the central estimate; the central 60% of scenarios still spanned an uncertainty range of 6%, over just 5 years. Such ranges would, of course, considerably increase if extended to the outlier scenarios and other modelling studies.

Other factors add to uncertainties, including questions about the reliability of historic data and the expected impact of other policies and measures to reduce emissions. The verified emissions data for the EU ETS in 2005 represent the best data available, and imply that the less accurate historic emissions used so far would have created additional (and biased) errors in the projections based on them.[2] Various policies and measures adopted by EU Member States in their efforts to comply with the Kyoto Protocol include sectors covered by the EU ETS, with the degree of response to these measures introducing additional uncertainties.

Even based on scenarios alone, this suggests a typical forecasting uncertainty of at least ±2%/year cumulative. The observation that the future is not certain due to uncertainty in underlying parameters is, of course, no surprise – though it is still not obvious how that is factored into allocation processes. More troubling is the possibility of *bias* in projections, on which other approaches to the issue shed light.

Statistical analyses of past forecasts

The most rigorous approach to assessing forecasting errors would be to analyse statistically the accuracy of past forecasts. There is a well-known history stemming from the 1970s debates about energy – both projections of oil depletion in the face of galloping demand, and forecasts of electricity consumption used to justify the planning of new power stations. In both cases, the 'energy establishment' was widely criticized for forecasts that turned out to be far too high. Of course, with hindsight there were plausible reasons: the oil world underestimated both the demand and supply responses to the price shocks; and electricity analyses 'projected the past' in terms of economic growth rates that with hindsight were clearly unrealistic, as well as underestimating the scope for improved efficiency.

The general aura of 'projection inflation' from that era is only partly true. As energy prices, markets and macroeconomic conditions stabilized, and energy economists absorbed the lessons, energy demand forecasts became more modest.

In one of the most interesting contributions of the time, Baumgartner and Midttun (1987) collected analyses of eight countries, together with the global forecasts by IIASA, to establish overwhelming evidence that 'largely because of the importance of forecasters in the policy process, they are subject to a variety of influences which combine to prevent their forecasts from being objective'. For example, in Denmark, the dominant coalition had in the 1970s reflected industrial interests which wanted, and projected, big growth. Not long afterwards, when a far more environmentally inclined government came to power, energy projections dropped dramatically in favour of 'low-growth' projections. The 'politics of energy forecasting' is a theme to which we return briefly below.

In a bid to make energy projections more objective, in the USA responsibility rests with the Energy Information Administration, a specialist arm of the US Department of Energy, which has over many years built up a track record of readily available, annually published projections. Unlike the sporadic, *ad hoc*, and sometimes unpublished projections in most other countries, the EIA series facilitate rigorous statistical analysis. A recent study (Winebrake and Sakva, 2006) reports:

> Low errors for total energy consumption are concealing much larger sectoral errors that cancel each other out when aggregated. For example, 5-year forecasts made between 1982 and 1998 demonstrate a mean percentage error for total energy consumption of 0.1%. Yet, this hides the fact that the industrial sector was overestimated by an average of 5.9%, and the transportation sector was underestimated by an average of 4.5%. We also find no evidence that forecasts within each sector have improved over the two decades studied here.

Unfortunately for schemes like the EU ETS, it is precisely the industrial sector, not the national total, that matters. And a consistent upward bias error of more than 5% in as many years, if translated into the European context, would imply huge problems where the regulatory system is seeking emission cutbacks from projections that are not much bigger than the systemic bias identified in US industrial energy forecasts.

The remarkable fact is that, despite a search in both the literature and in web-based data, we found neither published analyses nor a readily analysable data-set that would enable a similar analysis to be carried out for European countries.

Understanding the process

The third line of evidence is to understand the process of constructing official emission forecasts. The starting point is economic or sector modelling, which needs to be informed by projections of underlying driving forces (such as economic or sector output growth) and other influential parameters (such as fuel prices), together with estimates of response functions (notably, elasticities of fuel consumption with respect to changes in the various input parameters). Most of these can now be estimated econometrically, hence 'using the past' to project the future.

Such projections err to the extent either that input assumptions on driving forces prove wrong, or if future responses are not a continuation of past patterns. Energy price forecasting is notoriously uncertain, almost the only systematic feature being a tendency to place too much emphasis upon recent trends, and related 'groupthink' problems as the world cycles between high and low energy price periods. The request to revise UK allocations upwards for phase I of the EU ETS reflected to a large degree the impact of sharply rising gas prices, which drove generators back towards coal, sharply increasing emissions.

Economic growth and sector output projections are potentially more liable to systematic error, as there are strong pressures towards optimism. No government likes to predict a gloomy economic future, or imply that it will mismanage the economy. No company raises capital, justifies a new project, or energizes its workforce, by proclaiming a future of decline. Indeed, capitalism thrives on the optimism of those in the market. Yet not all can be winners: competitive markets are all about weeding out those whose optimism proves misplaced.

This introduces a paradox into forecasting. The more disaggregated the level of forecasting – the greater the level of sectoral and even plant-level detail – the more information is at hand, and the more precisely sector forecasts can match the detailed plans and projections of the actual players in the market. Such rich information is lost in aggregated, economic model-driven, forecasts. Yet only aggregated forecasts can capture the statistical fact that not all the individual plans and hopes will come to pass.

This paradox gives rise to real procedural dilemmas. For example, to support its allocation process, the UK put its model-based projections out for consultation, and established an expert advisory group to strengthen the independence of its response to industry representations. Unquestionably consultation reduces the risk of significant underprojection, as industry will have a strong incentive to avoid that. Yet the converse is lacking: if projections are used to inform allocation, what industry would interject to argue that its projected emissions are too high? The level of detailed knowledge required – and the intrinsic uncertainty – makes it impossible for any degree of independent oversight to be certain about the accuracy and objectivity of all evidence for revising sector projections.

In the case of the UK, this effect was balanced by maintaining an aggregated model-based cap across ETS sectors, derived from Treasury projections of economic growth, with the detailed consultations being used to inform the sector distribution; the overall process did result in some modest downward revisions (by 4% for the non-large electricity producers in aggregate; DTI, 2006b). Few other Member States have adopted such an extensive process, and considerable uncertainties remain.

The history of allocation negotiations

This brings us to the final line of evidence, namely, the actual *ex-post* history from cases where governments have sought to negotiate allocations of CO_2 emissions, in one form or another. The UK offers two clear examples.

The first concerns the pilot UK emissions trading scheme, a 'bid-in' scheme in which 32 companies were paid a total of £215m to accept binding caps (established though an auction process). Collectively, participants agreed targets to deliver emission reductions on a linear increase to 3.8 $MtCO_2$e by 2006, a reduction of around 14% relative to collective baseline of 27.8 $MtCO_2$e. In practice, trading prices peaked after a few months, and then fell towards zero as it became increasingly clear that the market was in surplus. The official assessment of the scheme (National

Audit Office, 2004) studied four of the biggest participants (which accounted for more than 50% of the incentive funding) and reported:

> In 2002 their emissions were 3.78 million tonnes below their baselines, nine times the target of 0.42 million tonnes ... approximately 66% of the reductions reported by these four companies is attributed to the Scheme while an estimated 34 per cent (1.28 million tonnes) is not.

By the end of the second year, 6.5 $MtCO_2e$ of surplus allowances were already banked forward (NERA Economic Consulting, 2004). Not surprisingly, the price had dwindled close to zero, and any discussion of extending the scheme was shelved as the EU ETS emerged.

On a larger scale, the UK Climate Change Agreements gave 44 industrial sectors discounts from the UK Climate Change Levy if they met a set of negotiated targets for emission reduction, defined biannually through to 2010. Despite the enormous effort expended in negotiating the original targets, the second target period assessment report is a testimony to the inherent difficulties:

> ... [since 2000] there have been widespread structural changes in UK industry, changes to products because of market forces and entrants and exits in many sectors ... the assumptions of growth and energy prices on which the original BAU forecasts were made are now outdated and of limited relevance.

This, it should be remembered, refers to a period generally hailed as being in the middle of the UK's longest period of sustained, stable, low-inflation economic growth and, in its early years, relatively stable fuel prices. Excluding the steel sector, in target period 1 (2002) the savings were about 40% greater than the targeted savings relative to base year; for the second period, the savings were more than double the target. Exceedence in the steel sector was much bigger still. As a result, the review process resulted in a tightening of targets for the final three target periods (compared to the original agreements) in all but four of the sectors.

Finally, the biggest test of all was the 2005 verification data on the EU ETS. The most recent and detailed analyses by Kettner et al. (2007) confirm that allowances issued for 2006 exceeded verified emissions by about 100 $MtCO_2$, or about 5% of the total.[3] Moreover, sectoral analyses demonstrated a highly skewed distribution, in that the 'net short' element was restricted to about a 60 $MtCO_2$ shortfall in the power sector of EU15 countries (dominated by the UK), set against the much larger surplus from other sectors, and in all sectors in the Accession countries. The percentage surplus in non-power sectors ranged from 5% to 30%, or higher in some cases.

The analysis by Kettner et al. (2007) also presents evidence from the 2005 verification data that the bigger facilities were more able to lobby effectively for allocations that turned out to be inflated – within just a year or two.

Ellerman and Buchner (2006) discuss the difficulty of estimating how much of the surplus was due to abatement, concluding that there was unquestionably *some*, but that any estimate of how much is 'arbitrary and must remain so until better data and more careful assessments can be made'. They develop a 'net ratio' indicator to assess likelihood of over-allocation. Whilst the previous examples in this Commentary focused on the UK, the UK and Ireland show the *least* evidence of aggregate over-allocation (with a significant net shortfall); whereas at least half the Member States have ratios (+0.4 or higher) that could be interpreted as suggesting a general pattern of over-allocation across all sectors.

Note that all three examples share the fundamental impossibility of knowing the 'counterfactual' – what would have happened if the schemes had not been introduced. Thus, they all embody the impact of the schemes on incentives to reduce emissions, as well as the possibility of projection inflation. All attempts to assess retrospectively who or what was responsible conclude that it has been some hard-to-apportion balance of actual abatement with inflation of the original projections. The corollary of estimates that emphasize the importance of abatement compared to projection inflation, however, is that they imply that abatement must have been much easier than originally anticipated during the course of allocation negotiations.

Conclusions and implications

These four lines of evidence – scenario projection ranges, statistical analyses of past forecasts, the process of forecasting, and the evidence from previous allocation and target-setting efforts – point to two fundamental conclusions:

- There is an intrinsic uncertainty in forecasting energy consumption and emissions, probably exceeding ±2%/year cumulative, that no amount of analytic sophistication, whether model-based or procedural consultation, is likely to remove.
- Underlying this, there is evidence of systematic upward bias in industrial energy and emission forecasts, particularly (but not only) when these form the basis of setting sector emission targets or caps, probably on the order of +1%/year.

Obviously, certain kinds of fluctuations can result in bigger uncertainties and biases, particularly in the short term. The numbers here are probably reasonable minimum estimates for forecasts relevant to the timescales of allocation decisions, and yield for example an 'expected error' in the range of at least –5% to +15% in forecasts for industry sector emissions for the EU ETS phase-II allocations (based on approx. 5-year forecasts). This may sound large; yet it is modest compared to the range of sector-level gaps between allocations and emissions in the EU ETS phase-II 2005 data, just 2–3 years after the underlying projections were made.

At least four implications flow from this.

First, any emissions trading scheme in which sector cutbacks are estimated relative to emissions projections, and are less than or comparable to the intrinsic forecasting error, risks a considerable degree of shortfall or surplus at the sector level, even prior to abatement. In the EU ETS phase II, most countries have proposed this approach for sectors other than electricity – given underlying bias errors, the a *priori* likelihood is that most such sectors stand to gain irrespective of their pricing and abatement strategies.

Second, even *aggregate* phase-II cutbacks across all sectors and countries on the order of 5–10% relative to projections risk creating an intrinsically unstable market, since there will be no way of knowing for sure whether in reality the cutbacks during the period are actually extremely modest (if the 'business-as-usual' trend is below that forecast), or severe (if it is higher than forecast).

Third, future development of trading schemes must acknowledge the importance of both irreducible uncertainty and projection inflation, and be designed accordingly. Avoiding projection-based allocation – e.g. through benchmarking – would reduce the direct incentive to projection inflation (although indirect incentives could remain). But even with this, a stable market can only be ensured if the cutbacks are much bigger than the intrinsic projection uncertainties. If this is deemed economically too severe, other approaches must be considered – for example with consideration of measures explicitly designed to contain price uncertainty within bounds, such as mechanisms for price floors and ceilings (see, e.g., Hepburn et al., 2006). Even if free allocations are cut back in line with declared European goals for deep emission reductions – which is clearly not the case for most proposed phase-II allocations at the time of writing – such mechanisms may still have a valuable role to play in increasing confidence, both that the costs are containable, and that prices will support low-carbon investment irrespective of other considerations (such as CDM inflow).

Finally, projections can only conceivably improve if data are reliable, consistent and accessible to independent analysis. This is not the case at present. The relevant data in Europe are scattered, varied and frequently opaque, even when technically accessible. Improving data quality and comparability, and encouraging independent scrutiny over extended time periods, is essential if the EU ETS is to evolve into a more stable incentive for low-carbon investment.

Acknowledgements

We are grateful to numerous colleagues for the information and guidance that informed this Commentary.

Notes

1 The expression (used in relation to EU ETS phase-I allocations in Grubb et al., 2005) derives from the Greek myth in which Achilles' mother gave the baby godly protection by dipping him into the magical waters of the river Styx – but held on to his heels, which thus became his only vulnerable point.
2 As the 2005 Verified Emissions have been consistently below most expectations.
3 See Note 3 in Betz and Sato 2006, this issue.

References

Baumgartner, T., Midttun, A. (Eds), 1987. The Politics of Energy Forecasting: A Comparative Study of Energy Forecasting in Western Europe and North America. Oxford University Press, New York. Specific citation from review by R.J. Jones, International Journal of Forecasting Policy 5 (1989), 133–145.

Betz, R., Sato, M., 2006. Emissions trading: lessons learnt from the 1st phase of the EU ETS and prospects for the 2nd phase. Climate Policy 6(4), 351–359.

DTI, 2006a. UK Energy and CO$_2$ Emissions Projections: Updated Projections to 2020. Department of Trade and Industry, February 2006.

DTI, 2006b. EU ETS Phase II CO$_2$ Emission Projections: Revisions to Projections following consultations. Department of Trade and Industry, August 2006.

Ellerman, D., Buchner, B., 2006. A preliminary analysis of the EU ETS based on the 2005 emissions data. Nota di Lavoro 139.2006 [also downloadable through http://www.climate-strategies.org/].

Grubb, M., Azar, C., Persson, M., 2005. Allowance allocation in the European emissions trading system: a commentary. Climate Policy 5(1), 127–136.

Hepburn, C., Grubb, M., Neuhoff, K., Matthes, F., Tse, M., 2006. Auctioning of EU ETS phase II allowances: how and why? Climate Policy 6(1), 137–160.

IPCC, 2001. Climate Change 2001: Mitigation. Cambridge University Press, Cambridge, UK.

IPCC, 2007. Climate Change 2007: Mitigation. Cambridge University Press, Cambridge, UK (forthcoming).

Kettner, C., Kopp, A., Schleicher, S., Thenius, G., 2007. Stringency and distribution in the EU Emissions Trading Scheme – the 2005 Evidence. Climate Policy, forthcoming.

National Audit Office, 2004. The UK Emissions Trading Scheme: A New Way to Combat Climate Change. HMSO Report HC-517, NAO, London.

NERA Economic Consulting, 2004. Review of First and Second Years of the UK Emissions Trading Scheme. NERA, London.

Neuhoff, K., Ferrario, F., Grubb, M., Gabel, E., Keats, K., 2006. Emission projections 2008–2012 versus national allocation plans II. Climate Policy 6(4), 395–410.

Winebrake, J.J., Savka, D., 2006. An evaluation of errors in US energy forecasts: 1982–2003. Energy Policy 34, 3475–3483.

T - #0196 - 270225 - C0 - 262/190/9 - PB - 9781138012202 - Gloss Lamination